Bazaar Bonanza in PLASTIC CANVAS

Edited by Laura Scott

HOUSE of
WHITE
BIRCHES
PUBLISHERS
SINCE 1947

Bazaar Bonanza in Plastic Canvas

Copyright © 2000 House of White Birches, Berne, Indiana 46711

All rights reserved. No part of this publication may be
reproduced or transmitted in any form or by any means,
electronic or mechanical, including photocopying,
recording, or any other information storage and retrieval
system, without the written permission of the publisher.

Editor: Laura Scott
Associate Editor: June Sprunger
Copy Editor: Mary Nowak
Publications Coordinator: Tanya Turner

Photography: Tammy Christian, Jeff Chilcote, Justin P. Wiard
Photography Stylist: Arlou Wittwer
Photography Assistant: Linda Quinlan

Production Coordinator: Brenda Gallmeyer
Graphic Arts Supervisor: Ronda Bechinski
Book Design: Vicki's Design Studio
Cover Design: Jessi Butler
Graphic Artist: Amy S. Lin
Production Assistants: Janet Bowers, Marj Morgan
Traffic Coordinator: Sandra Beres
Technical Artists: Leslie Brandt, Julie Catey, Chris Moorman, Chad Summers

Publishers: Carl H. Muselman, Arthur K. Muselman
Chief Executive Officer: John Robinson
Marketing Director: Scott Moss
Book Marketing Manager: Craig Scott
Product Development Director: Vivian Rothe
Publishing Services Manager: Brenda R. Wendling

Printed in the United States of America
First Printing: 2000
Library of Congress Number: 00-132493
ISBN: 1-882138-61-9

Every effort has been made to ensure the accuracy and completeness of the instructions
in this book. However, we cannot be responsible for human error or for the results when using
materials other than those specified in the instructions, or for variations in individual work.

Ready, Set, Stitch!

Dear Needlecrafter,

What is your favorite part of stitching plastic canvas projects? Is it picking out which projects to work on? Is it shopping at your local craft store for just the right colors of yarn you need? Is it spending your relaxation time working on your piece, stitch by stitch? Or is it seeing the look of pleasure on the person's face to whom you either gave or sold the project?

Each of us no doubt has favorite and least favorite aspects of our favorite hobby. (For example, my *least* favorite part is cutting out the canvas.) For each project in this book, we've included a gorgeous, close-up, full-color photo so you can see every last detail. Our instructions and graphs are written by the designers, edited by our technical editor, and double-checked by our proofreaders to make sure you don't have any troubles making any or all of the projects in this collection!

Because we've organized this book by seasons, it will take you just a couple minutes to flip open the book and find just the right project for the occasion at hand. Our spring and summer chapters give you dozens upon dozens of ideas for bringing nature's beauty indoors, and into your pocketbook with great sales! Many churches and schools have annual autumn and winter craft bazaars. These chapters are chock-full of great ideas for gift-giving and decorating, all sure to be successful moneymakers at your next fund-raising event.

So whether you use these projects as a source of income, or simply enjoy making quick-and-easy projects to share with family and friends, you're sure to love this collection of more than 150 all-new plastic canvas projects!

Happy Stitching,

Laura Scott

CONTENTS

Chapter 1
SPRING FLING

Chapter 2
SUMMER STITCHING

Chapter 3
AUTUMN COLORS

Chapter 4
WINTER WONDERS

CHAPTER ONE

Spring Fling

Put aside that spring cleaning
and jump into spring stitching!

Kick off your year of
craft bazaar success with
this collection of more than
40 easy-to-stitch and
fresh-as-spring projects!

Floral Gingham Keepsakes

Designs by Susan Leinberger

Stitch four sets of pretty gingham boxes with matching floral barrettes, perfect for gift-giving!

skill level • intermediate

✖ materials ✖

- ❑ 4 sheets Uniek Quick-Count 7-count plastic canvas
- ❑ Uniek Needloft plastic canvas yarn as listed in color key
- ❑ Worsted weight yarn as listed in color key
- ❑ #16 tapestry needle
- ❑ 4 (70mm) steel bow barrettes
- ❑ Hot-glue gun

finished size:

Box: 3 inches square x 2½ inches H, including flowers

Barrette: 3 inches L x 1¼ inches W, excluding flowers

boxes & barrettes

1 For each box, cut four box sides, four lid sides, one lid top and one barrette according to graphs (page 10). Cut one 17-hole x 17-hole piece for each box bottom. Box bottoms will remain unstitched.

2 Stitch forget-me-not box pieces and barrette following graphs. Work sail blue Backstitches on box sides when background stitching is completed.

3 Using sail blue throughout, Whipstitch lid sides together, then Whipstitch lid sides to lid top; Overcast bottom edges. Whipstitch box sides together, then Whipstitch box sides to unstitched box bottom; Overcast top edges.

4 Following steps 2 and 3 for remaining boxes, work wild rose box pieces and barrette, replacing sail blue with pink and baby blue with pale pink.

5 Work daisy box pieces and barrette replacing sail blue with yellow and baby blue with lemon.

6 Work violet box pieces and barrette replacing sail blue with purple and baby blue with lilac.

7 Overcast barrettes with white.

flowers & leaves

1 Cut pieces according to graphs (page 10).

2 Stitch leaves following graphs. Overcast with adjacent colors. Work Straight Stitches when stitching and Overcasting are completed.

3 Following graph, Overcast six forget-me-nots with sail blue and two with baby blue, then work lemon French Knots in center of each flower.

4 Stitch and Overcast wild roses with pink following graph. Work lemon Turkey Loop Stitches in flower centers, making loops approximately ⅛-inch to ¼-inch high.

5 Following graph, Overcast daisies with white, then work yellow French Knots in flower centers.

6 Following graph, stitch and Overcast violets with purple, then work yellow stitches and French Knots.

final assembly

1 Use photo as a guide throughout final assembly. For forget-me-not set, glue four leaves, four sail blue flowers and one baby blue flower to center top of lid; glue four leaves, two sail blue flowers and one baby blue flower to center top of barrette.

2 For wild rose set, glue two leaves and one flower each to center tops of lid and barrette.

3 For daisy set, glue two leaves and one flower each to center tops of lid and barrette.

4 For violets set, glue two leaves and four flowers to center top of lid; glue two leaves and one flower to center top of barrette.

5 Glue steel bow barrettes to the back of stitched barrettes. ❑

COLOR KEY

Plastic Canvas Yarn	Yards
▨ Pink #07	18
Lemon #20	16
■ Christmas green #28	7
■ Sail blue #35	16
▨ Baby blue #36	14
☐ White #41	42
Lilac #45	13
■ Purple #46	18
▨ Mermaid #53	5
▨ Yellow #57	18
✎ Christmas green #28 Straight Stitch	
✎ Sail blue #35 Backstitch	
✎ Mermaid #53 Straight Stitch	
○ Lemon #20 French Knot	
● Yellow #57 French Knot	
△ Lemon #20 Turkey Loop Stitch	
Worsted Weight Yarn	
Pale pink	13

Color numbers given are for Uniek Needloft plastic canvas yarn.

Violet
5 holes x 5 holes
Cut 5

Violet Leaf
5 holes x 6 holes
Cut 4

Wild Rose Leaf
5 holes x 6 holes
Cut 4

Daisy Leaf
6 holes x 6 holes
Cut 4

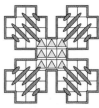

Wild Rose
9 holes x 9 holes
Cut 2

Forget-Me-Not Leaf
3 holes x 3 holes
Cut 8

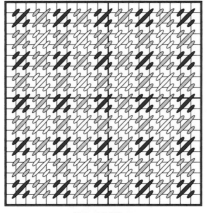

Box Lid Top
19 holes x 19 holes
Cut 1 for each box
Stitch forget-me-not top as graphed
Stitch wild rose top, replacing sail blue
with pink and baby blue with pale pink
Stitch daisy top, replacing sail blue
with yellow and baby blue with lemon
Stitch violet top, replacing sail blue
with purple and baby blue with lilac

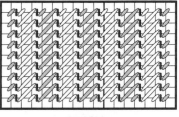

Box Side
17 holes x 10 holes
Cut 4 for each box
Stitch forget-me-not sides as graphed
Stitch wild rose sides, replacing sail blue
with pink and baby blue with pale pink
Stitch daisy sides, replacing sail blue
with yellow and baby blue with lemon
Stitch violet sides, replacing sail blue
with purple and baby blue with lilac

Forget-Me-Not
3 holes x 3 holes
Cut 8
Overcast 6 as graphed
Overcast 2 with baby blue

Box Lid Side
19 holes x 3 holes
Cut 4 for each box
Stitch forget-me-not lid sides as graphed
Stitch wild rose lid sides, replacing sail blue
with pink and baby blue with pale pink
Stitch daisy lid sides, replacing sail blue
with yellow and baby blue with lemon
Stitch violet lid sides, replacing sail blue
with purple and baby blue with lilac

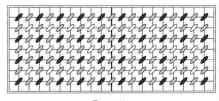

Barrette
20 holes x 8 holes
Cut 4
Stitch forget-me-not barette as graphed
Stitch wild rose barrette, replacing sail blue
with pink and baby blue with pale pink
Stitch daisy barette, replacing sail blue
with yellow and baby blue with lemon
Stitch violet barette, replacing sail blue
with purple and baby blue with lilac

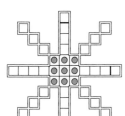

Daisy
11 holes x 11 holes
Cut 2

Tulip Tote

Design by Angie Arickx

Use this charming basket for this year's Easter egg hunt, or simply for adding a fresh-as-spring touch to your home!

skill level • beginner

✖ materials ✖

- ❑ 2 sheets Darice Ultra Stiff 7-count plastic canvas
- ❑ 2 sheets Darice Super Soft 7-count plastic canvas
- ❑ Uniek Needloft plastic canvas yarn as listed in color key
- ❑ #16 tapestry needle
- ❑ Basket, approximately 6¼ inches in diameter, with handle
- ❑ Craft glue

finished size:

Approximately 12 inches H x 6¾ inches in diameter, including handle

instructions

1 Cut plastic canvas according to graphs.

2 Stitch pieces following graphs, working six tulips as graphed and six replacing yellow with watermelon. Leave blue lines on ribbon tails unstitched at this time.

3 Overcast tulips with adjacent colors. Using watermelon throughout, Overcast ribbon tails and long edges on bow loops. Fold bow loops with wrong sides together; Whipstitch short edges of loops to ribbon tails where indicated with blue lines, forming the bow.

4 Using photo as a guide throughout, glue right side of tulips around inside of basket rim, alternating yellow and watermelon. Glue bow to basket handle. ❑

COLOR KEY	
Plastic Canvas Yarn	**Yards**
■ Fern #23	26
▨ Watermelon #55	18
☐ Yellow #57	6
Color numbers given are for Uniek Needloft plastic canvas yarn.	

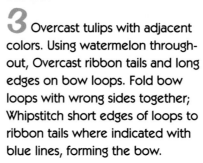

Tulip Tote Bow Loop
32 holes x 5 holes
Cut 2 from soft

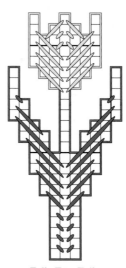

Tulip Tote Tulip
11 holes x 23 holes
Cut 12 from stiff
Stitch 6 as graphed
Stitch 6, replacing
yellow with watermelon

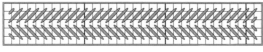

Tulip Tote Ribbon Tails
79 holes x 5 holes
Cut 1 from soft

Gardener's Plant Pokes

Design by Susan Leinberger

Tried-and-true gardeners will love this pair of whimsical plant pokes!

skill level • beginner

✖ materials ✖

- ❑ 1 sheet Uniek Quick-Count 7-count plastic canvas
- ❑ Small amount 10-count plastic canvas
- ❑ Uniek Needloft plastic canvas yarn as listed in color key
- ❑ Worsted weight yarn as listed in color key
- ❑ #16 tapestry needle
- ❑ #20 tapestry needle
- ❑ 2 (12-inch) lengths ⅛-inch dowel
- ❑ Tacky craft glue
- ❑ Hot-glue gun

finished size:

3⅞ inches W x 4½ inches H, excluding dowel

instructions

1 Cut one front and one back for each sign from 7-count plastic canvas; cut one caterpillar, one bee and two ladybugs from 10-count plastic canvas according to graphs.

2 With #16 tapestry needle, stitch front and back pieces following graphs, working uncoded areas with white Continental Stitches.

3 When background stitching is completed, work fern Backstitches for dandelion stem and Straight Stitches on dandelion leaves; work Christmas red French Knots for potted geraniums. For dandelion, work yellow Turkey Loop Stitches as indicated; snip loops and fluff yarn. Work letters with 1 ply forest.

4 Hot glue dowels to wrong side of front pieces where indicated on graphs with a blue dot, leaving 10 inches of dowel extending from bottom edge.

5 Whipstitch wrong sides of backs and fronts together with Christmas red and yellow, alternating colors and working stitches around dowels.

6 Using #20 tapestry needle and 1 ply yarn through step 7, stitch and Overcast 10-count plastic canvas following graphs. **Note:** *Bee's wings will remain unstitched.*

7 When background stitching and Overcasting are completed, work French Knots on caterpillar and lady–bugs and Straight Stitches on ladybugs. Wrap black yarn around caterpillar as indicated to make stripes.

8 Using photo as a guide, with tacky craft glue, attach caterpillar and one ladybug to "Weeds bug me!" front ; attach bee and remaining ladybug to "I dig gardening!" front. Allow to dry. ❑

COLOR KEY
I DIG GARDENING
Plastic Canvas Yarn	Yards
■ Black #00	1
■ Christmas red #02	9
▨ Fern #23	4
■ Forest #29	3
□ Yellow #57	6
Uncoded areas are white #41	
Continental Stitches	5
✎ Black #00 Straight Stitch	
● Christmas red #02 French Knot	
✎ Forest #29 Backstitch and Straight Stitch	
● Forest #29 French Knot	
Worsted Weight Yarn	
▨ Rust	2

Color numbers given are for Uniek Needloft plastic canvas yarn.

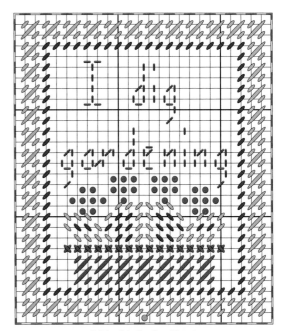

I Dig Gardening Front
25 holes x 29 holes
Cut 1 from 7-count

Plant Poke Back
25 holes x 29 holes
Cut 2 from 7-count

Caterpillar
5 holes x 14 holes
Cut 1 from 10-count

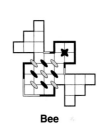

Bee
8 holes x 8 holes
Cut 1 from 10-count

Ladybug
4 holes x 4 holes
Cut 2 from 10-count

COLOR KEY
WEEDS BUG ME
Plastic Canvas Yarn	Yards
■ Black #00	1
■ Christmas red #02	6
▨ Fern #23	3
■ Forest #29	4
□ Yellow #57	7
Uncoded areas are white #41	
Continental Stitches	6
✎ Black #00 Straight Stitch	
✎ Fern #23 Backstitch and Straight Stitch	
✎ Forest #29 Backstitch	
● Black #00 French Knot	
● Forest #29 French Knot	
○ Yellow #57 French Knot	
△ Yellow #57 Turkey Loop Stitch	

Color numbers given are for Uniek Needloft plastic canvas yarn.

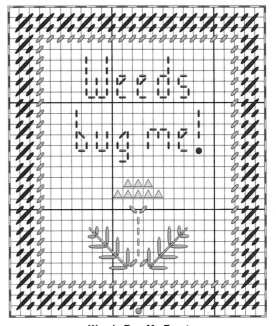

Weeds Bug Me Front
25 holes x 29 holes
Cut 1 from 7-count

Fun Frames

Design by Joan Green

This set of five magnetic frames is perfect for displaying special family photos on the refrigerator at home or on the filing cabinet at work!

skill level • beginner

✹ materials ✹

- ❑ 1 sheet 7-count plastic canvas
- ❑ Spinrite Bernat Berella "4" worsted weight yarn as listed in color key
- ❑ Plastic canvas yarn as listed in color key
- ❑ #16 tapestry needle
- ❑ 5 inches ⅛-inch-wide blue satin ribbon
- ❑ 5 (2½-inch) self-adhesive magnetic strips
- ❑ Photos to fit openings
- ❑ Lightweight white cardboard
- ❑ Fabric glue

finished size:

Balloon: 2¾ inches W x 8¾ inches H, including ribbon tail

Birdhouse: 3⅜ inches W x 4 inches H

Daisy: 3⅞ inches in diameter

Heart: 3⅞ inches W x 3¼ inches H

Ice Cream Cone: 2⅝ inches x 4¾ inches H

instructions

1 Cut plastic canvas according to graphs (pages 14,15 and 17). Cut lightweight cardboard slightly smaller than each plastic canvas piece.

2 Continental Stitch background on balloon with pale teal. Work Cross Stitches and Star Stitches with 2 plies white. Overcast with medium teal.

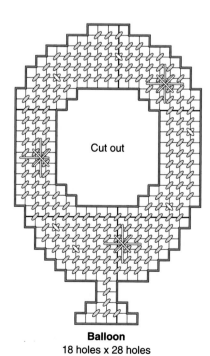

Cut out

Balloon
18 holes x 28 holes
Cut 1

COLOR KEY

Plastic Canvas Yarn	Yard
☐ Light brown	
☐ Yellow	
⁄ Dark blue green Backstitch	
⁄ Dark brown Backstitch	
● Dark brown French Knot	
Worsted Weight Yarn	
☐ Pale teal #8846	
◼ Medium teal #8884	
◼ Scarlet #8933	
☐ Winter white #8941	
☐ Baby pink #8943	1
Uncoded background on heart is baby pink #8943 Continental Stitches	
⁄ Light tapestry gold #8886 Overcasting	
⁄ Rose #8921 Overcasting	
⁄ Winter white # 8941 Straight Stitch	
⁄ Black #8994 Backstitch and Straight Stitch	
● Rose #8921 French Knot	

Color numbers given are for Spinrite Bernat Berell "4" worsted weight yarn.

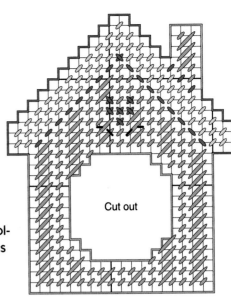

3 Stitch and Overcast birdhouse with scarlet, pale teal, medium teal and light brown following graph. Work Backstitches with 2 plies black.

Birdhouse
22 holes x 26 holes
Cut 1

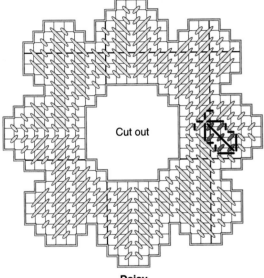

4 Stitch daisy with yellow and scarlet following graph. Overcast with light tapestry gold. Work black Backstitches and Straight Stitch with 2 plies black.

Daisy
25 holes x 25 holes
Cut 1

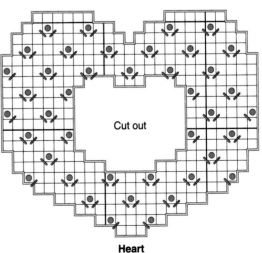

5 Work uncoded background on heart with baby pink Continental Stitches. Overcast with baby pink. Work dark blue–green Backstitches and rose French Knots with 2 plies yarn.

Heart
25 holes x 21 holes
Cut 1

continued on page 17

Tiny Treasures Pins

Designs by Ronda Bryce

In just 10 or 15 minutes, you can add
either of these darling pins to your wardrobe!

skill level • beginner

tulip teacup pin
✖ materials ✖

- Small amount 7-count plastic canvas
- Uniek Needloft plastic canvas yarn as listed in color key
- Uniek Needloft metallic craft cord as listed in color key
- #16 tapestry needle
- 3 inches ⅜-inch-wide light pink ruffled lace
- 6 (4mm) white pearl beads
- Sewing needle and light pink sewing thread
- 1-inch gold pin back

finished size:

2⅝ inches W x 1¾ inches H

instructions

1 Cut plastic canvas according to graph.

2 Stitch piece following graph, working uncoded area with white Continental Stitches. Overcast inside and outside edges with eggshell.

3 Using sewing needle and light pink thread through step 4, stitch lace to backside along rim edge of teacup, folding raw edges under.

4 Stitch pearl beads to teacup where indicated on graph. Sew pin back to backside. ❑

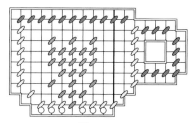

Teacup
17 holes x 10 holes
Cut 1

COLOR KEY	
Plastic Canvas Yarn	**Yards**
◼ Pink #07	1
◻ Eggshell #39	2
◼ Mermaid #53	1
Uncoded areas are white #41	
Continental Stitches	1
Metallic Craft Cord	
◼ Gold #01	1
○ Attach pearl bead	
Color numbers given are for Uniek Needloft plastic canvas yarn and metallic craft cord.	

fancy fan pin
✖ materials ✖

- ❏ 3-inch plastic canvas radial circle by Uniek
- ❏ Plastic canvas yarn as listed in color key
- ❏ #16 tapestry needle
- ❏ ½-inch light pink ribbon rose with leaves
- ❏ 4 inches ⅜-inch-wide light pink ruffled lace
- ❏ 7 (4mm) white pearl beads
- ❏ 1¼-inch light pink tassel
- ❏ Sewing needle and light pink sewing thread
- ❏ 1-inch gold pin back

finished size:
2⅝ inches W x 1¾ inches H

instructions

1 Cut plastic canvas according to graph, cutting away gray area.

2 Stitch piece following graph. Overcast with mermaid.

3 Using photo as a guide and sewing needle and pink thread through step 5, attach rose to green area at bottom front of fan.

4 Stitch lace to backside along curved edge, folding in edges. Attach pearl beads where indicated on graph.

5 Stitch tassel to green yarn on lower backside of fan. Stitch pin to backside of fan. ❏

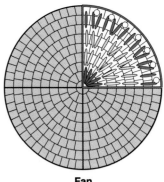

Fan
Cut 1
Cut away gray area

COLOR KEY	
Plastic Canvas Yarn	**Yards**
■ Pink	1
☐ Pale pink	1
☐ Cream	1
■ Green	1
○ Attach pearl bead	

Fun Frames continued from page 15

COLOR KEY	
Plastic Canvas Yarn	**Yards**
☐ Light brown	8
☐ Yellow	7
╱ Dark blue green Backstitch	2
╱ Dark brown Backstitch	1
● Dark brown French Knot	
Worsted Weight Yarn	
☐ Pale teal #8846	6
■ Medium teal #8884	6
■ Scarlet #8933	3
☐ Winter white #8941	1
☐ Baby pink #8943	10
Uncoded background on heart is baby pink #8943 Continental Stitches	
╱ Light tapestry gold #8886 Overcasting	4
╱ Rose #8921 Overcasting	4
╱ Winter white # 8941 Straight Stitch	
╱ Black #8994 Backstitch and Straight Stitch	1
● Rose #8921 French Knot	
Color numbers given are for Spinrite Bernat Berella "4" worsted weight yarn.	

7 Glue ribbon to back of balloon at center bottom.

8 Place photos on cardboard to fit in openings; glue photos in place. Glue cardboard to backs of frames.

9 Attach magnetic strips to cardboard on frame backs. ❏

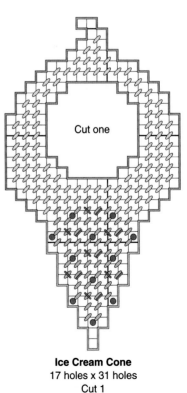

Ice Cream Cone
17 holes x 31 holes
Cut 1

6 Following graph, Continental Stitch ice cream cone with baby pink and light brown; Overcast with rose and light brown. Work Backstitches and French Knots with dark brown.

Spring Harvest Bunny

Design by Lee Lindeman

Bursting with personality and charm, this darling bunny will dress up any corner in your home!

skill level • intermediate

✖ materials ✖

- ❏ 1 sheet 7-count plastic canvas
- ❏ Coats & Clark Red Heart Super Saver worsted weight yarn Art. E300 as listed in color key
- ❏ 6-strand embroidery floss as listed in color key
- ❏ #16 tapestry needle
- ❏ 2 (3mm) black round beads
- ❏ 5mm black round cabochon
- ❏ 10 inches ½-wide white lace
- ❏ Sewing needle and white sewing thread
- ❏ Faux miniature carrot top foliage
- ❏ Small amount polyester fiberfill
- ❏ 1-inch white pompom
- ❏ 1-inch terra-cotta flowerpot
- ❏ 4½-inch terra-cotta flowerpot saucer
- ❏ Mini spade
- ❏ Hot-glue gun

finished size:

7¼ inches H x 4½ inches in diameter

cutting & stitching

1 Cut plastic canvas according to graphs.

2 Stitch pieces following graphs, working uncoded areas with white Continental Stitches. Work bunny head back entirely with white Continental Stitches, eliminating rose pink stitches.

3 Using 2 plies of black embroidery floss, work embroidery on face. With sewing needle and white sewing thread, attach beads for eyes where indicated on graph. For nose, glue black cabochon to face where indicated on graph.

assembly

1 Using photo as a guide throughout assembly, Whipstitch wrong sides of head front and back together with white, stuffing with small amount of fiberfill before closing.

2 Following graph, Overcast top edges of body front and back, then Whipstitch wrong sides together along side edges. Stuff with fiberfill. Whipstitch base to bottom edges with pale yellow.

3 Insert neck of head into top of body; glue in place. With sewing needle and white sewing thread, gather lace and wrap around neck, placing seam in back; glue in place.

4 Whipstitch wrong sides of arms and feet together with adjacent colors, forming two pairs of each; stuff feet with fiberfill before closing. Glue feet to bottom of body.

5 Invert flowerpot saucer and glue bunny to bottom. Glue miniature spade in front of bunny to saucer. Glue pompom to back of bunny for tail.

6 With orange, Whipstitch wrong sides of small carrot pieces and large carrot pieces together, forming two large and one small carrot. Glue faux foliage in top of each carrot.

7 Glue carrots in 1-inch flowerpot. Glue arms and pot to bunny so that bunny is holding pot. ❏

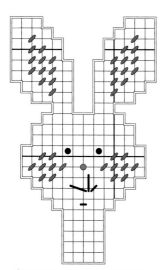

Spring Harvest Bunny Head
Front & Back
14 holes x 23 holes
Cut 2
Stitch front as graphed
Stitch back entirely with
white Continental Stitches

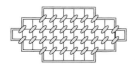

Spring Harvest Bunny Base
11 holes x 5 holes
Cut 1

Spring Harvest Bunny Foot
6 holes x 6 holes
Cut 4

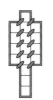

Spring Harvest Large Carrot
3 holes x 8 holes
Cut 4

Spring Harvest Bunny Arm
4 holes x 12 holes
Cut 4

Spring Harvest Small Carrot
3 holes x 7 holes
Cut 2

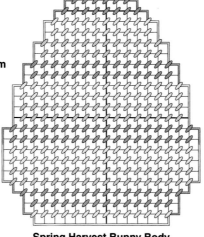

Spring Harvest Bunny Body
19 holes x 22 holes
Cut 2

COLOR KEY

Worsted Weight Yarn	Yards
☐ Orange #245	4
☐ Pale yellow #322	5
☐ Light mint #364	5
☐ Rose pink #372	1
☐ Baby pink #724	5
Uncoded areas are white #311	
Continental Stitches	10
✎ White #311 Whipstitching	

6-Strand Embroidery Floss
✎ Black Backstitch and
  Straight Stitch   1
● Attach black bead
● Attach black cabochon

Color numbers given are for Coats & Clark
Red Heart Super Saver worsted weight yarn
Art. E300.

Spring Welcome

Design by Celia Lange Designs

Welcome friends into your home with this enchanting sign!
The bunny can also be used as a plant poke
or refrigerator magnet.

skill level • beginner

✖ materials ✖

- ❑ 1 sheet Darice Ultra Stiff 7-count plastic canvas
- ❑ Coats & Clark Red Heart Classic worsted weight yarn Art. E267 as listed in color key
- ❑ DMC #3 pearl cotton as listed in color key
- ❑ #16 tapestry needle
- ❑ 2 (18-inch) lengths green 20-gauge florist wire
- ❑ 2 (12-inch) lengths mini ivy or leafy garland
- ❑ Small assorted silk flowers
- ❑ 6 inches ¼-inch dowel
- ❑ 7¼-inch x 3-inch piece yellow felt
- ❑ 4¾-inch x 1-inch piece brown felt
- ❑ 2 (¼-inch) white pompoms
- ❑ 2 (½-inch) carrot buttons
- ❑ Magnet (optional)
- ❑ Dowel for plant poke (optional)
- ❑ Hot-glue gun

finished size:

Sign: 7⅜ inches W x 7¾ inches H

Bunny Motif: 2⅜ inches W x 4½ inches H

cutting & stitching

1 Cut plastic canvas according to graphs (pages 21 and 23).

2 For lining, cut yellow felt slightly smaller than banner and brown felt slightly smaller than swing seat.

3 Stitch pieces following graphs, working uncoded areas with cornmeal Continental Stitches. Overcast pieces following graphs.

4 Stitch words on banner with purple yarn. Work pale rose yarn French Knots for bunnies' noses. Work dark topaz and black pearl cotton embroidery on chicks; work black pearl cotton embroidery on bunnies.

5 For chick pin feathers, work three loops of dark topaz pearl cotton, extending approximately ½ inch above tops of each head. Secure loops, then cut open.

assembly

1 Wrap each length of florist wire around 6-inch dowel length. Remove dowel and pull wire to form spiral, making lengths equal. Thread ends through holes on banner indicated with blue dots so that two lengths hang from banner; twist ends closed.

2 Thread opposite ends of wire through swing seat where indicated with blue dots; twist ends closed.

3 Glue yellow felt to backside of banner and brown felt to backside of swing seat.

4 Using photo as a guide through step 6, glue heads to chicks and arms to bunnies, gluing carrot buttons between bunnies' hands and bodies. Glue pompoms to bunnies for tails.

5 Wrap ivy or leafy garland around wire, then glue to banner and seat. Glue one bunny and both chicks to seat.

6 Glue flowers as desired to banner, ivy and bunnies.

7 If desired, glue magnet for fridgie or dowel for plant poke to back of remaining bunny. ❑

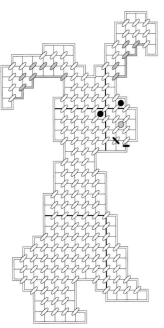

Spring Welcome Bunny
15 holes x 29 holes
Cut 2

Spring Welcome Chick Body
7 holes x 7 holes
Cut 2

Spring Welcome Chick Head
5 holes x 6 holes
Cut 2

COLOR KEY

Worsted Weight Yarn	Yards
☐ White #1	14
■ Mid brown #339	4
☐ Pale rose #775	1
Uncoded areas are cornmeal #220 Continental Stitches	15
∕ Cornmeal #220 Overcasting	
∕ Purple #596 Backstitch and Straight Stitch	2
○ Pale rose #755 French Knot	

#3 Pearl Cotton

∕ Black #310 Backstitch	1
∕ Dark topaz #782 Backstitch	1
● Black #310 French Knot	

Color numbers given are for Coats & Clark Red Heart Classic worsted weight yarn Art. E267 and DMC #3 pearl cotton.

continued on page 23

Miss Bunny Tissue Topper

Design by Angie Arickx

Nothing says "spring" more than hungry bunnies nibbling on your tender garden carrots!

✹ materials ✹

- ❏ 2 sheets Darice Ultra Stiff 7-count plastic canvas
- ❏ Uniek Needloft plastic canvas yarn as listed in color key
- ❏ DMC #3 pearl cotton as listed in color key
- ❏ #16 tapestry needle
- ❏ #18 tapestry needle

finished size:
Fits boutique-style tissue box

skill level • beginner

instructions

1 Cut plastic canvas according to graphs.

2 With #16 tapestry needle, stitch pieces with yarn following graphs, working uncoded areas with camel Continental Stitches. With #18 needle, work pearl cotton Cross Stitches for eyes and Backstitches for mouths.

3 Overcast bottom edges of sides with fern. Overcast inside edges of top with sail blue. Whipstitch sides together with sail blue and gray following graphs, then Whipstitch sides to top with sail blue. ❏

COLOR KEY	
Plastic Canvas Yarn	**Yards**
■ Lavender #05	4
■ Pumpkin #12	8
■ Fern #23	8
■ Sail blue #35	28
■ Gray #38	12
☐ White #41	22
☐ Camel #43	22
Uncoded areas are camel #43 Continental Stitches	
#3 Pearl Cotton	
■ Very dark beige brown #838	2
✎ Very dark beige brown #838 Backstitch	
Color numbers given are for Uniek Needloft plastic canvas yarn and DMC #3 Pearl Cotton.	

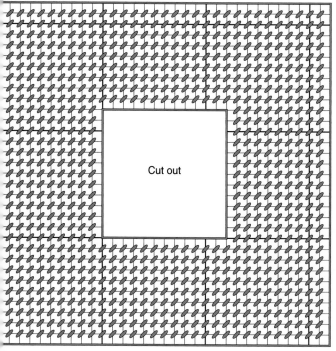

Tissue Topper Top
32 holes x 32 holes
Cut 1

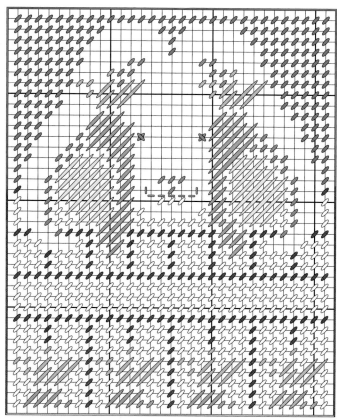

Tissue Topper Side
32 holes x 38 holes
Cut 4

Spring Welcome continued from page 21

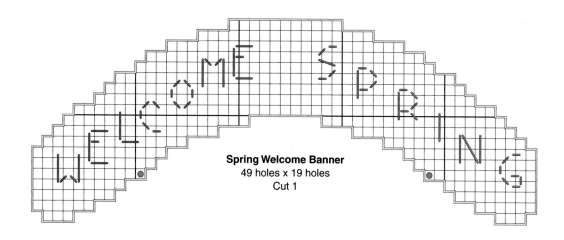

Spring Welcome Banner
49 holes x 19 holes
Cut 1

Spring Welcome Bunny Arm
7 holes x 7 holes
Cut 2

Continue pattern

Spring Welcome Swing Seat
31 holes x 5 holes
Cut 1

Wishing Well Tote

Design by Janelle Giese

This delightful tote is perfect for any gift-giving occasion
throughout the year, from birthdays to cheering a shut-in!

skill level
intermediate

✖ materials ✖

- ❏ ½ sheet clear 7-count plastic canvas
- ❏ 1 sheet almond 7-count plastic canvas
- ❏ Uniek Needloft plastic canvas yarn as listed in color key
- ❏ Worsted weight yarn as listed in color key
- ❏ Chenille yarn as listed in color key
- ❏ Kreinik ⅛-inch Ribbon as listed in color key
- ❏ DMC #5 pearl cotton as listed in color key
- ❏ #16 tapestry needle
- ❏ Large-eye needle
- ❏ 18 inches (4mm) light green twisted cording
- ❏ Thick white glue

finished size:

5¼ inches W x 8⅜ inches H x 2⅜ inches D

instructions

1 Cut tote front from clear plastic canvas according to graph.

2 From almond plastic canvas, cut two 15-hole x 40-hole pieces for tote sides, one 29-hole x 40-hole piece for tote back, one 29-hole x 15-hole piece for tote base and two 3-hole x 3-hole pieces for handle reinforcements. Almond pieces will remain unstitched.

3 With #16 tapestry needle, stitch front following graph, leaving pink Whipstitch lines unworked at this time. Work uncoded areas with light tan Continental Stitches. Work camel stitches on roof with two stitches per hole where indicated.

4 Overcast top edge of rainbow from dot to dot with lilac and lower edge with sail blue. For remaining inside edges, Overcast

roof edges with camel and sun edges with sunlight and gold.

5 With black pearl cotton, stitch bucket handle and facial features, passing over eyes, noses and "O" on mouths four times. Work remaining embroidery, omitting stitches on or along pink Whipstitch lines and edges at this time.

6 With moss, Whipstitch short edges of base to one short edge of each side.

7 Whipstitch front to sides and base where indicated with moss. Following graph, finish Whipstitching front to sides, by working remaining stitches along pink Whipstitch line, Overcasting extended edges while working

these stitches. Complete embroidery over Whipstitch lines.

8 With moss, Whipstitch back to sides and base; Overcast top edges of sides and back.

9 To attach handle, use large-eye needle to thread ends of twisted cording through sides, five holes from top and five holes from front, threading through handle reinforcements on inside of bag at the same time. Knot ends, trim and glue to secure. ❏

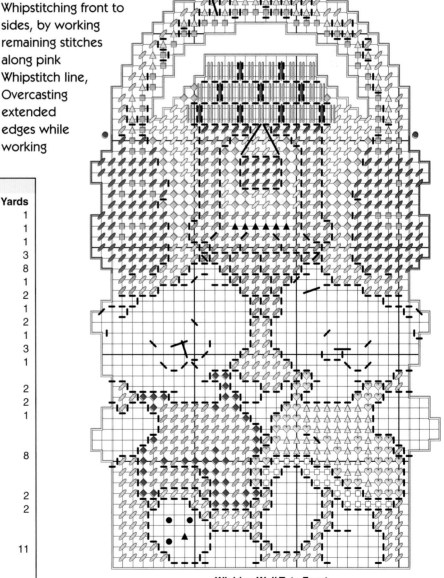

Wishing Well Tote Front
34 holes x 55 holes
Cut 1 from clear

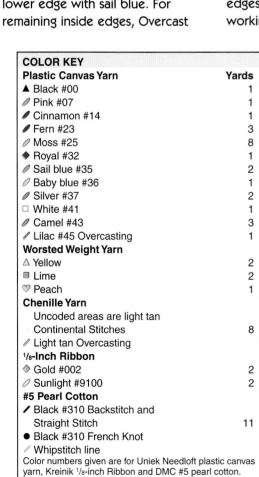

COLOR KEY	
Plastic Canvas Yarn	**Yards**
▲ Black #00	1
⬭ Pink #07	1
◢ Cinnamon #14	1
◢ Fern #23	3
⬭ Moss #25	8
◆ Royal #32	1
⬭ Sail blue #35	2
⬭ Baby blue #36	1
⬭ Silver #37	2
☐ White #41	1
⬭ Camel #43	3
◢ Lilac #45 Overcasting	1
Worsted Weight Yarn	
△ Yellow	2
■ Lime	2
♡ Peach	1
Chenille Yarn	
Uncoded areas are light tan	
Continental Stitches	8
◢ Light tan Overcasting	
⅛-Inch Ribbon	
◇ Gold #002	2
⬭ Sunlight #9100	2
#5 Pearl Cotton	
◢ Black #310 Backstitch and Straight Stitch	11
● Black #310 French Knot	
◢ Whipstitch line	
Color numbers given are for Uniek Needloft plastic canvas yarn, Kreinik ⅛-inch Ribbon and DMC #5 pearl cotton.	

Dresden Tea Bag Caddy

Design by Judy Collishaw

With just a few quick stitches on colored canvas, you can stitch up a dozen of these in a jiffy!

skill level • beginner

✱ materials ✱

- ☐ ½ sheet white 7-count plastic canvas
- ☐ 4¼-inch white Crafty Circle from Darice
- ☐ Worsted weight yarn as listed in color key
- ☐ #16 tapestry needle
- ☐ Safety pins (optional)
- ☐ Low-temperature glue gun

finished size:

2½ inches H x 4¼ inches in diameter

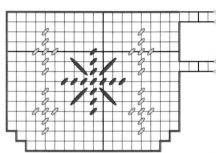

Teacup Front & Back
23 holes x 14 holes
Cut 2, reverse 1

instructions

1 Cut teacup pieces from white 7-count plastic canvas according to graph. Do not cut crafty circle, which is the saucer.

2 Stitch pieces following graphs, reversing teacup back before stitching.

3 Using blue through step 4, Overcast short edges of bottom and sides strip and top edges of teacup front and back, omitting handle edge. Overcast around outside edge of saucer.

4 With wrong sides facing, center bottom and sides strip along bottom edge of teacup front, then bring sides of strip up around sides of cup, using safety pins, if desired, to hold in place. Whipstitch together. Repeat with teacup back.

5 Glue stitches at bottom of teacup to center stitches on saucer. ☐

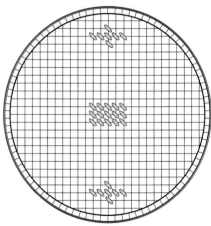

Teacup Saucer
Stitch 1

COLOR KEY	
Plastic Canvas Yarn	**Yards**
■ Blue	4
☐ Baby blue	2

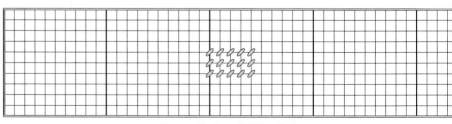

Teacup Bottom & Sides Strip
44 holes x 10 holes
Cut 1

Tulip Candle Ring

Design by Susan Leinberger

Dress up a large candle with this bright and cheery candle ring!

✖ materials ✖

- ❑ 1 sheet Uniek Quick-Count 7-count plastic canvas
- ❑ 5-inch Uniek plastic canvas hexagon
- ❑ Uniek Needloft plastic canvas yarn as listed in color key
- ❑ #16 tapestry needle

finished size:

3⅛ inches H x 5⅝ inches in diameter

skill level
beginner

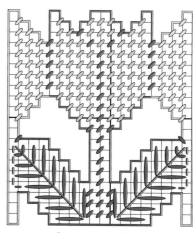

Candle Ring Tulips
18 holes x 20 holes
Cut 6

instructions

1 Cut and stitch six candle ring tulips according to graph.

2 Following graph throughout, Whipstitch tulips pieces together along side edges. Overcast all remaining edges except bottom edges.

3 Using Christmas green throughout, work Backstitches and Straight Stitches. Whipstitch bottom edges to plastic canvas hexagon, Overcasting edges of hexagon with no adjacent tulip pieces while Whipstitching. ❑

COLOR KEY

Plastic Canvas Yarn	Yards
■ Red #01	5
□ Christmas red #02	8
□ Lemon #20	4
■ Christmas green #28	12
□ Yellow #57	5
✎ Fern #23 Overcasting and Whipstitching	3
✎ Christmas green #28 Backstitch and Straight Stitch	

Color numbers given are for Uniek Needloft plastic canvas yarn.

Butterflies & Blooms Magnet

Design by Nancy Barrett

Tack notes to your refrigerator with this colorful magnet set that includes a large trellis magnet and four small flower magnets!

skill level • beginner

materials

- ❑ 1 sheet 10-count plastic canvas
- ❑ Worsted weight yarn as listed in color key
- ❑ #16 tapestry needle
- ❑ 4 (1-inch) and 3 (2-inch) pieces adhesive-backed magnets

finished size:

Trellis: 8¾ inches W x 7 inches H

Flower Magnets: 2 inches W x 1¾ inches H

Trellis Center Upright
4 holes x 71 holes
Cut 1

project notes

Refer to photo throughout. Separate yarn and complete all stitching using 2 plies unless instructed otherwise.

cutting & stitching

1 Cut plastic canvas according to graphs.

2 Stitch and Overcast eight small petals with bright purple as graphed and four with English rose. Stitch remaining pieces following graphs, working 12 large petals with bright purple as graphed and 12 with English rose.

3 Overcast all pieces with adjacent colors. Add black Backstitches at centers of butterflies, wrapping yarn over edges and securing yarn ends on wrong side by running them under several stitches.

assembly

1 Referring to Fig. 1 and using a single ply of off-white yarn throughout, assemble trellis uprights by tacking bottom ends of left and right pieces to wrong side of center at bottom. Tack trellis top, middle and bottom crosspieces in place, weaving them over and under uprights as shown.

2 Assemble large blooms using four matching petals and three leaves for each: Lay two petals tip to tip, then join across center tips with a 2-ply light pink or light lavender Straight Stitch. Without cutting yarn, join remaining petals to first two in same manner.

3 Attach three leaves between petals on wrong side of flower, tacking as needed on wrong side to hold flower together.

continued on page 31

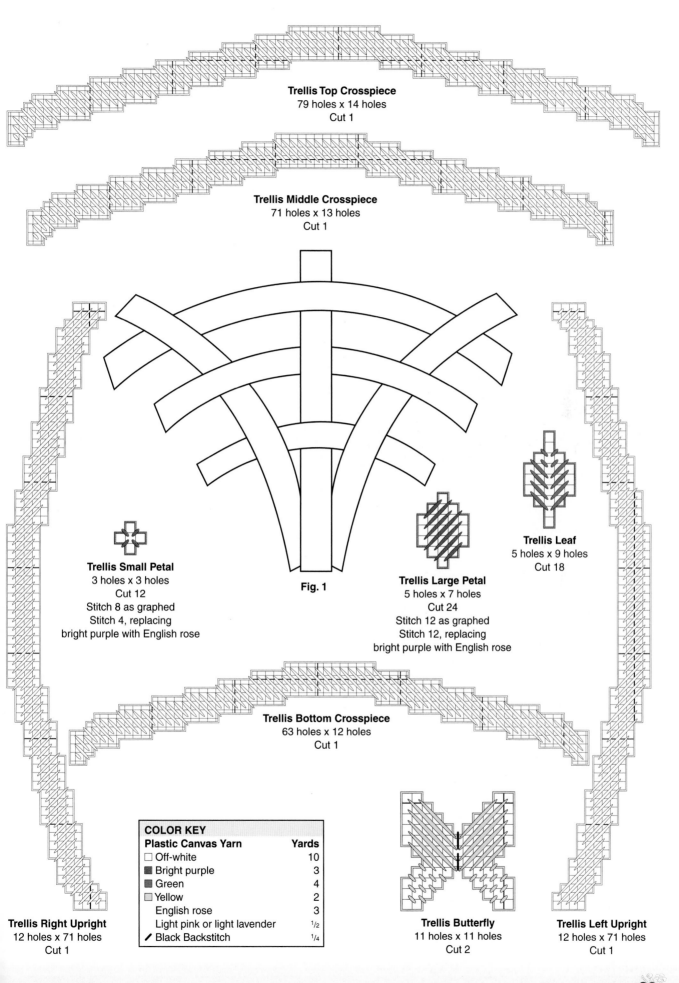

Trellis Top Crosspiece
79 holes x 14 holes
Cut 1

Trellis Middle Crosspiece
71 holes x 13 holes
Cut 1

Fig. 1

Trellis Leaf
5 holes x 9 holes
Cut 18

Trellis Small Petal
3 holes x 3 holes
Cut 12
Stitch 8 as graphed
Stitch 4, replacing
bright purple with English rose

Trellis Large Petal
5 holes x 7 holes
Cut 24
Stitch 12 as graphed
Stitch 12, replacing
bright purple with English rose

Trellis Bottom Crosspiece
63 holes x 12 holes
Cut 1

COLOR KEY	
Plastic Canvas Yarn	**Yards**
☐ Off-white	10
▨ Bright purple	3
▨ Green	4
☐ Yellow	2
English rose	3
Light pink or light lavender	1/2
✦ Black Backstitch	1/4

Trellis Right Upright
12 holes x 71 holes
Cut 1

Trellis Butterfly
11 holes x 11 holes
Cut 2

Trellis Left Upright
12 holes x 71 holes
Cut 1

Tulip Party Favor

Design by Lee Lindeman

Women's club members will be delighted
with this cheery table decoration and favor!

skill level • intermediate

materials

- ⅓ sheet 7-count plastic canvas
- Worsted weight yarn as listed in color key
- DMC 6-strand metallic embroi–dery floss as listed in color key
- #16 tapestry needle
- 10 inches ³⁄₁₆-inch-wide yellow satin ribbon
- 2-inch terra-cotta flowerpot
- Styrofoam plastic foam ball to fit in flowerpot
- 4 inches ⅛-inch dowel
- Green craft paint
- Paintbrush
- Craft knife
- Hot-glue gun

finished size:
2½ inches W x 5¼ inches H x 2¼ inches D

cutting & stitching

1 Cut plastic canvas according to graphs.

2 With craft knife, sharpen one end of dowel to a point. Paint dowel with green craft paint and paintbrush. Allow to dry.

3 Stitch pieces following graphs, reversing one of each leaf piece before stitching. Overcast base with green.

4 With a single strand (6 plies) gold embroidery floss, Overcast top edges of tulip pieces from dot to dot. With bright pink, Whipstitch wrong sides of tulip pieces together along one side. Glue unsharpened end of green dowel between center bottom of tulip pieces, then complete Whipstitching.

5 Using a single strand gold embroidery floss and matching edges, Whipstitch wrong sides of corresponding leaf pieces A and B together.

6 With a single strand gold embroidery floss, Whipstitch wrong sides of leaf C bottom together around side and bottom edges; Whipstitch wrong sides of leaf C top together around side and top

edges. Whipstitch remaining edges of leaf C top and bottom together with green.

7 Cut off approximately ⅓ of plastic foam ball; glue into pot with cut side facing up. Glue edges of base into pot over plastic foam ball. Insert sharpened end of dowel into center of base; glue to secure.

8 Using photo as a guide, glue leaves around stem and to base.

9 Tie yellow satin ribbon in a bow around top of pot; glue to secure. ❑

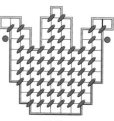

Tulip
11 holes x 10 holes
Cut 2

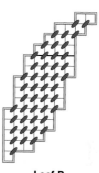

Leaf B
9 holes x 14 holes
Cut 2, reverse 1

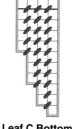

Leaf C Top
4 holes x 6 holes
Cut 2, reverse 1

Leaf C Bottom
4 holes x 11 holes
Cut 2, reverse 1

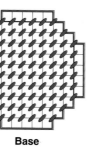

Base
11 holes x 11 holes
Cut 1

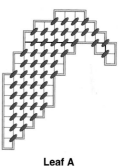

Leaf A
11 holes x 13 holes
Cut 2, reverse 1

COLOR KEY	
Worsted Weight Yarn	**Yards**
■ Bright pink	4
■ Green	8
6-Strand Metallic Embroidery Floss	
✎ Gold #5282 Overcasting and Whipstitching	8¾
Color number given is for DMC 6-strand metallic embroidery floss.	

Butterflies and Blooms Magnet continued from page 28

4 Assemble small blooms using four matching small petals: Lay two small petals tip to tip, then join across center tips with a 2-ply light pink or light lavender Straight Stitch. Without cutting yarn, join remaining flowers to first two in same manner, overlapping petals as needed.

5 Tack two butterflies, all small blooms and a large bloom of each color to trellis as shown. Peel backing from 2-inch magnet strips; press one to wrong side of each trellis upright.

6 For flower magnets, peel backing from 1-inch magnet strips and

press one to wrong side of each remaining large bloom. ❑

Baby Carriage Pins

Design by Ronda Bryce

Delight guests at a baby shower
with these easy-to-make party favors!

skill level • beginner

instructions

1 Cut plastic canvas according to graph, cutting away gray area on each circle.

2 Using cut-away pieces as templates, cut baby blue and baby pink felt.

3 Stitch pieces following graph, working one circle with sail blue and white as graphed; stitch remaining circle replacing sail blue with pink.

4 Overcast blue baby carriage with sail blue and pink baby carriage with pink.

5 Use photo as a guide throughout assembly. Using sewing needle and matching thread through step 9, stitch corresponding lace to backside along vertical edge of each carriage, folding raw edges under.

6 Stitch white buttons to bottom of carriages, then sew corresponding roses to middle of buttons. Attach remaining rose to center of each carriage.

7 Stitch felt to backside of carriage, allowing felt edge to extend above horizontal edge of carriage.

8 Stitch pearls to carriages where indicated on graphs. Sew pin back to backside of each carriage. ❏

✖ materials ✖

Each Pin
- ❏ 3-inch plastic canvas radial circle by Uniek
- ❏ Uniek Needloft plastic canvas yarn as listed in color key
- ❏ #16 tapestry needle
- ❏ 16 (4mm) white pearl beads
- ❏ Sewing needle
- ❏ 1-inch gold pin back
- ❏ 2 (⅞-inch) white pearl buttons

Blue Baby Carriage
- ❏ 3 (½-inch-wide) light blue ribbon roses with leaves
- ❏ 2 inches ¾-inch-wide light blue ruffled lace
- ❏ Small amount baby blue felt
- ❏ Light blue sewing thread

Pink Baby Carriage
- ❏ 3 (½-inch-wide) light pink ribbon roses with leaves
- ❏ 2 inches ⅜-inch-wide light pink ruffled lace
- ❏ Small amount baby pink felt
- ❏ Light pink sewing thread

finished size:
3 inches W x 3⅛ inches H

COLOR KEY

Plastic Canvas Yarn	Yards
Pink #07	3
■ Sail blue #35	3
☐ White #41	3
○ Attach pearl bead	

Color numbers given are for Uniek Needloft plastic canvas yarn.

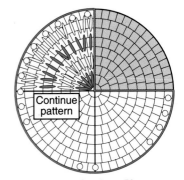

Baby Carriage Pin
Cut 2
Cut away gray area
Stitch 1 as graphed
Stitch 1, replacing
sail blue with pink

Teddy Bear Plant Poke

Design by Cera Thacker

This sweet teddy bear is just right for dressing up a lush, green plant!

skill level • beginner

instructions

1 Cut three flowers from plastic canvas according to graph.

2 Stitch pieces following graph, working one flower with pink as graphed, one with lemon and one with sail blue. Overcast with adjacent colors.

3 Paint terra-cotta flowerpot with pink craft paint. Allow to dry.

4 Cut two 1½-inch lengths and one 2-inch length from stem wire. Glue one topaz stone to center of each flower, then glue one flower to each length stem wire.

5 Cut two 1½–inch lengths and one 1–inch length from thin wire. Glue one heart-shaped stone to each length thin wire.

6 Glue plastic foam scraps in painted flowerpot. Glue Spanish moss in place over plastic foam. Insert flowers and hearts in pot.

7 Insert bamboo skewer into bottom of bear, cutting a small hole if necessary; glue to secure.

8 Glue flowerpot in bear's lap and to one arm. ❑

COLOR KEY	
Plastic Canvas Yarn	**Yards**
▦ Pink #07	1
Lemon #20	1
Sail blue #35	1
Color numbers given are for Uniek Needloft plastic canvas yarn.	

Plant Poke Flower
4 holes x 4 holes
Cut 3
Stitch 1 as graphed,
1 with lemon and
1 with sail blue

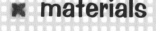

✖ materials ✖

- ❑ Small amount 7-count plastic canvas
- ❑ Uniek Needloft plastic canvas yarn as listed in color key
- ❑ #16 tapestry needle
- ❑ 3 (10mm x 11mm) heart-shaped faceted stones: crystal, pink and dark sapphire
- ❑ 3 (5mm) topaz round faceted stones
- ❑ 4-inch jointed bear
- ❑ 9 inches bamboo skewer or ⅛-inch dowel
- ❑ 5 inches 20-gauge green covered stem wire
- ❑ 4 inches thin wire
- ❑ 1-inch terra-cotta flowerpot
- ❑ Pink craft paint
- ❑ Paintbrush
- ❑ Spanish moss
- ❑ Scraps Styrofoam plastic foam
- ❑ Hot-glue gun

finished size:

Flower: ⅝ inches W x ⅝ inches H

Completed Plant Poke: 2½ inches W x 11¼ inches H

Miniature Teddy Bear Ornaments

Design by Cera Thacker

Celebrate the arrival of the newest family member with this charming pair of ornaments!

✖ materials ✖

Each Ornament
- ¼ sheet 10-count plastic canvas
- 6-strand embroidery floss as listed in color key
- #20 tapestry needle
- White-and-black alphabet beads
- 8 (4mm) beads in coordinating color
- Gold lamé thread
- ¾-inch pink satin bow
- Hot-glue gun

Crib
- 1-inch sitting or standing teddy bear
- 6 (⅜-inch) ribbon roses: 3 light blue and 3 burgundy

High Chair
- 1-inch sitting teddy bear
- ¼-inch white button
- 7 green seed beads

finished size:

Crib: 1 inch W x 1½ inches L x 1⅜ inches H, excluding beads and hanger

High Chair: 1 inch W x 1¾ inches H x 1 inch D, excluding beads and hanger

skill level • intermediate

crib

1 Cut plastic canvas according to graphs.

2 Using pink for all stitching, Continental Stitch pieces following graphs, leaving blue Whipstitch lines unworked at this time.

3 Whipstitch headboard to sides and canopy, easing around curve. Whipstitch footboard in place.

4 Whipstitch bottom to sides, headboard and footboard where indicated with blue Whipstitch line.

5 Using photo as a guide through step 7, glue teddy bear in crib. Alternating colors, glue ribbon roses to canopy; glue bow to footboard.

6 For hanger, cut desired length of gold lamé thread and attach one end to center top edge of footboard and tie off. Repeat with remaining end, threading through center top of canopy and headboard.

7 Thread a length of gold lamé thread with alphabet beads, spelling desired name. Thread four coordinating round beads on both sides of name, then attach ends to center bottom edges of headboard and footboard.

high chair

1 Cut plastic canvas according to graphs.

2 Using blue for all stitching, Continental Stitch and Overcast all but the Whipstitch edges indicated on tray sides.

3 Stitch all remaining pieces, leaving pink and yellow Whipstitch lines unworked at this time.

4 Beginning with legs, Whipstitch wrong sides of chair sides to right side of chair back. With wrong sides facing, Whipstitch chair front to chair sides.

5 Whipstitch chair seat to sides, front and back where indicated with yellow line.

6 Whipstitch tray to sides where indicated with pink line. Overcast all remaining edges.

7 Using photo as a guide, glue bear in seat and bow to chair front. Glue button to crib tray for dish, then green seed beads to button for peas.

8 Thread a length of gold lamé thread with alphabet beads, spelling desired name. Thread four coordinating round beads on both sides of name, then attach ends to bottom of seat at chair sides.

9 For hanger, thread desired length of gold lamé thread through top of piece. Tie ends in a knot to form a loop for hanging. ❑

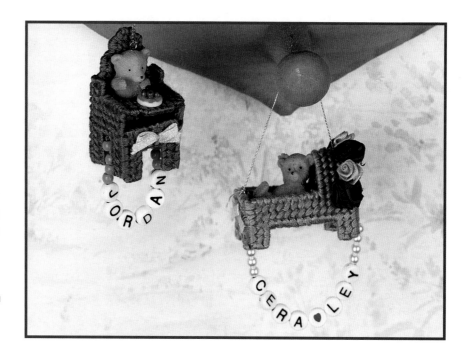

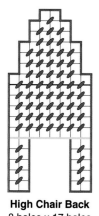

High Chair Back
8 holes x 17 holes
Cut 1

High Chair Seat
8 holes x 7 holes
Cut 1

High Chair Tray
8 holes x 7 holes
Cut 1

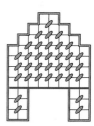

Crib Headboard
8 holes x 10 holes

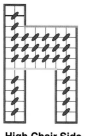

High Chair Side
7 holes x 11 holes
Cut 2, reverse 1

High Chair Front
8 holes x 6 holes
Cut 1

Crib Footboard
8 holes x 6 holes
Cut 1

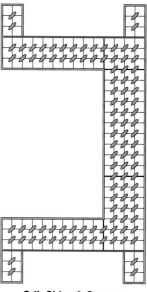

Crib Sides & Canopy
14 holes x 26 holes
Cut 1

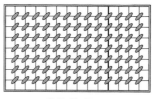

Crib Bottom
14 holes x 8 holes
Cut 1

COLOR KEY	
6-Strand Embroidery Floss	**Yards**
▦ Pink	9
▦ Blue	8
╱ Whipstitch to crib bottom	
╱ Whipstitch to seat	
╱ Whipstitch tray to chair	

Craft Room Accents

Designs by Judy Collishaw

Dress up your craft room with a pair of plant pokes and a pincushion sachet!

skill level • beginner

✵ materials ✵

- 1 sheet 7-count plastic canvas
- Worsted weight yarn as listed in color key
- #16 tapestry needle
- 18 inches ⅛-inch-wide dark green double-sided satin ribbon
- 6-inch square white tulle
- Sewing needle or sewing machine
- White sewing thread
- 2 tablespoons potpourri
- 2 (12-inch lengths) ³⁄₁₆-inch wooden dowels
- Low-temperature glue gun

finished size:

Sachet: 6¼ inches W x 3½ inches H

Scissors Motif for Plant Poke: 2⅜ inches W x 3½ inches H

Thread Spools Motif for Plant Poke: 1⅞ inches W x 3¾ inches H

sachet

pincushion

1 Cut two pincushion pieces from plastic canvas according to graph.

2 Stitch pieces following graph, working uncoded areas with scarlet Continental Stitches.

3 Separate black yarn, then work Straight Stitches with 2 plies. Work French knots with 4 plies white yarn, wrapping yarn around needle two times.

4 Overcast around top edges with sage green following graph. Whipstitch wrong sides together along remaining edges with scarlet.

5 Fold tulle in half. With sewing needle or sewing machine and white sewing thread, stitch a ½-inch seam along 6-inch side opposite fold and across 3-inch bottom, forming a pouch.

6 Trim seam; turn pouch inside out and fill with potpourri. Cut a 9-inch length of dark green satin

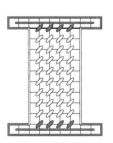

Thread Spool
9 holes x 11 holes
Cut 1 for sachet
Stitch as graphed
Cut 2 for plant poke
Stitch 1 as graphed
Stitch 1, replacing white with royal blue

Cut out

Scissors Blade
6 holes x 23 holes
Cut 2, reverse 1, for sachet
Cut 2, reverse 1, for plant poke

ribbon and tie in a bow around top of pouch. Insert pouch inside pincushion.

7 Glue ends of remaining ribbon inside pincushion to form hanger.

scissors & thread spool

1 Cut two scissors blades and one thread spool from plastic canvas according to graphs.

2 Stitch and Overcast scissors following graphs, reversing one scissors blade before stitching. Place one blade over the other and secure through both layers with gray French Knot where indicated on graph. Lightly glue between blades to hold in position.

3 Stitch and Overcast spool following graph. Work tan Straight Stitches on spool, then wrap white yarn around white

area of spool in straight lines to resemble thread, tucking end of yarn in under wrapping on back of spool. *Note: Do not wrap too tightly or plastic canvas will bend.*

4 Using photo as a guide, glue spool to back left side of pincushion and scissors to right front side.

plant pokes

instructions

1 Cut two scissors blades and two thread spools from plastic canvas accord ing to graphs.

2 Stitch and assemble scissors following step 2 of scissors and thread spool in sachet instructions.

3 Stitch thread spools following step 3 of scissors and thread spool in sachet instructions, working one spool with white as graphed and one replacing white with royal blue.

4 Using photo as a guide, glue scissors to top of one dowel. Glue spools at opposite angles to top of remaining dowel. ❑

COLOR KEY
PLANT POKE

Plastic Canvas Yarn	Yards
☐ Yellow	3
☐ White	2
■ Tan	2
Royal blue	2
✏ Gray Overcasting	1
✏ Tan Straight Stitch	
● Gray French Knot	

COLOR KEY
SACHET

Plastic Canvas Yarn	Yards
■ Sage green	3
☐ Yellow	3
☐ White	2
■ Tan	1
Uncoded areas are scarlet Continental Stitches	
✏ Scarlet Whipstitching	5
✏ Gray Overcasting	
✏ Sage green Straight Stitch	1
✏ Tan Straight Stitch	
✏ Black Straight Stitch	
○ White French Knot	1
● Gray French Knot	

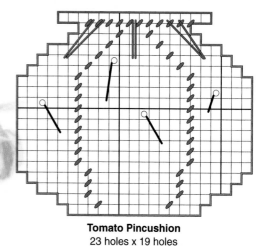

Tomato Pincushion
23 holes x 19 holes
Cut 2

Road Royalty Key Chains

Design by Susan Leinberger

With this pair of jeweled key chains,
there will be no doubt about
who is king (or queen) of the road!

skill level • beginner

✖ materials ✖

- ❑ 1 sheet Uniek Quick-Count 7-count plastic canvas
- ❑ Uniek Needloft plastic canvas yarn as listed in color key
- ❑ Kreinik ⅛-inch Ribbon as listed in color key
- ❑ #16 tapestry needle
- ❑ 6mm x 8mm octagon faceted acrylic jewels #7460 from Westrim Crafts:
  - 2 red #8
  - 2 aqua #18
  - 3 amethyst #612
  - 3 emerald #616
- ❑ 2 (32mm) silver split key rings
- ❑ Tacky craft glue

finished size:

2¾ inches W x 3⅛ inches H, excluding key ring

instructions

1 Cut plastic canvas according to graphs.

2 Stitch pieces following graphs, working uncoded areas with white Continental Stitches. Overcast inside edges with white.

3 When background stitching is completed, work embroidery with ⅛-inch ribbon, keeping ribbon smooth and flat.

4 Whipstitch wrong sides of corresponding fronts and backs together following graphs.

5 Glue aqua and emerald jewels evenly spaced to top part of dad's crown. Glue red and amethyst jewels evenly spaced to top part of mom's crown.

6 Insert silver key rings into holes at top of each assembled piece. ❑

COLOR KEY
DAD
Plastic Canvas Yarn	Yards
Uncoded areas are white #41 Continental Stitches	9
⬦ White #41 Overcasting	
✦ Dark royal #48 Whipstitching	2
⅛-Inch Ribbon	
■ Gold #002	2
✦ Gold #002 Backstitch and Straight Stitch	
✦ Royal blue #033 Backstitch	3
✦ Silver night #393 Backstitch	1

Color numbers given are for Uniek Needloft plastic canvas yarn and Kreinik ⅛-inch Ribbon

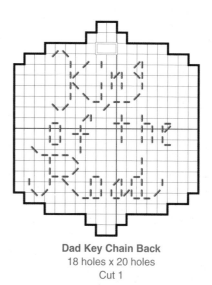

Dad Key Chain Back
18 holes x 20 holes
Cut 1

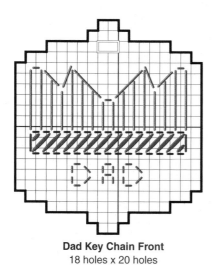

Dad Key Chain Front
18 holes x 20 holes
Cut 1

COLOR KEY
MOM
Plastic Canvas Yarn	Yards
Uncoded areas are white #41 Continental Stitches	9
⬦ White #41 Overcasting	
✦ Red #01 Whipstitching	2
⅛-Inch Ribbon	
■ Gold #002	2
✦ Gold #002 Backstitch and Straight Stitch	
✦ Red #003 Backstitch	3
✦ Flame #203 Backstitch	1

Color numbers given are for Uniek Needloft plastic canvas yarn and Kreinik ⅛-inch Ribbon

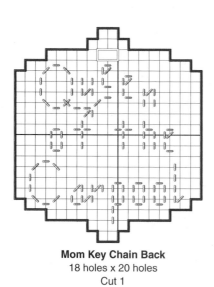

Mom Key Chain Back
18 holes x 20 holes
Cut 1

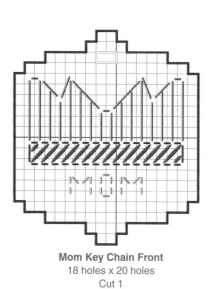

Mom Key Chain Front
18 holes x 20 holes
Cut 1

Pansy Button Bookmark

Design by Carol Krob

Select your favorite shades of ribbon
with coordinating buttons,
then stitch pretty bookmarks for Mom,
Sis and Grandma!

skill level • beginner

✖ materials ✖

- ❑ Small amount 10-count plastic canvas
- ❑ Kreinik ⅛-inch Ribbon as listed in color key
- ❑ Anchor #3 pearl cotton from Coats & Clark as listed in color key
- ❑ #22 tapestry needle
- ❑ 3 lavender pansy buttons #86048 from Mill Hill Products/Gay Bowles Sales Inc.
- ❑ Hot-glue gun

finished size:
1¾ inches W x 7 inches H

instructions

1 Cut plastic canvas according to graph.

2 Stitch vase with ⅛-inch ribbon, working uncod–ed areas with pearl ribbon Continental Stitches. To prevent ribbon from twisting and tangling, guide it between thumb and forefinger of free hand.

3 Using light baby pink pearl cotton, fill in back-ground with Slanting Gobelin Stitches; Overcast edges.

4 Using photo as a guide, sew or glue buttons to bookmark at top of stem. ❑

COLOR KEY	
⅛-Inch Ribbon	**Yards**
■ Green #008	1
☐ Pearl #032	2
▨ Star pink #092	2
■ Star mauve #093	2
Uncoded areas are pearl #032 Continental Stitches	
#3 Pearl Cotton	
☐ Light baby pink #73	5
Color numbers given are for Kreinik 1/8-inch Ribbon and Coats & Clark Anchor #3 pearl cotton.	

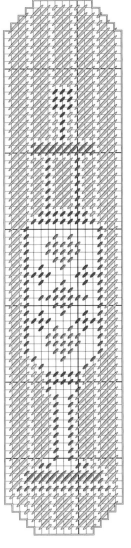

Bookmark
16 holes x 70 holes
Cut 1

Cottage Note Holder

Design by Janelle Giese

Stitch a dozen of these pretty cottage note holders and watch them sell like hotcakes at your local bazaar!

skill level • intermediate

Cottage
30 holes x 37 holes
Cut 1

instructions

1 Cut cottage from plastic canvas according to graph.

2 Stitch piece following graph, working vertical stitches at top of chimney with two stitches per hole where indicated. **Note:** *Notepad opening and bar below it are left unstitched.*

3 Overcast chimney with peach, roof with straw and cottage with pink. When stitching and Overcasting are completed, work pearl cotton embroidery first, then work yarn embroidery.

4 Glue magnet strips to back and insert notepad into slot. ❏

✖ materials ✖

- ❏ ¼ sheet 7-count plastic canvas
- ❏ Worsted weight yarn as listed in color key
- ❏ DMC #8 pearl cotton as listed in color key
- ❏ #16 tapestry needle
- ❏ 2 (3–inch) lengths ½–inch–wide magnet strip
- ❏ 3-inch x 5-inch notepad
- ❏ Thick white glue

finished size:

4⅝ inches W x 5⅝ inches H, excluding notepad

COLOR KEY	
Worsted Weight Yarn	**Yards**
☐ Baby yellow	5
☐ Baby pink	4
▨ Pink	2
☐ Yellow	2
☐ Baby blue	2
☐ White	2
▨ Peach	2
╱ Chartreuse Straight Stitch	1
╱ Pink Straight Stitch	
● Pink French Knot	
● Peach French Knot	
#8 Pearl Cotton	
╱ Black #310 Backstitch and Straight Stitch	11
Color number given is for DMC #8 pearl cotton.	

Sunbonnet Sweethearts Door Chime

Design by Janelle Giese

Overall Bill and Sunbonnet Sue will dress up your door
with a sweet, romantic touch!

skill level • intermediate

instructions

1 Cut plastic canvas according to graph.

2 Stitch and Overcast piece following graph, then work black pearl cotton Backstitches.

3 Using a double strand of invisible thread, attach wind chimes to five bottom points of stitched motif, allowing 1 inch between chimes and motif.

4 For hanger, attach jump rings to ends of chain and to top of motif as shown in photo. ❑

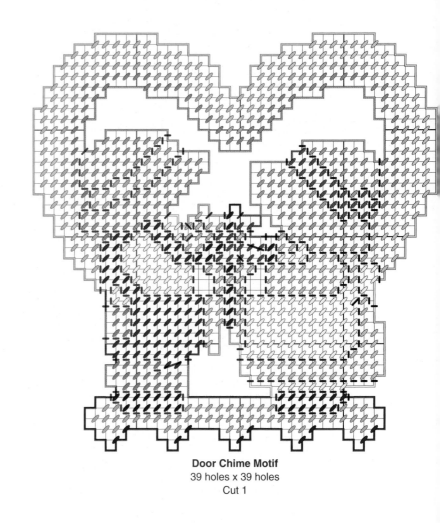

Door Chime Motif
39 holes x 39 holes
Cut 1

COLOR KEY	
Plastic Canvas Yarn	**Yards**
▨ Pink #07	5
■ Cinnamon #14	1
▨ Sail blue #35	3
☐ Eggshell #39	3
▨ Beige #40	4
▨ Lilac #45	1
▨ Yellow #57	2
Worsted Weight Yarn	
▨ Lime	2
■ Parrot green	2
■ Dark country blue	2
Uncoded areas are flesh tone Continental Stitches	1
#5 Pearl Cotton	
✔ Black #310 Backstitch	6
Color numbers given are for Uniek Needloft plastic canvas yarn and DMC #5 pearl cotton.	

✖ materials ✖

❑ ¼ sheet 7-count plastic canvas

❑ Uniek Needloft plastic canvas yarn as listed in color key

❑ Worsted weight yarn as listed in color key

❑ DMC #5 pearl cotton as listed in color key

❑ #16 tapestry needle

❑ 5 (6mm) gold-tone wind chimes

❑ 2 (7mm) gold jump rings

❑ 6½-inch length gold chain

❑ Invisible thread

finished size:

Motif: 6 inches W x 5⅞ inches H

Completed Chime: 6 inches W x 13⅛ inches H

Daisy Pincushion

Design by Terry Ricioli

Quick-to-stitch petals with a soft, felt center
make this pretty and practical project a snap to make!

skill level • intermediate

✖ materials ✖

- ½ sheet 7-count plastic canvas
- 3-inch plastic canvas radial circle by Darice
- Uniek Needloft plastic canvas yarn as listed in color key
- #16 tapestry needle
- 1 sheet yellow felt
- Small amount polyester fiberfill
- Sewing needle and yellow sewing thread
- Hot-glue gun

finished size:

2 inches H x 7⅛ inches in diameter

instructions

1 Cut and stitch plastic canvas according to graph.

2 Overcast petals around side and top edges from dot to dot with white.

3 Whipstitch bottom edges of petals to 3-inch plastic canvas radial circle, overlapping as necessary so there are five petals in each quarter circle.

4 For pincushion flower center, cut a 6-inch circle from yellow felt. Sew a running stitch with sewing needle and yellow sewing thread ¼ inch from edge. Stuffing with fiberfill, pull ends to gather so center will fit over plastic canvas radial circle. Knot ends and glue in place. ❑

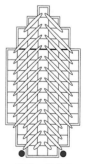

Daisy Petal
7 holes x 14 holes
Cut 20

COLOR KEY	
Plastic Canvas Yarn	**Yards**
☐ White #41	40
Color number given is for Uniek Needloft plastic canvas yarn.	

God Bless Card

Design by Alida Macor

skill level
beginner

✖ materials ✖

- ❑ ⅓ sheet 10-count plastic canvas
- ❑ DMC #3 pearl cotton as listed in color key
- ❑ Trifold needlework card with 3½-inch x 2½-inch heart-shaped opening from Yarn Tree Designs Inc.
- ❑ Matching envelope
- ❑ Craft glue or glue stick

finished size

Stitched Motif: 4¼ inches W x 3 inches H

Completed Card: 5½ inches W x 3¾ inches H

Instructions

1 Cut and stitch plastic canvas according to graph. Overcast edges with very light peach.

2 Glue stitched heart inside card so design is centered in heart-shaped opening. Allow to dry.

3 Glue entire backside of heart to flap adjacent to bottom of heart. Insert in envelope. ❑

Share the blessing of spring with this special, hand-stitched card.

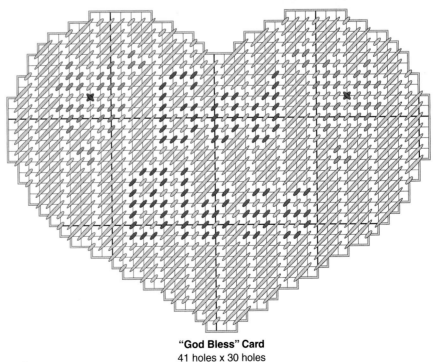

"God Bless" Card
41 holes x 30 holes
Cut 1

COLOR KEY	
#3 Pearl Cotton	**Yards**
■ Very dark lavender #208	3
■ Light lavender #211	2
■ Medium terra cotta #356	1
■ Chartreuse #703	1
☐ Very light peach #948	9
Color numbers given are for DMC #3 pearl cotton.	

Ewes Special Eyeglasses Case

Design by Judy Collishaw

Make a young girl who wears eyeglasses feel special with this cute eyeglasses case!

skill level • beginner

✻ materials ✻

- ❏ 1 sheet 7-count plastic canvas
- ❏ Worsted weight yarn as listed in color key
- ❏ #5 pearl cotton as listed in color key
- ❏ #8 pearl cotton as listed in color key
- ❏ #16 tapestry needle
- ❏ Low-temperature glue gun

finished size:

4⅛ inches W x 7⅛ inches H

instructions

1 Cut plastic canvas according to graphs.

2 Overcast flowers with burgundy, but do not work yellow French Knots at this time.

3 Stitch case pieces and lambs' heads following graphs, making white Turkey Loop Stitches approximately ⅝ inches long. Work uncoded areas on case front and back with mint Continental Stitches and uncoded background on lambs' heads with black Continental Stitches.

4 Overcast lambs' heads with black and white following graph. When Overcasting is completed, Straight Stitch nose with rose #5 pearl cotton; work Backstitches and

French Knots for eyes with royal blue #8 pearl cotton.

5 Work stems and letters on case front and back with forest Backstitches and Straight Stitches. Attach burgundy flowers where indicated with a yellow French Knot.

6 Using mint throughout, Overcast top edges of case front and back. Whipstitch wrong sides together around side and bottom edges.

7 Using photo as a guide, glue heads to tops of lambs' bodies at a slight angle. ❏

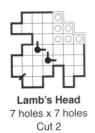

Lamb's Head
7 holes x 7 holes
Cut 2

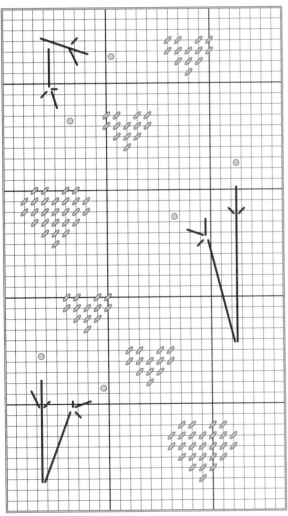

Eyeglasses Case Flower
3 holes x 3 holes
Cut 8

Eyeglasses Case Back
27 holes x 47 holes
Cut 1

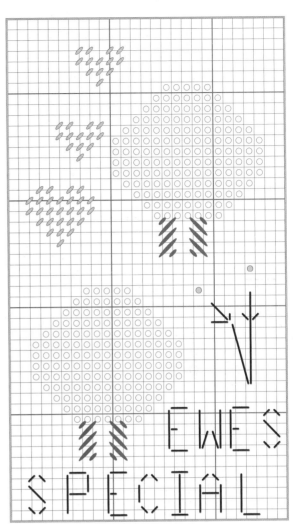

Eyeglasses Case Front
27 holes x 47 holes
Cut 1

COLOR KEY	
Plastic Canvas Yarn	**Yards**
◻ Rose	3
◼ Black	3
Uncoded areas on case are mint Continental Stitches	28
Uncoded areas on lambs' heads are black Continental Stitches	
╱ Mint Overcasting and Whipstitching	
╱ Burgundy Overcasting	3
╱ Forest Backstitch and Straight Stitch	2
○ White Turkey Loop Stitch	26
● Yellow French Knot	1
#5 Pearl Cotton	
╱ Rose Straight Stitch	1
#8 Pearl Cotton	
╱ Royal blue Backstitch	1
● Royal blue French Knot	

Bee & Butterfly Suncatchers

Design by Christina Laws

Hang these flying critters in a sunny window and watch them sparkle!

skill level • intermediate

materials

- ❑ 1 sheet clear 7-count plastic canvas
- ❑ Small amount black 7-count plastic canvas
- ❑ Plastic canvas yarn as listed in color key
- ❑ #16 tapestry needle
- ❑ 4 (10mm) movable eyes
- ❑ 4 (8mm) yellow faceted beads
- ❑ 10 (8mm) clear faceted beads
- ❑ Yellow and white sewing thread
- ❑ Hot-glue gun

finished size:

Butterfly: 6¾ inches W x 5¼ inches H, excluding hanger

Bee: 4⅞ inches W x 4¾ inches H, excluding hanger

instructions

1 Cut two butterflies and two bees from clear plastic canvas; cut four antennae from black plastic canvas according to graphs, cutting away blue lines on antennae.

2 Antennae will remain unstitched. Stitch butterfly and bee fronts following graphs.

3 On butterfly back, work head and body with black Reverse Continental Stitches; work wings as graphed. On bee back, work head and body with yellow and black Continental Stitches; work wings as graphed.

4 When background stitching is completed, Backstitch mouths on head fronts only. ❑

5 Whipstitch wrong sides of corresponding pieces together along inside and outside edges following graphs, leaving top edges on heads from blue dot to blue dot unworked at this time.

6 Using photo as a guide through step 7, lightly glue antennae between fronts and backs at top corners of heads, then com-

plete Whipstitching, working around antennae. Glue on eyes.

7 Using yellow thread, attach yellow beads to openings in bee body. Using white thread, attach clear beads to openings in butterfly wings.

8 For hangers, thread desired

length of white thread from back to front through holes indicated at top of heads; tie ends in a knot to form a loop. ❑

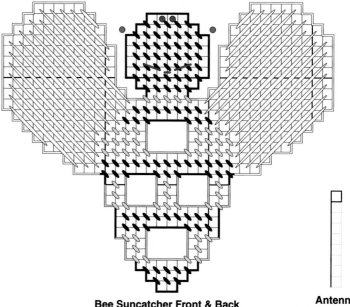

Bee Suncatcher Front & Back
32 holes x 27 holes
Cut 2 from clear
Stitch front as graphed
Stitch head and body on back
with yellow and black
Continental Stitches

Antenna
1 holes x 9 holes
Cut 4 from black,
cutting away blue lines
Do not stitch

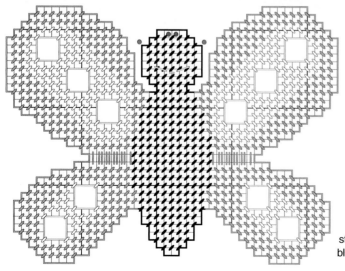

COLOR KEY

Plastic Canvas Yarn	Yards
☐ White	14
▨ Bright pink	12
■ Black	11
☐ Yellow	5
✐ Red Backstitch	1
⬭ White Backstitch	
✐ Bright pink Straight Stitch	
● Attach hanger	

Butterfly Suncatcher
Front & Back
44 holes x 33 holes
Cut 2 from clear
stitch front as graphed
stitch head and body on back with
black Reverse Continental Stitches

CHAPTER TWO

Summer Stitching

Catch the stitching bug
with easy and fun projects!

Capture all the fun, color and relaxation of summertime with this collection of more than two dozen fun-to-stitch projects! From rainbows and watermelons, to light-houses and flowers, this chapter of delightful projects will remind you of everything you love about summer!

Friendly Finger Puppets

Designs by Lee Lindeman

Spark your child's imagination with this set of three **delightful** animal finger puppets!

skill level • intermediate

lion
✖ materials ✖

- ½ sheet 7-count plastic canvas
- Worsted weight yarn as listed in color key
- #3 pearl cotton as listed in color key
- #16 tapestry needle
- 12mm triangular black animal nose
- 2 (5 mm) round black cabochons
- Small red bow tie button or ribbon bow
- Small amount polyester fiberfill
- Hot-glue gun

finished size:

3½ inches W x 4¾ inches H, excluding tail

cutting & stitching

1 Cut plastic canvas according to graphs.

2 Stitch pieces following graphs, working head back, body back and outside arms entirely with tan Continental Stitches. Add ⅝-inch loop for ears where indicated on head front.

3 Work black pearl cotton Backstitches on head front. Glue cabochons to head for eyes where indicated on graph. Glue nose to head as in photo.

4 Using tan, Overcast top edges on body front and back from dot to dot; Overcast bottom edges.

assembly

1 Using tan through step 2, Whipstitch wrong sides of body front and back together along side edges.

2 Whipstitch wrong sides of head front and back together, stuffing with a small amount of fiberfill before closing. Whipstitch wrong sides of corresponding arm pieces together.

3 For tail, cut a 36-inch length of tan yarn. Tie ends together in a knot, forming a large circle. Loop circle over index fingers of both hands. Twist fingers in opposite directions, twisting cord until it begins to loop back on itself.

4 Place both loops on one index finger, folding yarn in half; allow halves to twist around each other. Knot about 3½ inches from fold. Trim excess, leaving enough to fringe cut ends. Center and glue folded end to body back, ½ inch from bottom edge.

5 For bottom fringe, cut 24 (6-inch) lengths of tan yarn. Thread yarn through holes indicated at bottom of body pieces. Tie each in a knot and fringe; evenly trim.

6 Repeat procedure for mane, using two strands in each hole.

7 Glue neck on head into neck opening on body. Glue arms to shoulders.

8 Glue bow tie button or ribbon bow to center top of body front.

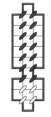

Lion Right Arm
3 holes x 10 holes
Cut 2
Stitch inside arm as graphed
Stitch outside arm entirely
with tan Continental Stitches

COLOR KEY	
LION	
Worsted Weight Yarn	**Yards**
■ Tan	15
☐ Natural	2
■ Bright pink	1
#3 Pearl Cotton	
✒ Black Backstitch	½
● Attach cabochon	
○ Attach yarn for mane and fringe	

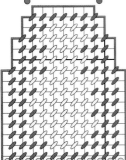

Lion Body Front & Back
12 holes x 15 holes
Cut 2
Stitch front as graphed
Stitch back entirely with
tan Continental Stitches

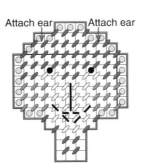

Attach ear   Attach ear

Lion Head Front & Back
11 holes x 13 holes
Cut 2
Stitch front as graphed
Stitch back entirely with
tan Continental Stitches

Lion Left Arm
7 holes x 8 holes
Cut 2, reverse 1
Stitch inside arm as graphed
Reverse outside arm
and stitch entirely with tan
Continental Stitches

tiger
✖ materials ✖

- ½ sheet 7-count plastic canvas
- Worsted weight yarn as listed in color key
- #3 pearl cotton as listed in color key
- #16 tapestry needle
- 12mm triangular black animal nose
- 2 (6mm) round black cabochons
- Small amount white craft fur
- Small amount polyester fiberfill
- Hot-glue gun

finished size:
2¾ inches W x 4¼ inches H, excluding tail

cutting & stitching

1 Cut plastic canvas according to graphs.

2 Stitch pieces following graphs, working uncoded areas with orange Continental Stitches.

3 Work black pearl cotton Backstitches on head front. Glue cabochons to head for eyes where indicated on graph. Glue nose to head as in photo.

4 Using orange, Overcast top edges on body front and back from dot to dot; Overcast bottom edges.

assembly

1 Use photo as a guide throughout assembly. Using orange through step 2, Whipstitch wrong sides of body front and back together along side edges.

2 Whipstitch wrong sides of head front and back together, stuffing with a small amount of fiberfill before closing. Whipstitch wrong sides of corresponding arm pieces together. For each ear, Whipstitch wrong sides of one front and one back together.

3 For tail, cut a 36-inch length of orange yarn. Tie ends together in a knot, forming a large circle. Loop circle over index fingers of both hands. Twist fingers in opposite directions, twisting cord until it begins to loop back on itself.

4 Place both loops on one index finger, folding yarn in half; allow halves to twist around each other. Wrap black yarn around twisted tail then knot orange and black tail about 4¾ inches from fold. Trim excess, leaving enough to fringe cut ends.

5 Center and glue folded end to body back ¼ inch from bottom edge, placing black yarn under fold.

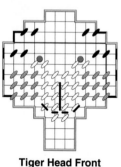

Tiger Head Front
11 holes x 13 holes
Cut 1

Tiger Ear Front & Back
3 holes x 2 holes
Cut 4
Stitch 2 front pieces as graphed
Stitch 2 back pieces, replacing white with orange

Tiger Left Outside Arm
3 holes x 10 holes
Cut 1

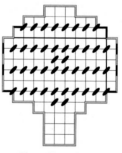

Tiger Head Back
11 holes x 13 holes
Cut 1

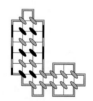

Tiger Right Outside Arm
7 holes x 8 holes
Cut 1

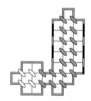

Tiger Right Inside Arm
7 holes x 8 holes
Cut 1

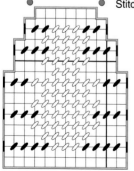

Tiger Body Front
12 holes x 15 holes
Cut 1

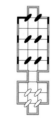

Tiger Left Inside Arm
3 holes x 10 holes
Cut 1

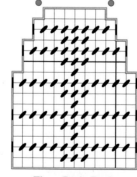

Tiger Body Back
12 holes x 15 holes
Cut 1

COLOR KEY	
TIGER	
Worsted Weight Yarn	**Yards**
■ Orange	9
■ Black	7
■ Bright pink	1
Uncoded areas are orange Continental Stitches	
#3 Pearl Cotton	
╱ Black Backstitch	½
● Attach cabochon	

6 Glue neck on head into neck opening on body. Glue ears to top corners on head. Glue arms to shoulders.

7 Cut a 2½ inch strip of fur and glue around neck. Glue a small tuft of fur to center top of head. Glue a short strip around tuft on tail. Trim fur as necessary.

elephant ✖ materials ✖

- ❑ ½ sheet 7-count plastic canvas
- ❑ Worsted weight yarn as listed in color key
- ❑ #16 tapestry needle
- ❑ 2 (3 mm) round black beads
- ❑ ⅝-inch gold star button
- ❑ Small amount white craft foam
- ❑ Small amount felt: gray and red
- ❑ Pinking shears
- ❑ Small amount polyester fiberfill
- ❑ Hot-glue gun

finished size:
3¼ inches W x 5⅝ inches H, excluding tail

cutting & stitching

1 Cut plastic canvas according to graphs.

2 Using patterns given, cut two tusks from white craft foam, two ears from gray felt and one hat from red felt, cutting rounded edge of hat with pinking shears.

3 Stitch pieces following graphs, working head back and body back entirely with light gray Continental Stitches and reversing one trunk and one left arm before stitching.

4 Glue beads to head for eyes where indicated on graph.

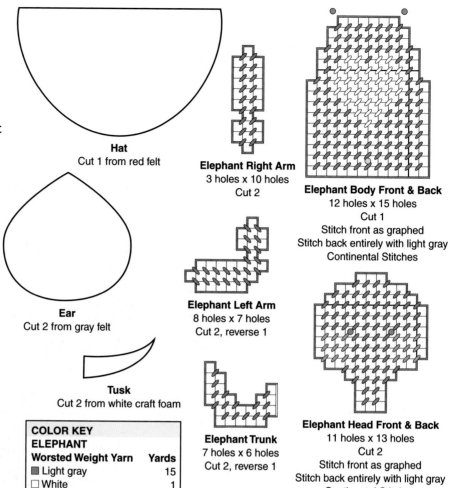

Hat
Cut 1 from red felt

Ear
Cut 2 from gray felt

Tusk
Cut 2 from white craft foam

COLOR KEY	
ELEPHANT	
Worsted Weight Yarn	**Yards**
▮ Light gray	15
☐ White	1
▨ Bright pink	1
● Attach bead	
○ Attach tail	

Elephant Right Arm
3 holes x 10 holes
Cut 2

Elephant Left Arm
8 holes x 7 holes
Cut 2, reverse 1

Elephant Trunk
7 holes x 6 holes
Cut 2, reverse 1

Elephant Body Front & Back
12 holes x 15 holes
Cut 1
Stitch front as graphed
Stitch back entirely with light gray
Continental Stitches

Elephant Head Front & Back
11 holes x 13 holes
Cut 2
Stitch front as graphed
Stitch back entirely with light gray
Continental Stitches

5 Using light gray, Overcast top edges on body front and back from dot to dot; Overcast bottom edges.

assembly

1 Use photo as a guide throughout assembly. Using light gray through step 2, Whipstitch wrong sides of body front and back together along side edges. Whipstitch wrong sides of corresponding arm pieces together.

2 Whipstitch wrong sides of head front and back together, stuffing with a small amount of fiberfill before closing.

3 Whipstitch wrong sides of

trunk pieces together with white and light gray following graph.

4 For tail, braid gray yarn until braid is approximately ½-inch long; tie ends in a knot, fringe and evenly trim. Sew to body back with gray where indicated on graph.

5 Glue neck on head into neck opening on body. Center and glue star button above heart on body front.

6 Glue arms to body back at shoulders.

7 Glue trunk to face, then glue tusks to face at trunk sides. Glue ears to top corners of head.

8 Form hat into a cone; glue to secure. Fold up rim and glue to top of head. ❑

Buggy Bag Clips

Designs by Nancy Marshall

Close your chip bags tightly with this pair of whimsical bag clips!

skill level • beginner

✖ materials ✖

- ☐ ⅓ sheet Uniek Quick-Count 7-count plastic canvas
- ☐ Uniek Needloft plastic canvas yarn as listed in color key
- ☐ 2 inches red 6-strand embroidery floss
- ☐ #16 tapestry needle
- ☐ 4 (7mm) movable eyes
- ☐ 4 (½-inch) black pompoms
- ☐ 4 (5mm) pink pompoms
- ☐ Black chenille stem
- ☐ 3¼-inch x 4¼-inch piece red self-adhesive Presto felt from Kunin Felt
- ☐ 3½-inch x 4¼-inch piece white self-adhesive Presto felt from Kunin Felt
- ☐ 2 spring clothespins
- ☐ Craft glue

finished size:

Bee: 3½ inches W x 5 inches H

Ladybug: 3¼ inches W x 5 inches H

instructions

1 Cut plastic canvas according to graphs. Cut white felt to fit bee; cut red felt to fit ladybug.

2 Stitch pieces following graphs, working uncoded areas on bee with white Continental Stitches and uncoded areas on ladybug with black Continental Stitches.

3 Work black Backstitches on ladybug when background stitching is completed. Overcast pieces following graphs.

4 Cut 6-strand embroidery floss in half so there are two 1-inch lengths. Glue one length to each bug for mouth where indicated on graphs.

5 Using photo as a guide through step 6, glue pink pompoms at corners of mouths. Center and glue eyes above mouths.

6 Cut four 1½-inch lengths from black chenille stem. Glue one black pompom to one end of each stem. Glue opposite ends to back of bugs' heads.

7 Attach felt to back of bugs. Glue one clothespin at an angle to back of each bug. ☐

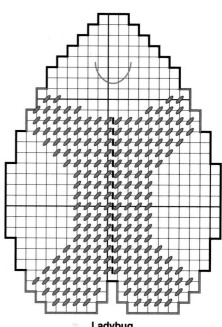

Ladybug
21 holes x 28 holes
Cut 1

COLOR KEY	
LADYBUG	
Plastic Canvas Yarn	**Yards**
■ Christmas red #02	3
Uncoded areas are black #00 Continental Stitches	5
╱ Black #00 Backstitch and Overcasting	
╱ Attach mouth	
Color numbers given are for Uniek Needloft plastic canvas yarn.	

COLOR KEY	
BEE	
Plastic Canvas Yarn	**Yards**
■ Black #00	2
▨ Tangerine #11	2
Uncoded areas are white #41 Continental Stitches	6
╱ White Overcasting	
╱ Attach mouth	
Color numbers given are for Uniek Needloft plastic canvas yarn.	

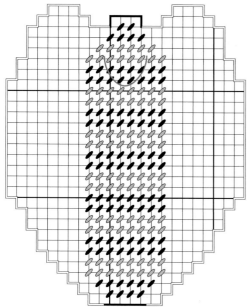

Bee
23 holes x 28 holes
Cut 1

Watermelon Napkin Holder

Design by Angie Arickx

Perk up your picnic table with this bright and colorful watermelon napkin holder!

skill level • beginner

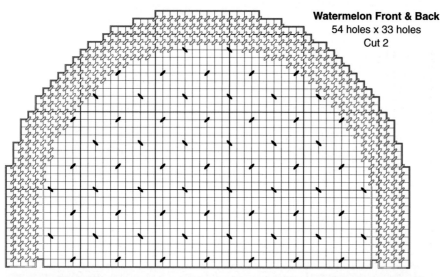

Watermelon Front & Back
54 holes x 33 holes
Cut 2

☀ materials ☀

❏ 1 sheet 7-count plastic canvas

❏ Uniek Needloft plastic canvas yarn as listed in color key

❏ #16 tapestry needle

finished size:

8¼ inches W x 5 inches H x 2¼ inches D

instructions

1 Cut plastic canvas according to graph. Cut one 44-hole x 14-hole piece for holder bottom and two 14-hole x 11-hole pieces for holder sides.

2 Continental Stitch holder sides with watermelon. Holder bottom will remain unstitched.

3 Stitch watermelon front and back following graph, working uncoded areas with watermelon Continental Stitches and leaving bars indicated with blue lines unworked at this time. Overcast fern, lemon, white and pink edges at bottom of watermelon front and back while stitching.

4 Overcast around side and top edges of watermelon front and back with holly.

5 Using watermelon throughout, Whipstitch bottom to front, back and sides. Continental Stitch sides to front and back where indicated with blue lines. ❏

COLOR KEY	
Plastic Canvas Yarn	**Yards**
■ Black #00	6
☐ Pink #07	4
☐ Lemon #20	4
■ Fern # 23	4
☐ White #41	4
Uncoded areas are watermelon #55 Continental Stitches	40
✎ Holly #27 Overcasting	4
✎ Watermelon #55 Overcasting and Whipstitching	

Color numbers given are for Uniek Needloft plastic canvas yarn.

Rocky Coast Basket

Design by Janelle Giese

Capture the rugged beauty of the rocky coast with this decorative basket filled with unique coastal treasures.

✖ materials ✖

- ¼ sheet 7-count plastic canvas
- Uniek Needloft plastic canvas yarn as listed in color key
- Worsted weight yarn as listed in color key
- DMC #5 pearl cotton as listed in color key
- Kreinik Fine (#8) Glow-in-the-Dark Braid as listed in color key
- #16 tapestry needle
- Wall basket
- Twisted paper ribbon in coordinating color 1½ times the width of basket
- Raffia straw
- Excelsior
- Seashore articles to fit in basket: driftwood, sand dollar, etc.
- Carpet thread
- Thick white glue

finished size:

Stitched Motif: 4½ inches W x 4⅞ inches H

This project is designed after the oldest lighthouse in Washington state, Cape Disappointment, Ilawaco, Wash. It was built in 1856. Be sure to use glow-in-the-dark braid for the light rays so your lighthouse "lights" up the dark.

instructions

1 Cut plastic canvas according to graph (page 61).

2 Stitch and Overcast piece following graph, working uncoded areas with camel Continental Stitches.

3 When background stitching and Overcasting are completed, work fine (#8) braid Straight Stitches. Add pearl cotton Backstitches and Straight Stitches, working Straight Stitch in house window four times.

continued on page 61

Ballooning Bear

Design by Angie Arickx

Dress up a **child's** room or door with **teddy** taking a **ride** in his **rainbow-colored** hot-air balloon!

skill level • beginner

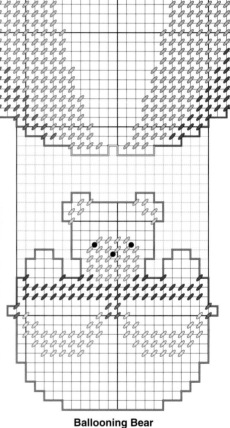

Ballooning Bear
39 holes x 68 holes
Cut 1
Cut away blue lines

✖ materials ✖

- ❏ 1 sheet 7-count plastic canvas
- ❏ Uniek Needloft plastic canvas yarn as listed in color key
- ❏ #16 tapestry needle

finished size:

6 inches W x 10¼ inches H

instructions

1 Cut plastic canvas according to graph, cutting away blue lines.

2 Stitch piece following graph, working uncoded areas on bear and basket with maple Continental Stitches and uncoded areas on balloon with lemon Continental Stitches.

3 Work black French Knots for eyes and nose when background stitching is completed. Overcast edges following graph, leaving "rope" edges unworked.

4 Hang as desired. ❑

<table>
<thead>
<tr><th colspan="2">COLOR KEY</th></tr>
<tr><th>Plastic Canvas Yarn</th><th>Yards</th></tr>
</thead>
<tbody>
<tr><td>■ Red #01</td><td>4</td></tr>
<tr><td>▨ Tangerine #11</td><td>5</td></tr>
<tr><td>▢ Lemon #20</td><td>7</td></tr>
<tr><td>▨ Fern #23</td><td>5</td></tr>
<tr><td>■ Royal #32</td><td>5</td></tr>
<tr><td>▢ Beige #41</td><td>1</td></tr>
<tr><td>Uncoded areas on bear and basket are maple #13 Continental Stitches</td><td>5</td></tr>
<tr><td>Uncoded area on balloon is lemon #20 Continental Stitches</td><td>1</td></tr>
<tr><td>╱ Maple #13 Overcasting</td><td></td></tr>
<tr><td>● Black #00 French Knot</td><td></td></tr>
<tr><td colspan="2">Color numbers given are for Uniek Needloft plastic canvas yarn.</td></tr>
</tbody>
</table>

Rocky Coast Basket continued from page 59

4 Open twisted paper ribbon and gather at center. Split a length of raffia straw lengthwise into several fine pieces. Place lengths together and tie in a bow. Center bow over twisted paper ribbon, then wrap centers of each together with carpet thread and knot. Do not cut off thread ends.

5 Center bow and ribbon over front of basket, draw thread to inside of basket and knot. Add glue to bow assembly.

6 Glue stitched piece over center of bow and tie to basket with thread as in step 5.

7 Glue paper ribbon tails to sides of basket, allowing paper to puff slightly on each side of stitched motif. Trim ends at an angle.

8 Fill basket with excelsior and seashore articles. ❑

<table>
<thead>
<tr><th colspan="2">COLOR KEY</th></tr>
<tr><th>Plastic Canvas Yarn</th><th>Yards</th></tr>
</thead>
<tbody>
<tr><td>■ Black #00</td><td>2</td></tr>
<tr><td>■ Red #01</td><td>1</td></tr>
<tr><td>■ Cinnamon #14</td><td>2</td></tr>
<tr><td>▨ Gray #38</td><td>1</td></tr>
<tr><td>▢ Eggshell #39</td><td>2</td></tr>
<tr><td>▨ Beige #40</td><td>1</td></tr>
<tr><td>Uncoded areas are camel #43 Continental Stitches</td><td>3</td></tr>
<tr><td>╱ Camel #43 Overcasting</td><td></td></tr>
<tr><td>Worsted Weight Yarn</td><td></td></tr>
<tr><td>▢ Light aqua</td><td>1</td></tr>
<tr><td>Fine (#8) Glow-in-the-Dark Braid</td><td></td></tr>
<tr><td>╱ Grapefruit #052F Straight Stitch</td><td></td></tr>
<tr><td>#5 Pearl Cotton</td><td></td></tr>
<tr><td>╱ Black #310 Backstitch and Straight Stitch</td><td>2</td></tr>
<tr><td colspan="2">Color numbers given are for Uniek Needloft plastic canvas yarn, Kreinik Fine (#8) Glow-in-the-Dark Braid and DMC #5 pearl cotton.</td></tr>
</tbody>
</table>

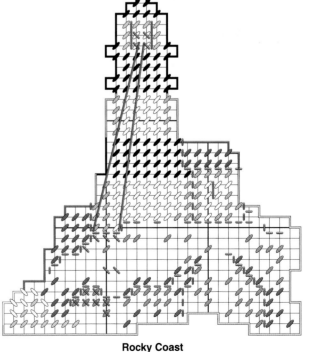

Rocky Coast
29 holes x 32 holes
Cut 1

Pet ID Tags

Designs by Vicki Blizzard

Keep your precious pets safe by including your pet's name
and your home telephone number
on these handy collar slides!

skill level • beginner

✖ materials ✖

Each Tag
❑ Small amount 14-count plastic canvas
❑ DMC 6-strand embroidery floss as listed in color key
❑ #26 tapestry needle

Dog ID Tag
❑ 8mm ruby glass heart bead
❑ Dog collar up to ⅝ inches-wide

Cat ID Tag
❑ 6mm transparent glass heart bead
❑ Cat collar up to ⅜ inches-wide

finished size:

Dog ID Tag: 2 inches W x 1 inch H, fitting dog collar up to ⅝ inches-wide

Cat ID Tag: 2 inches W x ¾ inches H, fitting cat collar up to ⅜ inches-wide

dog ID tag

1 Cut for front and back from plastic canvas according to graphs.

2 Stitch pieces following graphs, working all uncoded areas, including entire slide back, with ultra pale yellow Continental Stitches.

3 Referring to graph for alphabet and numbers and using 3 plies Christmas red floss, center and Backstitch pet's name on back in area shaded with blue on graph; center and Backstitch phone number in area shaded with yellow. Add French Knots as needed.

4 Using 3 plies ultra pale yellow, attach ruby bead to front where indicated on graph. Proceed, following instructions for assembly.

cat ID tag

1 Cut slide front and back from plastic canvas according to graphs.

2 Stitch pieces following graphs and steps 2 and 3 for dog ID tag, replacing ultra pale yellow with ultra very light blue and Christmas red with electric blue.

3 Work Straight Stitches and French Knots on fish when background stitching is completed.

4 Using 3 plies ultra very light blue, attach transparent bead to front where indicated on graph. Proceed, following instructions for assembly.

assembly

1 Following graphs, Overcast side edges on fronts and backs with 6-strand embroidery floss.

2 For buckle-style collar, with wrong sides facing, Whipstitch top and bottom edges of corresponding slide pieces together. Insert end of collar into assembled slide and pull through.

3 For clip-style collar, with wrong sides facing, Whipstitch top edges of corresponding slide pieces together. Insert collar between front and back. Whipstitch bottom edges together. ❑

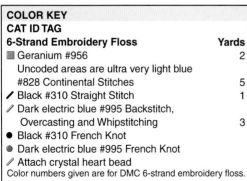

COLOR KEY	
CAT ID TAG	
6-Strand Embroidery Floss	**Yards**
▨ Geranium #956	2
Uncoded areas are ultra very light blue #828 Continental Stitches	5
╱ Black #310 Straight Stitch	1
╱ Dark electric blue #995 Backstitch, Overcasting and Whipstitching	3
● Black #310 French Knot	
● Dark electric blue #995 French Knot	
╱ Attach crystal heart bead	
Color numbers given are for DMC 6-strand embroidery floss.	

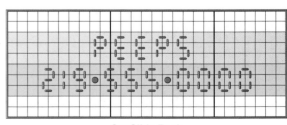

Cat Slide Back
27 holes x 10 holes
Cut 1

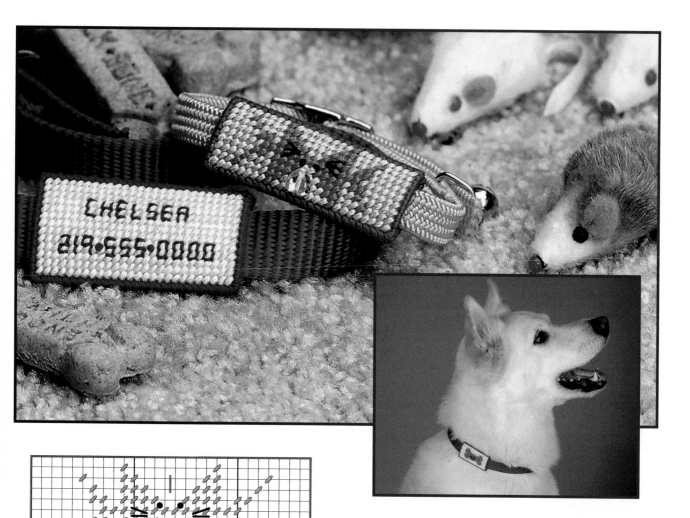

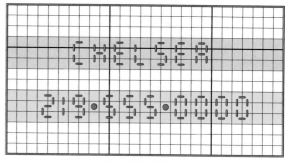

Cat Slide Front
27 holes x 10 holes
Cut 1

COLOR KEY
DOG ID TAG

6-Strand Embroidery Floss	Yards
■ Very light brown #435	2
Uncoded areas are ultra pale yellow #3823 Continental Stitches	9
⁄ Christmas red #321 Backstitch, Overcasting and Whipstitching	3
⁄ Attach ruby heart bead	

Color numbers given are for DMC 6-strand embroidery floss.

Dog Slide Back
27 holes x 14 holes
Cut 1

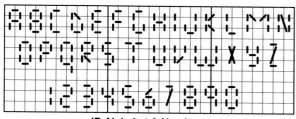

ID Alphabet & Numbers
Stitch dog slide with Christmas red
Stitch cat slide with dark electric blue

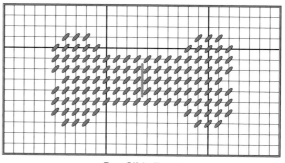

Dog Slide Front
27 holes x 14 holes
Cut 1

skill level
beginner

✖ materials ✖

- ❏ 1 sheet 7-count plastic canvas
- ❏ Uniek Needloft plastic canvas yarn as listed in color key
- ❏ Worsted weight yarn as listed in color key
- ❏ DMC #5 pearl cotton as listed in color key
- ❏ Kreinik ⅛-inch Ribbon as listed in color key
- ❏ #16 tapestry needle
- ❏ 5 (6mm) gold wind chimes
- ❏ 5 (6mm) silver wind chimes
- ❏ 9 inches gold chain
- ❏ 8 inches silver chain
- ❏ 2 (7mm) gold jump rings
- ❏ 2 (7mm) silver jump rings
- ❏ Needle-nose pliers
- ❏ Monofilament

finished size:

Sun: 6 inches W x 6 inches H, excluding chimes

Moon: 5½ inches W x 5⅛ inches H, excluding chimes

Sun & Moon Wind Chimes

Designs by Janelle Giese

Promise your **sweetheart** the sun, moon and stars, then give him or her this pair of **tinkling** wind chimes!

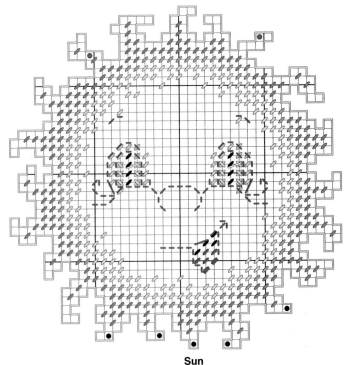

Sun
39 holes x 39 holes
Cut 1

COLOR KEY	
SUN	
Plastic Canvas Yarn	**Yards**
■ Black #00	1
■ Burgundy #03	1
■ Tangerine #11	2
■ Gold #17	4
☐ Eggshell #39	
Uncoded areas are baby yellow #21	
Continental Stitches	7
⁄ White #41 Straight Stitch	1
Worsted Weight Yarn	
☐ Yellow	3
⅛-Inch Ribbon	
☐ Gold #002	8
#5 Pearl Cotton	
⁄ Black #310 Backstitch and Straight Stitch	3
● Attach wind chime	
● Attach jump ring	

Color numbers given are for Uniek Needloft plastic canvas yarn, Kreinik ⅛-inch Ribbon and DMC #5 pearl cotton.

COLOR KEY	
MOON	
Plastic Canvas Yarn	**Yards**
■ Black #00	1
■ Burgundy #03	1
Uncoded areas are eggshell #39	
Continental Stitches	4
⁄ White #41 Straight Stitch	1
Worsted Weight Yarn	
☐ Light aqua	4
■ Aqua	3
⁄ Aqua Straight Stitch	
⅛-Inch Ribbon	
☐ Silver #001	6
#5 Pearl Cotton	
⁄ Black #310 Backstitch and Straight Stitch	1
● Attach wind chime	
● Attach jump ring	

Color numbers given are for Uniek Needloft plastic canvas yarn, Kreinik ⅛-inch Ribbon and DMC #5 pearl cotton.

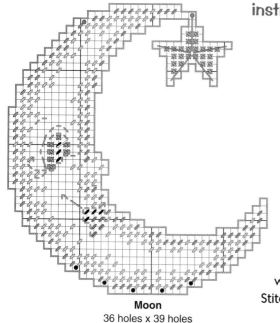

Moon
36 holes x 39 holes
Cut 1

instructions

1 Cut plastic canvas according to graphs.

2 Stitch pieces following graphs. Overcast sun with gold ribbon and moon with silver ribbon.

3 When background stitching and Overcasting are completed, Backstitch features with pearl cotton. Straight Stitch eye highlights with 2 plies white yarn. Work aqua Straight Stitches on star with 4 plies yarn.

4 Using gold chimes with sun and silver chimes with moon and using monofilament, attach chimes where indicated on graphs, allowing 1¼ inches between chimes and bottom edge of stitched piece.

5 For hangers, use gold chain and jump rings for sun; use silver chain and jump rings for moon. Using needle-nose pliers, attach jump rings to ends of chains and to stitched pieces where indicated on graphs. ❑

materials ✖

- ½ sheet 7-count plastic canvas
- Plastic canvas yarn as listed in color key
- #16 tapestry needle
- 8 miniature plastic, spring clothespins: 2 yellow, 2 blue, 2 pink and 2 green
- 8 (5mm) movable eyes
- 4 (1½-inch) lengths magnetic strip
- Hot-glue gun

finished size:

Cat: 4⅛ inches W x 3¾ inches H

Dog: 3¾ inches W x 3⅝ inches H

Pig: 3¼ inches W x 3¼ inches H

Frog: 2¾ inches W x 3¼ inches H

Fridgie Clips

Designs by Christina Laws

You'll never forget those **important** reminders on the **fridge** again when they're clipped onto this set of four **eye-catching** critters!

skill level • beginner

instructions

1 Cut plastic canvas according to graphs.

2 Stitch and Overcast cat, dog and pig pieces following graphs, working Backstitches on cat and dog muzzles while Overcasting.

3 Stitch and Overcast frog pieces following graphs, working entire body and head pieces with green Continental Stitches. Work light green Smyrna Crosses over Continental Stitches on body. Work red Backstitches on head.

Fridgie Cat Ears
3 holes x 4 holes each
Cut 1 set

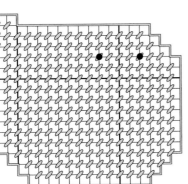

Fridgie Cat Body
26 holes x 21 holes
Cut 1

Fridgie Cat Muzzle
5 holes x 4 holes
Cut 1

COLOR KEY	
CAT	
Plastic Canvas Yarn	**Yards**
☐ Yellow	4
☐ White	1
☐ Pink	1
✏ Pink Backstitch	
● Attach eye	

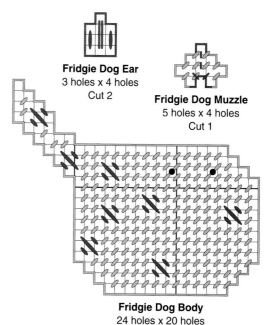

Fridgie Dog Ear
3 holes x 4 holes
Cut 2

Fridgie Dog Muzzle
5 holes x 4 holes
Cut 1

Fridgie Dog Body
24 holes x 20 holes
Cut 1

COLOR KEY	
DOG	
Plastic Canvas Yarn	**Yards**
☐ Light blue	4
■ Blue	1
╱ Blue Backstitch	
● Attach eye	

COLOR KEY	
PIG	
Plastic Canvas Yarn	**Yards**
☐ Pink	4
■ Rose	1
● Attach eye	

Fridgie Pig Snout
5 holes x 4 holes
Cut 1

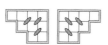

Fridgie Pig Ears
4 holes x 3 holes each
Cut 1 set

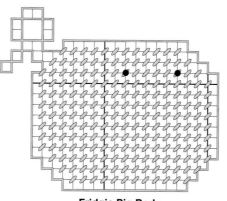

Fridgie Pig Body
21 holes x 17 holes
Cut 1

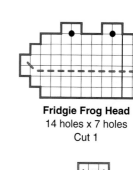

Fridgie Frog Head
14 holes x 7 holes
Cut 1

Fridgie Frog Tongue
3 holes x 3 holes
Cut 1

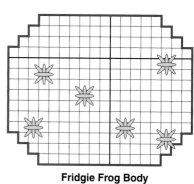

Fridgie Frog Body
18 holes x 14 holes
Cut 1

4 Glue eyes to frog head and to dog, cat and pig bodies where indicated on graphs.

5 Using photo as a guide through step 6, glue ears and muzzles to dog and cat. Glue ears and snout to pig. Glue tongue to frog head, then glue head to frog.

6 Glue one magnetic strip to back of each body. Matching colors, glue clothespins to lower part of bodies. ❏

COLOR KEY	
FROG	
Plastic Canvas Yarn	**Yards**
☐ Light green	1
■ Red	1
Uncoded background on body and head are green Continental Stitches	4
╱ Green Overcasting	
╱ Red Backstitch	
● Attach eye	

Tea-Time Wind Chime

Design by Susan Leinberger

Hang this **delightful** wind chime
near an **open** kitchen window as a **sweet** accent!

skill level • beginner

✖ materials ✖

- ☐ 1 sheet Uniek Quick-Count 7-count plastic canvas
- ☐ 2 Uniek 3-inch plastic canvas radial circles
- ☐ Uniek Needloft plastic canvas yarn: 5 inches in color resembling tea and as listed in color key
- ☐ 8 inches white Uniek Needloft iridescent craft cord
- ☐ 1 yard white #5 pearl cotton
- ☐ #16 tapestry needle
- ☐ 14 (4mm) round crystal transparent beads
- ☐ 5 (6mm) gold wind chimes
- ☐ Hot-glue gun

finished size:

Teapot: 4¾ inches W x 4¼ inches H

Cup & Saucer: 2¼ inches H x 3 inches in diameter

Completed Wind Chime: 6 inches W x 16¼ inches H

cutting & stitching

1 Cut teapots, tea cups, leaves and flowers from plastic canvas according to graphs. Do not cut plastic canvas radial circles which are the saucer pieces.

2 Stitch saucer top following graph, working uncoded areas with white Continental Stitches and leaving pink Whipstitch line unworked at this time. Saucer bottom will remain unstitched.

3 Stitch teapot and cup pieces following graphs, reversing one teapot and one cup before stitching. Stitch and Overcast flowers and leaves with 1 ply yarn.

assembly

1 Use photo as a guide throughout assembly. Glue tea-colored yarn to wrong side of one teapot spout where indicated on graph. Following graph, Whipstitch wrong sides of teapot together along inside and outside edges.

2 Glue remaining end of tea-colored yarn to wrong side of one cup at center top. Following graph, Whipstitch wrong sides of cup together along all edges except bottom edge. With white, Whipstitch bottom edge of cup to saucer top through all three thicknesses along pink Whipstitch line.

3 Secure white pearl cotton at center of saucer bottom where indicated on graph with blue dot. Thread pearl cotton through longest chime, then bring up through center of circle, wrapping pearl cotton around center bar so chime hangs about 2 inches from saucer bottom.

4 Following Fig. 1 and beginning at top of circle, wrap pearl cotton around bar indicated with red dot, thread on chime and wrap pearl cotton around next bar indicated with green dot, allowing chime to hang 2 inches from saucer bottom.

5 Following step 4, continue process until all chimes are attached, ending back at red dot. secure pearl cotton on top of circle.

6 With white, Whipstitch saucer top and bottom together.

7 To make large flowers, glue one small flower to center of each large flower, then center and glue one large flower to each side of teapot, gluing two leaves under each large flower; glue two small flowers to each side of large flower.

8 Glue three small flowers to each side of cup. Glue two small leaves and one small flower to each side of saucer. Glue one bead to center of each flower.

9 Attach white iridescent cord to top of teapot where indicated on graph with a Lark's Head Knot. Tie ends in a knot to form a loop for hanging. ☐

COLOR KEY	
Plastic Canvas Yarn	**Yar**
■ Moss #25	
☐ White #41	2
■ Bright blue #60	
Uncoded areas on saucer top are white #41 Continental Stitches	
⁄ Bright blue #60 Backstitch and Straight Stitch	
○ Attach white iridescent cord	

Color numbers given are for Uniek Needloft plastic canv yarn.

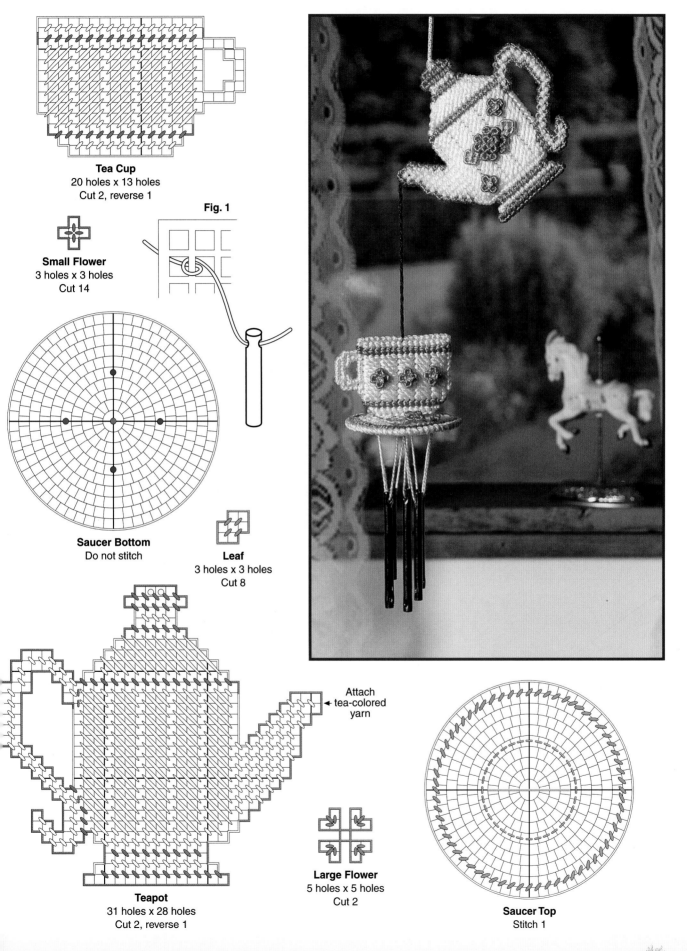

Tea Cup
20 holes x 13 holes
Cut 2, reverse 1

Small Flower
3 holes x 3 holes
Cut 14

Fig. 1

Saucer Bottom
Do not stitch

Leaf
3 holes x 3 holes
Cut 8

← Attach
tea-colored
yarn

Teapot
31 holes x 28 holes
Cut 2, reverse 1

Large Flower
5 holes x 5 holes
Cut 2

Saucer Top
Stitch 1

Patriotic Bear Welcome Sign

Design by Celia Lange Designs

Invite friends and family into your home for this year's Fourth of July reunion with this festive sign!

skill level • beginner

✖ materials ✖

- ❏ 1 sheet Darice Ultra Stiff 7-count plastic canvas
- ❏ Coats & Clark Red Heart Classic worsted weight yarn Art. E267 as listed in color key
- ❏ Coats & Clark Red Heart Super Saver worsted weight yarn Art. E300 as listed in color key
- ❏ Chenille acrylic yarn as listed in color key
- ❏ #16 tapestry needle
- ❏ 2 (15mm) movable oval eyes
- ❏ 2 yards 4mm red cording
- ❏ Gold metallic stars and strands pick
- ❏ Scissors
- ❏ 2 (⅝-inch) gold star buttons #20817 from JHB International Inc.
- ❏ ⅝-inch red star button #20825 from JHB International Inc.
- ❏ ³⁄₁₆-inch round metallic gold shank button
- ❏ Scraps Fun Foam craft foam by Westrim Crafts: white, blue and brown
- ❏ Hot-glue gun

finished size:

9¼ inches W x 12½ inches H, excluding hanging cord

instructions

1 Cut plastic canvas according to graphs (this page, and pages 71 and 73).

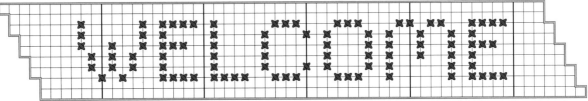

Patriotic Bear Banner
57 holes x 9 holes
Cut 1

2 From blue craft foam, cut two 1½-inch x ⅜-inch pieces. From white craft foam cut one 1⅛-inch x ⅜ inch piece. From brown craft foam cut one ⅞-inch x ⅜ inch piece and one 1⅜-inch x 1-inch piece.

3 Stitch plastic canvas following graphs, working uncoded areas on banner, arm and hat top with off-white Continental Stitches. Overcast banner with gold and all remaining edges with adjacent colors. Work embroidery on head with black yarn.

4 Use photo as a guide through step 9. With gold yarn, sew gold button to cuff where indicated on graph. With matching yarn, stitch gold and red star hearts to Olympic blue area on left side of heart.

5 Center and glue brim to bottom of hat. Cut one 4½-inch length of star wire strand from pick. Wrap length around hat above hat brim; gluing in back.

6 Gently curl plain gold strands of pick with scissors; coil remaining wire strands. Wrap 1 inch of pick with Olympic blue yarn approximately 3½ inches from top of curled strands. Cut off excess wire from bottom of pick, then glue pick to back of paw. Glue arm to back of heart.

7 Glue white strip of craft foam to back of cuff on arm over pick. Glue small brown strip of craft foam to back of paw over pick.

8 Glue hat and movable eyes to head, then glue head to front of heart. Glue welcome banner across middle of heart at a slight angle.

9 Glue cording to back of heart. To secure cording, glue blue pieces of craft foam and remaining brown piece over cording to matching color. ❏

Patriotic Bear Heart
45 holes x 43 holes
Cut 1

COLOR KEY	
Chenille Acrylic Yarn	**Yards**
■ Brown	10
Worsted Weight Yarn	
□ Off-white #3	19
■ Black #12	1
■ Olympic blue #849	18
■ Country red #914	14
Uncoded areas on arm, hat top and banner are off-white #3 Continental Stitches	
✎ Gold #321 Overcasting	1
✏ Black #12 Backstitch	
◉ Attach gold button	
Color numbers given are for Coats & Clark Red Heart Classic worsted weight yarn Art. E267 and Super Saver worsted weight yarn Art. E300.	

Patriotic Bear Hat Brim
26 holes x 3 holes
Cut 1

Graphs continued on page 73

Beach Bear Sunglasses Case

Design by Janelle Giese

Protect your **favorite** pair of "shades" with this **super-cool sunglasses case!**

skill level • beginner

COLOR KEY

Chenille Acrylic Yarn   Yard
☐ Light tan
Plastic Canvas Yarn
☐ Black #00
■ Christmas red #02
■ Sandstone #16
■ Sail blue #35
☐ White #41
■ Mermaid #53
☐ Watermelon #55
☐ Yellow #57
☐ Bright orange #58
   Uncoded areas are baby blue #36
   Continental Stitches
╱ Christmas red #02 Straight Stitch
#5 Pearl Cotton
╱ Black #310 Backstitch and Straight Stitch
Color numbers given are for Uniek Needloft plastic canvas
yarn and DMC #5 pearl cotton.

✖ materials ✖

- ☐ ½ sheet 7-count plastic canvas
- ☐ Chenille acrylic yarn as listed in color key
- ☐ Uniek Needloft plastic canvas yarn as listed in color key
- ☐ DMC #5 pearl cotton as listed in color key
- ☐ #16 tapestry needle

finished size:
4⅜ inches W x 7 inches H

instructions

1 Cut plastic canvas according to graphs.

2 Stitch pieces following graphs, working uncoded areas with baby blue Continental Stitches. Overcast top edges of back from dot to dot with sail blue.

3 Work black pearl cotton embroidery on front, working vertical stitch for each eye three times, then work Christmas red Straight Stitches on kite tail with 2 plies yarn.

4 Align bottom edges of front and back, then Whipstitch together with sail blue; Overcast remaining edges of front. ❑

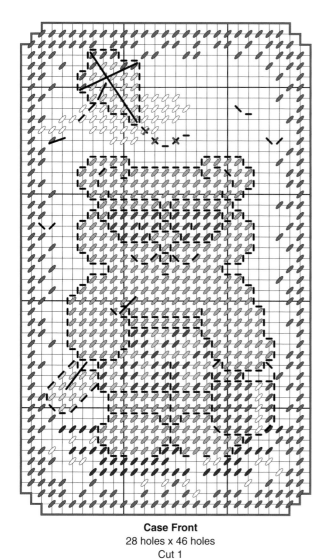

Case Front
28 holes x 46 holes
Cut 1

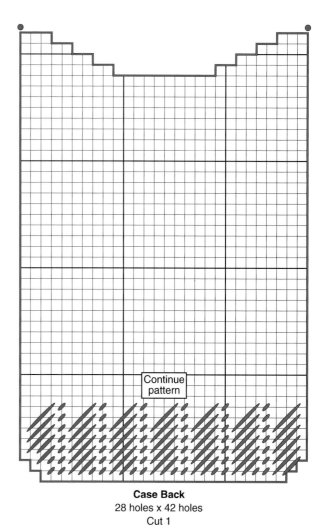

Case Back
28 holes x 42 holes
Cut 1

Patriotic Bear Welcome Sign continued from page 71

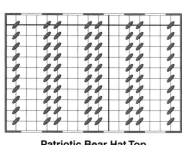

Patriotic Bear Hat Top
17 holes x 11 holes
Cut 1

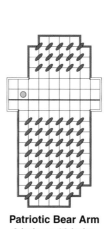

Patriotic Bear Arm
9 holes x 16 holes
Cut 1

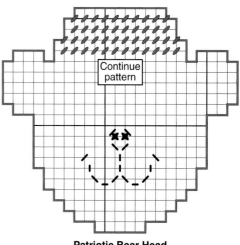

Continue pattern

Patriotic Bear Head
23 holes x 21 holes
Cut 1

Wedding Hearts Sachets

Designs by Deborah Scheblein

Need a **bridal shower gift** in a hurry?
Stitch this **pair** of fragrant sachets for the **bride-to-be!**

skill level • begnner

❧ materials ❧

- ⅓ sheet white 7-count plastic canvas
- ⅓ sheet black 7-count plastic canvas
- Plastic canvas yarn as listed in color key
- #16 tapestry needle
- 4 (5mm) round black cabochons
- 6 (5mm) white pearl beads
- White heavy-duty thread
- 6 inches ⅛-inch-wide white satin ribbon
- 6 inches ⅛-inch-wide satin ribbon in desired color
- 6 inches ⅜-inch-wide black satin ribbon
- 12 inches ½-inch-wide white lace
- ½-inch-wide satin ribbon rose: white or color of bridesmaids' dresses.
- Potpourri pearls
- Hot-glue gun

finished size:

Bridal Heart: 4¼ inches W x 4⅛ inches H
Tuxedo Heart: 3¾ inches W x 3¾ inches H

instructions

1 Cut two bridal hearts and one tuxedo collar from white plastic canvas; cut two tuxedo hearts from black plastic canvas according to graphs.

2 Do not stitch heart backs. Stitch heart fronts and collar following graphs.

3 With white thread, attach pearl beads to bridal heart front where indicated on graph. Glue black cabochons to tuxedo heart front where indicated on graph.

Tuxedo Heart Front & Back
24 holes x 24 holes
Cut 2 from black
Stitch front only

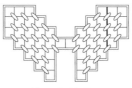

Tuxedo Collar
12 holes x 7 holes
Cut 1 from white

COLOR KEY	
BRIDAL HEART	
Plastic Canvas Yarn	**Yards**
☐ White	6
● Attach pearl bead	

COLOR KEY	
TUXEDO HEART	
Plastic Canvas Yarn	**Yards**
■ Black	5
☐ White	2
● Attach black cabochon	

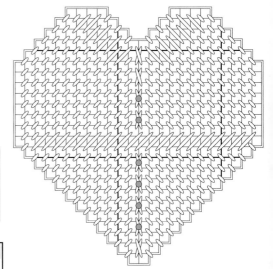

Bridal Heart Front & Back
24 holes x 24 holes
Cut 2 from white
Stitch front only

4 Whipstitch bridal heart front and back together with white, filling with potpourri pearls before closing. Whipstitch tuxedo heart front and back together with black, filling with potpourri pearls before closing.

5 Using photo as a guide through step 6, for bridal heart, glue white lace around edges of heart back. Place both lengths of ⅛-inch-wide ribbon together and tie in a bow. Glue to center top of heart front.

6 For tuxedo heart, glue collar to top front of heart. Tie ⅜-inch black satin ribbon a bow for bow tie and glue to collar. Glue ribbon rose to heart front for boutonniere. ❑

Wedding Accents

Designs by Deborah Scheblein

Treat your **guests** to a wedding dinner accented with a **diminutive** church **party** favor, and eyelet and roses napkin **ring**.

skill level • beginner

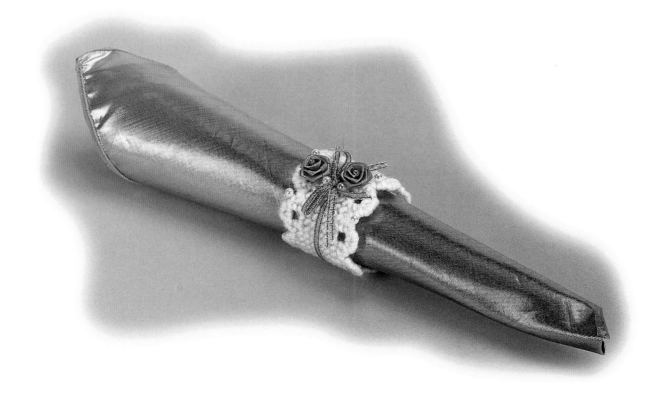

✖ materials ✖

- ❑ ⅓ sheet 7-count plastic canvas
- ❑ Plastic canvas yarn as listed in color key
- ❑ Metallic craft cord as listed in color key
- ❑ #16 tapestry needle
- ❑ 15 inches ⅛-inch-wide gold ribbon
- ❑ 2 (⅝-inch) satin ribbon roses in desired color
- ❑ Pearl spray
- ❑ Craft glue

finished size:

Napkin Ring: 1¾ inches W x 2 inches in diameter
Church Party Favor: 1¾ inches W x 4 inches H x 1⅝ inches D

instructions

1 Cut plastic canvas according to graphs. Cut one 9-hole x 10-hole piece for church bottom. Bottom will remain unstitched.

2 Stitch church favor pieces following graphs, working uncoded areas with white Continental Stitches. Work white gold Straight Stitches when background stitching is completed.

3 Overcast church roof edges and cross edges with white gold and white following graph.

4 Using white throughout, Overcast top edges of sides and back. Whipstitch front and back to sides, then Whipstitch front, back and sides to bottom.

5 Stitch and Overcast napkin ring following graph, overlapping four holes where indicated before stitching.

6 Using photo as a guide through step 7, center and wrap gold ribbon around circumference of napkin ring; tie in a knot, leaving ¾-inch tails. Tie remaining length of ribbon in a bow and glue on top of knot; trim tails as desired.

7 Cut several lengths of pearl spray; glue around bow as desired. Glue ribbon roses above and below bow. ❑

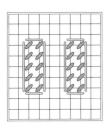

Church Back
9 holes x 10 holes
Cut 1

COLOR KEY	
CHURCH PARTY FAVOR	
Plastic Canvas Yarn	**Yards**
▨ Light blue	1
▧ Tan	1
Uncoded areas are white	
Continental Stitches	4
⁄ White Overcasting and Whipstitching	
Metallic Cord	
☐ White/gold	
⁄ White/gold Straight Stitch	3

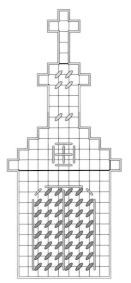

Church Front
11 holes x 25 holes
Cut 1

COLOR KEY	
NAPKIN RING	
Plastic Canvas Yarn	**Yards**
☐ White	5

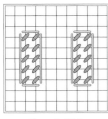

Church Side
10 holes x 10 holes
Cut 2

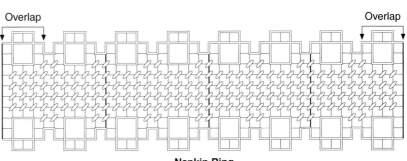

Overlap   Overlap

Napkin Ring
39 holes x 11 holes
Cut 1

Picnic-Time Memo Magnets

Designs by Susan Leinberger

Liven up your **refrigerator** with this set of sandwich, chips and soda magnets, which can be tucked into the magnetic picnic basket memo pad holder when not in use!

skill level • beginner

cutting & stitching

1 Cut sandwich, chips and soda from clear plastic canvas according to graphs (pages 79 and 80).

2 From green plastic canvas, cut basket back, front, sides and handles according to graphs. Also cut one 3-hole x 9-hole piece for pencil holder loop and one 31-hole x 3-hole piece for basket bottom.

3 Stitch basket back, sides and front following graphs. On front and sides, work maple vertical Long Stitches first, then work horizontal stitches. Handles, pencil holder loop and basket bottom will remain unstitched.

4 Following graphs through step 7, stitch and Overcast sandwich, working uncoded areas with camel Continental Stitches.

5 Stitch and Overcast chips working uncoded area with Christmas red Continental Stitches.

6 Stitch and Overcast soda working uncoded bottle cap and uncoded background in center of bottle with white Continental Stitches.

7 When background stitching and Overcasting are completed, work Backstitches and Straight Stitches.

assembly

1 Using maple throughout basket assembly, fold pencil holder loop in half, then working through all three thicknesses, Whipstitch to basket back where indicated on graph.

2 Whipstitch sides to bottom, then Whipstitch sides and bottom to front; Overcast top edges. Whipstitch sides and bottom to basket back where indicated on graph.

3 Insert brass brads through cut-out areas of basket handles, then insert to inside of basket through front and back pieces where indicated on graphs.

4 Cut magnetic strip into three pieces and attach to backsides of sandwich, chips and soda. Glue ceramic magnets to backside of basket.

5 Insert memo pad through cut-out slit at bottom of basket; insert pencil through loop.

6 Store sandwich, chips and soda magnets inside basket until ready to use. ❑

✖ materials ✖

- ❑ 1 sheet Uniek Quick-Count green 7-count plastic canvas
- ❑ ½ sheet Uniek Quick-Count clear 7-count plastic canvas
- ❑ Uniek Needloft plastic canvas yarn as listed in color key
- ❑ #16 tapestry needle
- ❑ 4 brass brads
- ❑ 2 (¾-inch) round ceramic magnets
- ❑ 6½-inch length self-adhesive magnetic strip
- ❑ 3-inch x 5-inch memo pad
- ❑ Pencil
- ❑ Hot-glue gun

finished size:
Picnic Basket: 4⅞ inches W x 5¼ inches H
Sandwich: 4 inches W x 1¾ inches H
Soda: 2 inches W x 4⅝ inches H
Chips: 2⅜ inches W x 3⅜ inches H

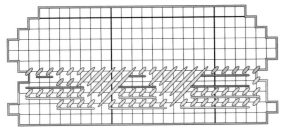

Sandwich
26 holes x 11 holes
Cut 1 from clear

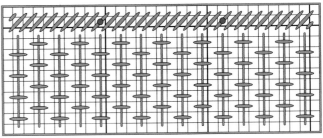

Basket Front
31 holes x 12 holes
Cut 1 from green

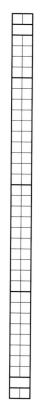

Basket Handle
2 holes x 36 holes
Cut 2 from green
Do not stitch

Soda
13 holes x 30 holes
Cut 1 from clear

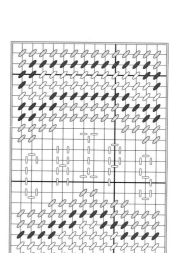

Basket Side
3 holes x 12 holes
Cut 2 from green

Chips
15 holes x 23 holes
Cut 1 from clear

COLOR KEY	
Plastic Canvas Yarn	**Yards**
■ Black #00	1
■ Christmas red #02	6
☐ Pink #07	1
■ Maple #13	6
■ Brown #15	2
■ Fern #23	1
■ Royal #32	3
■ Silver #37	1
☐ White #41	5
☐ Yellow #57	4
Uncoded area on chips is Christmas red #02 Continental Stitches	
Uncoded areas on soda are white #41 Continental Stitches	
Uncoded areas on sandwich are camel #43 Continental Stitches	3
⁄ Camel #43 Overcasting	
⁄ Christmas red #02 Backstitch and Straight Stitch	
⁄ Pink #07 Straight Stitch	
⁄ Royal #32 Backstitch	
⁄ White #41 Backstitch	
⁄ Whipstitch to pencil holder loop	
⁄ Whipstitch to basket bottom	
● Attach brad	
Color numbers given are for Uniek Needloft plastic canvas yarn.	

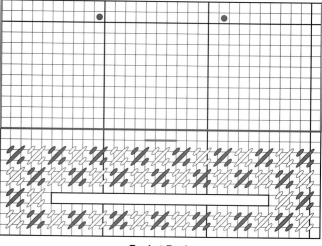

Basket Back
22 holes x 31 holes
Cut 1 from green

✖ materials ✖

❑ Small amount 7-count plastic canvas

❑ Uniek Needloft plastic canvas yarn as listed in color key

❑ #16 tapestry needle

❑ 2-inch paper clip

❑ Sewing needle and navy sewing thread

finished size:

1⅞ inches W x 6¼ inches H

Tie Clip

Design by Ronda Bryce

Give the man who has **everything** something he doesn't—this **handy** paper clip tie! It makes a **great** bookmark or paper organizer.

skill level • beginner

instructions

1 Cut plastic canvas according to graph.

2 Stitch tie following graph.

Overcast with dark royal.

3 With sewing needle and navy sewing thread, attach paper clip to yarn on center backside of tie near top edge. ❑

Tie
12 holes x 40 holes
Cut 1

COLOR KEY	
Plastic Canvas Yarn	**Yards**
■ Christmas red #02	2
■ Dark royal #48	2
□ Yellow #57	7
Color numbers given are for Uniek Needloft plastic canvas yarn.	

Tropical Fish Curtain Accents

Designs by Nanette M. Seale

Jazz up your **bathroom** with this set of 12 vibrant tropical fish holding up your **shower curtain!**

skill level
beginner

🐟 materials 🐟

- ❏ 1 sheet 7-count plastic canvas
- ❏ Plastic canvas yarn as listed in color key
- ❏ #16 tapestry needle
- ❏ Clear plastic shower curtain rings
- ❏ Hot-glue gun

finished size:

Long-Nosed Fish: 2 inches W x 2 inches H, excluding shower curtain ring

Short-Nosed Fish: 2⅜ inches W x 2 inches H, excluding shower curtain ring

instructions

1 Cut fish from plastic canvas according to graphs.

2 Stitch fish following graphs. Overcast with black.

3 Glue fish to shower curtain rings, placing closures at the bottom and attaching fish to sides. ❏

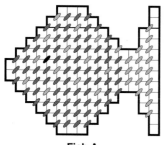

Fish A
15 holes x 12 holes
Cut 1

COLOR KEY	
FISH A	
Plastic Canvas Yarn	**Yards**
■ Bright purple	2
■ Black	2
▢ Lilac	1

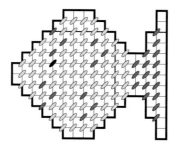

Fish B
15 holes x 12 holes
Cut 1

COLOR KEY	
FISH B	
Plastic Canvas Yarn	**Yards**
■ Black	2
▢ Yellow	1
■ Red	1

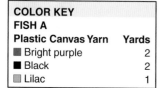

Fish C
15 holes x 12 holes
Cut 1

COLOR KEY	
FISH C	
Plastic Canvas Yarn	**Yards**
■ Black	2
■ Bright pink	1
▢ Bright yellow-green	1

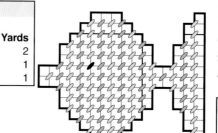

Fish D
16 holes x 12 holes
Cut 1

COLOR KEY	
FISH D	
Plastic Canvas Yarn	**Yards**
■ Black	2
▢ Bright yellow-green	1
▢ Light green	1

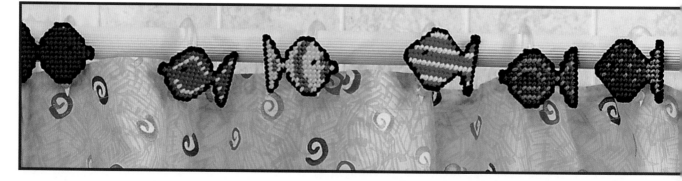

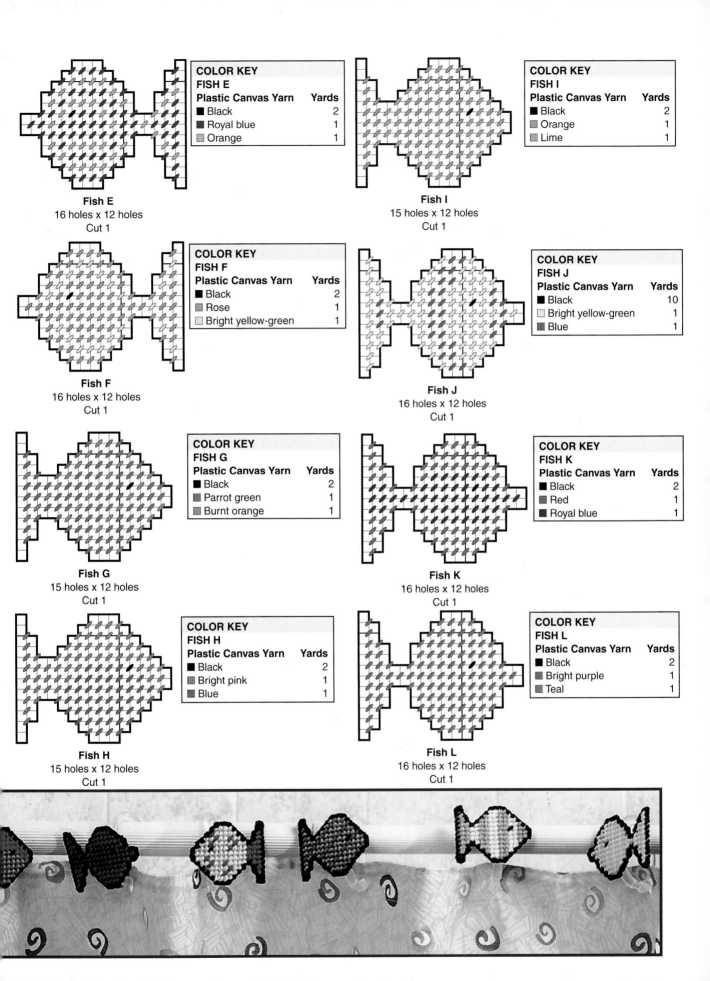

COLOR KEY
FISH E

Plastic Canvas Yarn	Yards
■ Black	2
■ Royal blue	1
□ Orange	1

Fish E
16 holes x 12 holes
Cut 1

COLOR KEY
FISH I

Plastic Canvas Yarn	Yards
■ Black	2
□ Orange	1
□ Lime	1

Fish I
15 holes x 12 holes
Cut 1

COLOR KEY
FISH F

Plastic Canvas Yarn	Yards
■ Black	2
□ Rose	1
□ Bright yellow-green	1

Fish F
16 holes x 12 holes
Cut 1

COLOR KEY
FISH J

Plastic Canvas Yarn	Yards
■ Black	10
□ Bright yellow-green	1
■ Blue	1

Fish J
16 holes x 12 holes
Cut 1

COLOR KEY
FISH G

Plastic Canvas Yarn	Yards
■ Black	2
■ Parrot green	1
□ Burnt orange	1

Fish G
15 holes x 12 holes
Cut 1

COLOR KEY
FISH K

Plastic Canvas Yarn	Yards
■ Black	2
■ Red	1
■ Royal blue	1

Fish K
16 holes x 12 holes
Cut 1

COLOR KEY
FISH H

Plastic Canvas Yarn	Yards
■ Black	2
■ Bright pink	1
■ Blue	1

Fish H
15 holes x 12 holes
Cut 1

COLOR KEY
FISH L

Plastic Canvas Yarn	Yards
■ Black	2
■ Bright purple	1
□ Teal	1

Fish L
16 holes x 12 holes
Cut 1

Loopy Flowers Frame

Design by Debi Schmitz

Here's a **project** that's super **quick-and-easy** to make,
and **friends** will love it!

skill level • beginner

※ materials ※

❏ 1 sheet pink 7-count plastic canvas

❏ #5 pearl cotton: 10 yards each light yellow and green, 7 yards white and as listed in color key

❏ #16 tapestry needle

❏ 46 inches ½-inch-wide white satin ribbon

❏ ½-inch buttons: 3 purple, 2 pink and 2 white

❏ 2-inch long piece heavy cardboard

❏ Fabric glue

finished size:

6⅛ inches W x 7⅞ inches H, excluding hanging ribbon

instructions

1 Cut frame front from plastic canvas according to graph. Cut one 40-hole x 50-hole piece for frame back. Frame back will remain unstitched.

2 Using a double strand of pearl cotton throughout, Overcast inside edges of frame front, working two stitches per hole as necessary to cover edge. Following graph, work Cross Stitches around frame opening.

3 Using four plies dark pink, work Backstitches across top of Cross Stitches, then place frame back behind frame front and continue backstitching around sides and bottom of Cross Stitches.

4 Using a double strand, Whipstitch frame front and back together from dot to dot around side and bottom edges. Overcast remaining top edges between dots.

5 Cut a 10-inch length of white satin ribbon. Place buttons over rib-bon ends and using dark pink pearl cotton, stitch to frame back approximately 8 bars from side edges and 3 bars from top edge.

6 Thread a 24-inch length of ribbon under Cross Stitches on frame, beginning and ending in upper left-hand corner; glue to secure, trimming ends as needed. Tie a bow with remaining ribbon and glue to upper left-hand corner.

7 Using photo as a guide through step 9, for flowers, wrap a 3-yard length of white pearl cotton around 2-inch length of heavy cardboard 20 times. Slip pearl cotton off cardboard and tie a 6-inch length around center. Glue pink button to center of flower.

8 Following step 7, make one more white flower, three light yellow flowers and three green leaves, gluing remaining pink button to white flower and purple buttons to light yellow flowers.

9 Glue leaves and flowers to frame front. ❏

COLOR KEY	
#5 Pearl Cotton	**Yards**
■ Dark pink	109

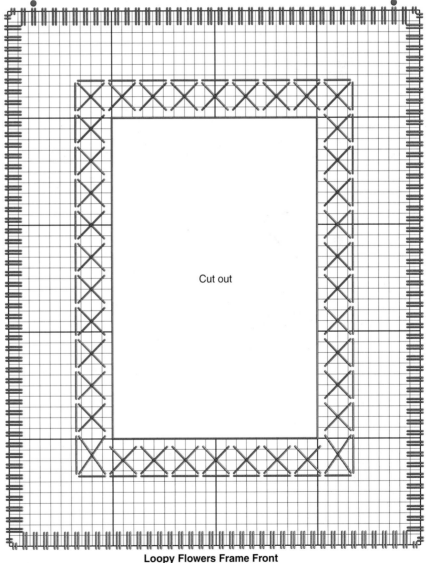

Loopy Flowers Frame Front
40 holes x 50 holes
Cut 1 from pink

Victorian Pretties

Designs by Ronda Bryce

This set of three pretty-as-a-picture pins is sure to sell like hotcakes at your local bazaar!

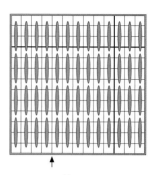

Purse
13 holes x 13 holes
Cut 1

COLOR KEY	
PURSE & HANKIE	
Plastic Canvas Yarn	**Yards**
☐ White #41	1
■ Camel #43	5
Color numbers given are for Uniek Needloft plastic canvas yarn.	

skill level • beginner

purse & hankie ✳ materials ✳

- ☐ Small amount 7-count plastic canvas
- ☐ Uniek Needloft plastic canvas yarn as listed in color key
- ☐ #16 tapestry needle
- ☐ ½-inch ribbon roses with leaves: 2 white and 1 light pink
- ☐ 4 (4mm) white pearl beads
- ☐ 12 inches ⅜-inch-wide light pink lace
- ☐ 4½ inches ¼-inch-wide light pink satin ribbon
- ☐ Sewing needle and light pink sewing thread
- ☐ 7mm gold spring ring
- ☐ 6mm gold jump ring
- ☐ 1-inch gold pin back
- ☐ Needle-nose pliers

finished size:
2¼ inches W x 4¾ inches H

instructions

1 Cut plastic canvas according to graphs, (this page and page 97). Cut one 5-hole x 5-hole piece for hankie.

2 Continental Stitch and Overcast hankie with white. Stitch remaining pieces following graphs.

3 With camel, Overcast around side and bottom edges of purse and purse flap. With wrong side of flap on right side of purse, Whipstitch top edges of flap and purse together.

4 Using photo as a guide and using sewing needle and light pink sewing thread through step 9, sew ribbon roses to bottom right of purse. Attach one pearl bead to bottom point of flap, then attach remaining beads in and around ribbon roses.

5 Cut one 5-inch and one 7-inch length from light pink lace. Sew 5-inch length around outside edge of hankie on backside, turning under raw edges and trimming as necessary to fit.

6 Sew 7-inch length around side and bottom edges of purse on backside, turning under raw edges and trimming as necessary to fit.

7 For handle, stitch light pink ribbon ends to top backside of purse.

8 With needle-nose pliers, attach one jump ring through a corner hole of hankie. Stitch spring ring to bottom backside of purse at arrow. Hook jump ring on hankie to spring ring on purse.

9 Stitch pin back to center top backside of purse.

key ✳ materials ✳

- ☐ Small amount 7-count plastic canvas
- ☐ Uniek Needloft plastic canvas yarn as listed in color key
- ☐ #16 tapestry needle
- ☐ ½-inch ribbon roses with leaves: 1 white, 1 light pink and 1 gold
- ☐ 6 (4mm) white pearl beads
- ☐ 12 inches ⅜-inch-wide light pink lace
- ☐ 1¼-inch light pink tassel
- ☐ Sewing needle and light pink sewing thread
- ☐ 1-inch gold pin back

finished size:
1¼ inches W x 3 inches H, excluding tassel

instructions

1 Cut plastic canvas according to graph.

2 Stitch and Overcast key following graph.

3 Using photo as a guide and using sewing needle and light pink sewing thread through step 5, sew ribbon roses to right side of key handle.

4 Attach pearl beads to key where indicated on graph.

5 Stitch tassel to backside of key handle on right side.

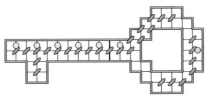

Key
19 holes x 8 holes
Cut 1

COLOR KEY
KEY
Plastic Canvas Yarn	Yards
■ Camel #43	2
○ Attach white pearl bead	
○ Attach tassel	

Color number given is for Uniek Needloft plastic canvas yarn.

hat & gloves ✖ materials ✖

- ❑ Small amount 7-count plastic canvas
- ❑ 2 (3-inch) plastic canvas radial circles
- ❑ Uniek Needloft plastic canvas yarn as listed in color key
- ❑ DMC 6-strand embroidery floss as listed in color key
- ❑ #16 tapestry needle
- ❑ 5 (½-inch) light blue ribbon roses with leaves
- ❑ 2 (4mm) white pearl beads
- ❑ 2 (2-inch) lengths ½-inch-wide light blue lace
- ❑ Sewing needle and light blue sewing thread
- ❑ 2 (7mm) gold spring rings
- ❑ 2 (6mm) gold jump rings
- ❑ 1-inch gold pin back
- ❑ Needle-nose pliers

finished size:

2⅜ inches W x 4 inches H x 1 inch D

instructions

1 Cut plastic canvas according to graphs (page 97), cutting away gray areas on hat top and hat brim.

2 Stitch pieces following graphs, reversing one glove before stitching.

3 Overcast gloves with white, then work Backstitches with light beige-brown embroidery floss.

4 Using camel throughout, Overcast around edge of hat brim. Whipstitch short edges of hat side together. Whipstitch top edge of side to hat top; Whipstitch bottom edge to brim where indicated on graph with blue line.

continued on page 97

Carryall Baskets

Designs by Marianne Telesca

You'll find **dozens** of **uses** for this set of **summer** baskets! They're **perfect** for taking snacks to the pool, carrying your **latest** plastic canvas **project**, or giving as hostess **gifts!**

skill level • beginner

instructions

1 Cut plastic canvas according to graphs, (this page and page 90) cutting away gray areas on hearts and stars.

2 Stitch basket sides following graphs, overlapping where indicated on graphs. Stitch and Overcast seagulls with white. Stitch remaining pieces following graphs, reversing one lighthouse before stitching.

3 Overcast handles, stars, lighthouses and watermelon slices following graphs. Work Backstitches and French Knots on lighthouses and Straight Stitches and French Knots on watermelon slices.

4 Use plastic canvas yarn through step 5. Holding wire around top edge of each basket, Overcast top edge and wire, using red for patriotic basket, medium blue for lighthouse basket and baby green for watermelon basket.

5 Overlap two bottom pieces of each basket where indicated on graph. Whipstitch to bottom edge of baskets, centering each basket seam at overlap and using royal blue for patriotic basket, green for lighthouse basket and baby green for watermelon basket.

6 Use photo as a guide through step 7. Placing handle ends along bottom edge, center and glue handles inside corresponding basket long sides.

7 Glue stars around patriotic basket. Glue lighthouses to one long side of lighthouse basket; glue one sea gull between lighthouses and one on each basket end. Glue watermelon pieces to one long side of watermelon basket. ❑

✖ materials ✖

Each Basket
- ❑ 1 artist-size sheet 7-count plastic canvas
- ❑ 2 (6-inch) Uniek QuickShape plastic canvas heart shapes
- ❑ Plastic canvas yarn as listed in color key
- ❑ ⅛ inch-wide Plastic Canvas 7 Metallic Needlepoint Yarn by Rainbow Gallery as listed in color key
- ❑ #16 tapestry needle
- ❑ 22 inches craft wire
- ❑ Hot-glue gun

Patriotic Basket
- ❑ 8 (6-inch) Uniek QuickShape plastic canvas star shapes

finished size:
8⅞ inches W x 8½ inches H x 4⅛ inches D

COLOR KEY
WATERMELON BASKET

Plastic Canvas Yarn	Yards
☐ White	26
☐ Baby green	21
■ Watermelon	6
■ Pink	4
☐ Baby pink	4
■ Green	4

⅛-Inch-Wide Metallic Needlepoint Yarn

■ Pink #PC8	12
╱ Black #PC11 Straight Stitch	1
● Black #PC11 French Knot	

Color numbers given are for Rainbow Gallery Plastic Canvas 7 Metallic Needlepoint Yarn.

Watermelon Slice
21 holes x 20 holes
Cut 2

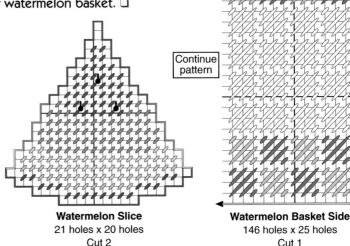

Continue pattern

Watermelon Basket Side
146 holes x 25 holes
Cut 1

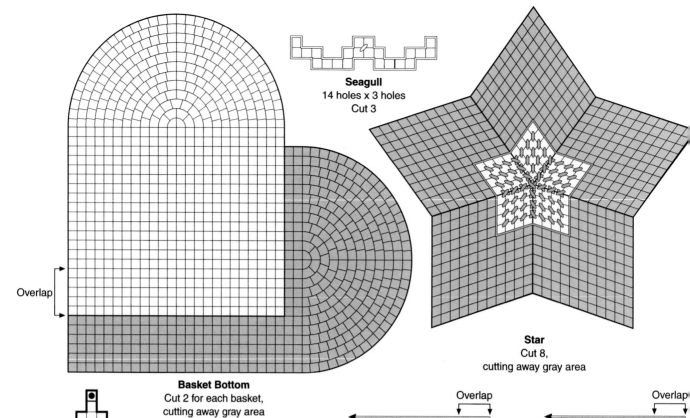

Seagull
14 holes x 3 holes
Cut 3

Overlap

Basket Bottom
Cut 2 for each basket,
cutting away gray area
Do not stitch

Star
Cut 8,
cutting away gray area

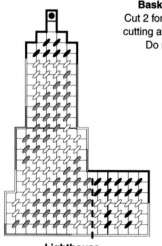

Lighthouse
14 holes x 21 holes
Cut 2, reverse 1

Continue
pattern

Basket Handle
4 holes x 118 holes
Cut 1 for each basket
Stitch patriotic and
watermelon handles as graphed
Stitch lighthouse handle
with beige

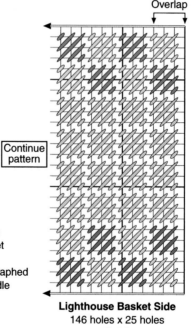

Overlap

Continue
pattern

Lighthouse Basket Side
146 holes x 25 holes
Cut 1

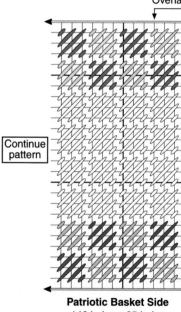

Overlap

Continue
pattern

Patriotic Basket Side
146 holes x 25 holes
Cut 1

COLOR KEY	
LIGHTHOUSE BASKET	
Plastic Canvas Yarn	**Yards**
☐ Beige	26
☐ Medium blue	9
☐ Green	9
☐ White	4
■ Red	2
■ Black	2
✎ Black Backstitch	
● Black French Knot	
⅛-Inch-Wide Metallic Needlepoint Yarn	
■ Green #PC4	6
■ Lite blue #PC14	6
Color numbers given are for Rainbow Gallery Plastic Canvas 7 Metallic Needlepoint Yarn.	

COLOR KEY	
PATRIOTIC BASKET	
Plastic Canvas Yarn	**Yards**
☐ White	26
☐ Red	9
☐ Royal blue	9
⅛-Inch-Wide Metallic Needlepoint Yarn	
■ Gold #PC1	20
■ Red #PC5	6
■ Navy #PC6	6
Color numbers given are for Rainbow Gallery Plastic Canvas 7 Metallic Needlepoint Yarn.	

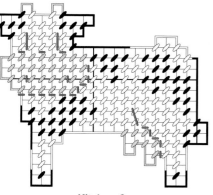

Kitchen Cow
21 holes x 17 holes
Cut 2, reverse 1

Kitchen Cows

Designs by Janelle Giese

Give your kitchen a **down-home country look** with this set of **decorative** projects!

skill level • beginner

✖ materials ✖

- ☐ ½ sheet Uniek Quick-Count white 7-count plastic canvas
- ☐ Chenille acrylic yarn as listed in color key
- ☐ Coats & Clark Red Heart Classic worsted weight yarn Art. E267 as listed in color key
- ☐ DMC #5 pearl cotton as listed in color key
- ☐ #16 tapestry needle
- ☐ 12 inches ¼-inch-wide red satin ribbon
- ☐ 10½-inch wooden spoon
- ☐ Red and white gingham twisted paper ribbon
- ☐ ½-inch plastic ring
- ☐ 2 inches ½-inch-wide magnetic tape
- ☐ Carpet thread
- ☐ Thick white glue

finished size:

Kitchen Cow: 3⅜ inches W x 2⅝ inches H

Cook's Bookmark: 3⅜ inches W x 7⅝ inches H

cutting & stitching

1 Cut plastic canvas according to graphs (this page and page 91), carefully cutting apart plastic canvas on bookmark where indicated with blue lines.

2 Stitch pieces following graphs, reversing one kitchen cow before stitching and working light colors of chenille yarn first, then black. Bottom of bookmark will remain unstitched. Overcast pieces following graphs.

3 When background stitching and Overcasting are completed, work pearl cotton Backstitches and Straight Stitches, working Straight Stitch for eyes four times.

assembly

1 Cut red satin ribbon into three 4-inch lengths. Tie each length in a tiny bow, trimming ends as desired. Using photo as a guide, glue one bow to tail of each cow.

2 For spoon, fold a long double strand of carpet thread in half and attach to plastic ring with a Lark's Head Knot. Place plastic ring on back of handle approximately 2 inches from end of handle and wrap thread tightly several times around handle; knot off.

3 Wrap a narrow length of unopened twisted paper ribbon around thread area, gluing while wrapping and overlapping end at front.

4 From twisted paper ribbon, cut two 6½-inch lengths, one 8½-inch length and one 3-inch length.

5 Use photo as a guide through step 8. To form bow, open two 6½-inch lengths and fold each length in half, placing ends together in center. Apply a small amount of glue to inside and pinch.

6 Open 8½-inch length and cut an inverted "V" in both ends. Crimp in center and glue to back of bow.

7 Wrap unopened 3-inch length around assembled bow, gluing in back. Glue bow to paper on front of handle.

8 Center right-facing kitchen cow over bow; glue in place. If extra stability is desired, thread a length of carpet thread through motif and bow, knotting ends at back of spoon handle.

9 Glue magnet to back of remaining kitchen cow. ☐

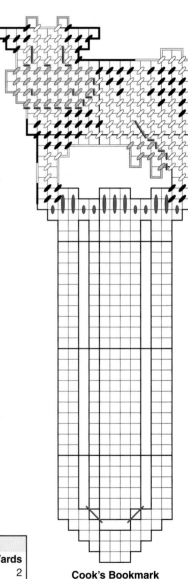

Cook's Bookmark
21 holes x 51 holes
Cut 1

COLOR KEY	
Chenille Acrylic Yarn	**Yards**
☐ White	2
■ Black	2
▨ Light peach	1
Worsted Weight Yarn	
■ Kiwi #651	1
#5 Pearl Cotton	
╱ Black #310 Backstitch and Straight Stitch	1
Color numbers given are for Coats & Clark Red Heart Classic worsted weight yarn Art. E267 and DMC #5 pearl cotton.	

Fun On Wheels

Designs by Lee Lindeman

Your **youngsters** will discover hours of **playtime fun**
with this set of three **colorful** toys on wheels!

skill level • intermediate

car
✖ materials ✖

- ❏ 1½ sheets 7-count plastic canvas
- ❏ Coats & Clark Red Heart Super Saver worsted weight yarn Art. E301 as listed in color key
- ❏ Metallic craft cord as listed in color key
- ❏ #5 pearl cotton as listed in color key
- ❏ #16 tapestry needle
- ❏ 4 (1½-inches in diameter x ½-inch) wooden toy wheels
- ❏ 4 (³⁄₁₆-inch x 1⅜-inch) axle pegs
- ❏ Acrylic craft paint: red and silver
- ❏ Paintbrush
- ❏ 2 (12mm) round crystal acrylic faceted stones
- ❏ 2 (11mm) round ruby acrylic faceted stones
- ❏ 5mm round black cabochon
- ❏ Polyester fiberfill
- ❏ Hot-glue gun

finished size:
3½ inches W x 6¼ inches L x 3½ inches H

instructions

1 Cut plastic canvas according to graphs. Cut one 11-hole x 34-hole piece for car bottom and two 18-hole x 2-hole pieces for bumpers.

2 Paint wooden toy wheels with red acrylic craft paint and axles with silver acrylic craft paint. Allow to dry.

3 Continental Stitch car bottom with bright yellow. Continental Stitch and Overcast car bumpers with silver.

4 Stitch remaining pieces following graphs, reversing one car side before stitching and working uncoded areas with bright yellow Continental Stitches.

5 When background stitching is completed, work black pearl cotton Backstitches on grill.

6 Following graphs, Overcast inside edges on car sides, then Whipstitch car top to car sides from dot to dot.

7 Stuff car with fiberfill, then Whipstitch to car bottom with bright yellow.

8 Using photo as a guide

through step 9, insert one axle through each wheel, then glue axles into side holes on car.

9 Glue crystal stones to front of car for headlights and ruby stones to back of car for tail lights. Center and glue black cabochon above grill on car front for ornament. Wrap bumpers around front and back of car, gluing ends to car sides.

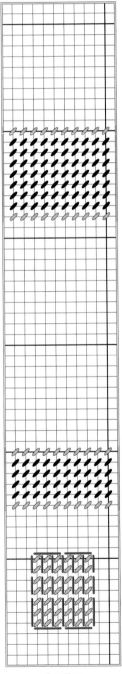

Car Top
11 holes x 62 holes
Cut 1

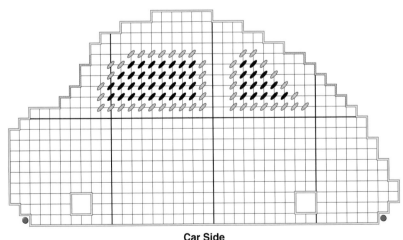

Car Side
38 holes x 20 holes
Cut 2, reverse 1

COLOR KEY
CAR

Worsted Weight Yarn   **Yards**

■ Black #312   8

   Uncoded areas are bright yellow
   #324 Continental Stitches   41

╱ Bright yellow #324 Whipstitching

Metallic Craft Cord

▨ Silver   10

#5 Pearl Cotton

╱ Black Backstitch   1

Color numbers given are for Coats & Clark Red Heart Super Saver worsted weight yarn Art. E301.

COLOR KEY
BIRD

Worsted Weight Yarn   **Yards**

☐ White #1   2

■ Black #312   2

▨ Medium clay #280   20

☐ Tan #334   7

■ Coffee #365   27

Color numbers given are for Coats & Clark Red Heart Classic worsted weight yarn Art. E267.

bird ✹ materials ✹

- ❑ 1½ sheets 7-count plastic canvas
- ❑ Coats & Clark Red Heart Classic worsted weight yarn Art. E267 as listed in color key
- ❑ #16 tapestry needle
- ❑ Small amount natural raffia
- ❑ Pencils
- ❑ 4 (1½-inches in diameter x ½-inch) wooden toy wheels
- ❑ 4 (³⁄₁₆-inch x 1⅜-inch) axle pegs
- ❑ 2 (9mm) round brown animal eyes
- ❑ Small amount black craft foam
- ❑ Polyester fiberfill
- ❑ Hot-glue gun

finished size:

3⅜ inches W x 6¼ inches L x 5¾ inches H

instructions

1 Cut plastic canvas according to graphs (this page and page 96). Cut beak pieces from black craft foam using patterns given.

2 Moisten eight strands of natural raffia and wrap around pencils. Allow to dry.

3 Stitch pieces following graphs,

reversing one body and one wing before stitching.

4 Following graphs through step 5, Overcast wings and inside edges of body pieces. Whipstitch body pieces together from blue dot at tip of tail across back and around head to blue dot at front of body.

5 Whipstitch gusset to body from blue dot on front of body around bottom and back to green dot at end of tail, stuffing with fiberfill before closing.

6 Using photo as a guide through step 8, glue wing edges from dot to dot to body sides.

7 Place top beak on bottom beak, then glue to front edge of head where indicated on graph, placing edge in indent.

8 Unwind natural raffia from pencils and tie strands together at one end. Glue tied end into tip of tail.

9 Insert one axle through each wheel, then glue axles into side holes on duck. Glue eyes to head.

Bird Beak Bottom
Cut 1 from
black craft foam

Bird Beak Top
Cut 1 from
black craft foam

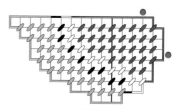

Bird Wing
15 holes x 8 holes
Cut 2, reverse 1

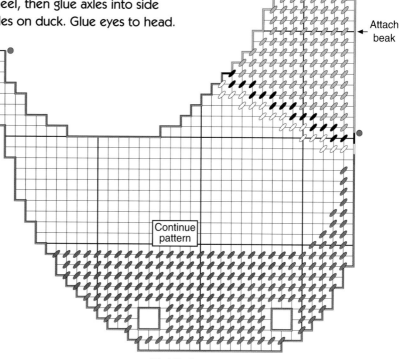

← Attach beak

Continue pattern

Bird Body
35 holes x 36 holes
Cut 2, reverse 1

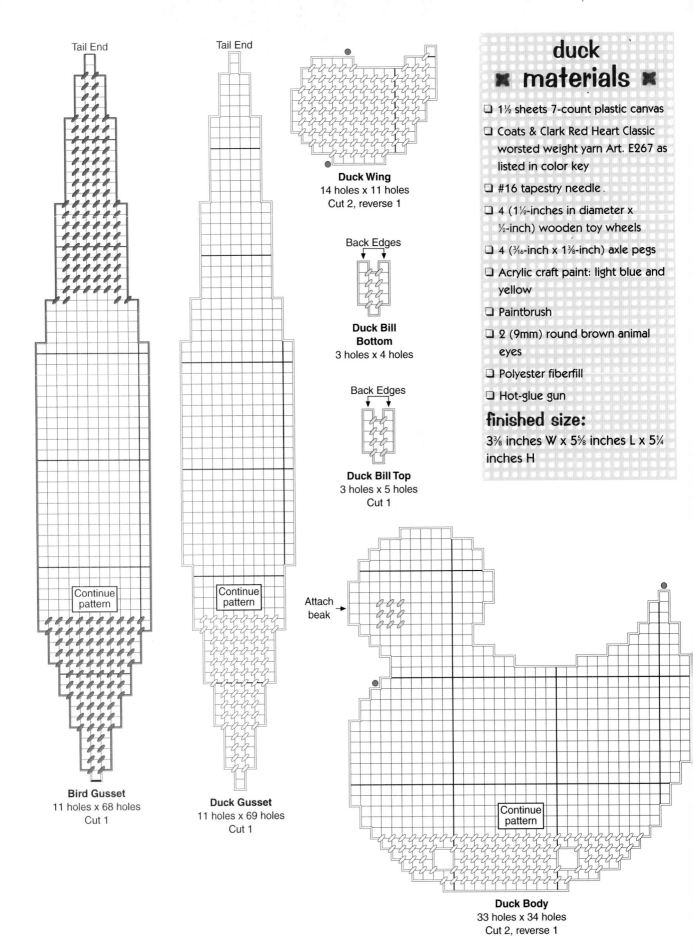

Tail End

Tail End

Duck Wing
14 holes x 11 holes
Cut 2, reverse 1

Back Edges

Duck Bill Bottom
3 holes x 4 holes

Back Edges

Duck Bill Top
3 holes x 5 holes
Cut 1

duck
✖ materials ✖

❑ 1½ sheets 7-count plastic canvas

❑ Coats & Clark Red Heart Classic worsted weight yarn Art. E267 as listed in color key

❑ #16 tapestry needle

❑ 4 (1½-inches in diameter x ½-inch) wooden toy wheels

❑ 4 (³⁄₁₆-inch x 1⅜-inch) axle pegs

❑ Acrylic craft paint: light blue and yellow

❑ Paintbrush

❑ 2 (9mm) round brown animal eyes

❑ Polyester fiberfill

❑ Hot-glue gun

finished size:
3⅜ inches W x 5⅝ inches L x 5¼ inches H

Continue pattern

Continue pattern

Bird Gusset
11 holes x 68 holes
Cut 1

Duck Gusset
11 holes x 69 holes
Cut 1

Attach beak →

Continue pattern

Duck Body
33 holes x 34 holes
Cut 2, reverse 1

COLOR KEY
DUCK

Worsted Weight Yarn	Yards
☐ White #1	50
☐ Yellow #230	1
☐ Pale rose #755	1

Color numbers given are for Coats & Clark Red Heart Classic worsted weight yarn Art. E267.

instructions

1 Cut plastic canvas according to graphs.

2 Paint wooden toy wheels with light blue acrylic craft paint and axles with yellow acrylic craft paint. Allow to dry.

3 Stitch pieces following graphs, reversing one body and one wing before stitching.

4 Using white through step 5, Overcast wings and inside edges of body pieces. Whipstitch body pieces together from dot to dot around top of body.

5 Whipstitch gusset around bottom of body from dot to dot, stuffing with fiberfill before closing.

6 Using photo as a guide through step 8, glue wing edges from dot to

dot to body sides.

7 With yellow, Overcast all but back edges of bill pieces, Overcasting indents adjacent to back edges. Whipstitch wrong sides of bill pieces together along back edges. Glue to front edge of head where indicated on graph, placing edge in indent.

8 Insert one axle through each wheel, then glue axles into side holes on duck. Glue eyes to head. ❏

Victorian Pretties continued from page 87

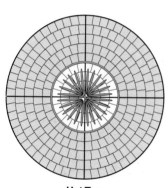

Hat Top
Cut 1,
cutting away gray area

Continue pattern

Hat Brim
Cut 1,
cutting away gray area

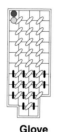

Glove
4 holes x 10 holes
Cut 2, reverse 1

COLOR KEY
HAT & GLOVES

Plastic Canvas Yarn	Yards
☐ White #41	3
■ Camel #43	6

6-Strand Embroidery Floss
✐ Light beige brown #841 Backstitch	
✐ Whipstitch to hat side	1
○ Attach white pearl bead	
● Attach jump ring	

Color numbers given are for Uniek Needloft plastic canvas yarn and DMC 6-strand embroidery floss.

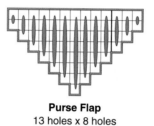

Purse Flap
13 holes x 8 holes
Cut 1

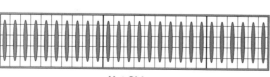

Hat Side
26 holes x 5 holes
Cut 1

5 Using sewing needle and light blue sewing thread through step 9, attach one length of lace around top of each glove, turning raw edges under and trimming to fit as necessary on backside.

6 Attach pearl bead to each glove where indicated on graph.

7 Evenly space and sew light blue ribbon roses around brim of hat at hat side.

8 With needle-nose pliers, attach one jump ring to each glove where indicated on graph. Stitch spring rings to bottom edge of hat approximately 1¼ inches apart. Hook jump rings on gloves to spring rings on hat.

9 Stitch pin back to center top backside of hat. ❏

CHAPTER THREE

Autumn Colors

Enjoy beautiful design and color

with these fantastic fall projects!

Savor the sights and
stitches of autumn in this
collection of charming
fall projects!
Vibrant leaves,
friendly spooks and
whimsical back-to-school
projects will give you dozens
of great ideas for sharing
with customers at this
year's autumn bazaar!

Bookworm Book Holder

Design by Susan Leinberger

Prop open your book with this personable bookworm!
He's a great helper while cooking, stitching or just reading!

skill level • beginner

instructions

1 Cut front from clear plastic canvas and back from green plastic canvas according to graph. Back will remain unstitched.

2 Stitch front following graph, working uncoded areas with fern Continental Stitches.

3 When background stitching is completed, work white French Knots and solid gold Backstitches and Straight Stitches.

4 For antennae, insert yellow chenille stem through hole indicated on graph, pulling through to middle of stem; bend up into a "V".

5 With sandstone, Overcast bottom of mushroom stems. Whipstitch front to back along remaining edges with adjacent colors, placing antenna located on backside between front and back pieces.

6 For eye, glue cabochon to head where indicated on graph. Glue pompoms to ends of antennae.

7 For book holder, bend wire hanger by first squeezing sides together and bending down (Fig. 1). Bend two ends up in the front; bend hook down in the back. (Fig. 2) Hook will help support the book holder.

8 Secure forest yarn with a dot of glue at end of hanger hook. Wrap yarn around hanger, securing with dots of glue as needed and wrapping just past the fold on the two ends.

9 Slide mushroom stems onto hanger ends when glue is dry. ❏

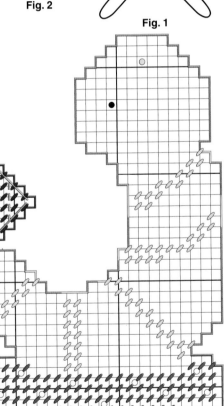

Fig. 2

Fig. 1

Worm Front & Back
50 holes x 43 holes
Cut 1 front from clear
stitch as graphed
Cut 1 back from green
Do not stitch

COLOR KEY

Plastic Canvas Yarn	Yards
■ Christmas red #02	5
■ Sandstone #16	3
□ Yellow #57	3
■ Dark royal #58	2
Uncoded areas are fern #23 Continental Stitches	10
✎ Fern #23 Whipstitching	
○ White #41 French Knot	1

Metallic Craft Cord
✎ Solid gold #55020 Backstitch and Straight Stitch
○ Insert chenille stem
● Attach black cabochon

Color numbers given are for Uniek Needloft plastic canvas yarn and metallic craft cord.

✖ materials ✖

- ❏ 1 sheet Uniek Quick-Count clear 7-count plastic canvas
- ❏ 1 sheet green 7-count plastic canvas
- ❏ Uniek Needloft plastic canvas yarn: 3 yards forest #29 and as listed in color key
- ❏ Uniek Needloft metallic craft cord as listed in color key
- ❏ #16 tapestry needle
- ❏ 4 inches yellow chenille stem
- ❏ 2 (7mm) green pompoms
- ❏ 6mm round black cabochon
- ❏ Wire coat hanger
- ❏ Tacky craft glue

finished size:

7½ inches W x 6¾ inches H x 6¾ inches D

Schoolkids Slate & Tote

Designs by Janelle Giese

Delight you child's teacher with this decorative
and practical set just right for the classroom!

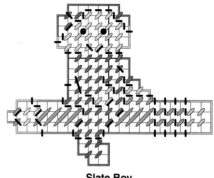

Slate Boy
20 holes x 15 holes
Cut 1

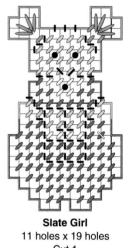

Slate Girl
11 holes x 19 holes
Cut 1

skill level • beginner

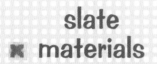

slate
✖ materials ✖

- ❑ Small amount 7-count plastic canvas
- ❑ Coats & Clark Red Heart Classic worsted weight yarn Art. E267 as listed in color key
- ❑ DMC #5 pearl cotton as listed in color key
- ❑ #16 tapestry needle
- ❑ Framed slate (sample used 5⅜ inches W x 11¼ inches H)
- ❑ ¾ yard ⅜-inch-wide emerald green grosgrain ribbon
- ❑ Sawtooth hanger
- ❑ Wood glue
- ❑ Thick white glue

finished size:

Boy: 3⅛ inches W x 2⅜ inches H

Girl: 1¾ inches W x 3 inches H

instructions

1 Cut plastic canvas according to graphs (this page and page 104).

2 Stitch and Overcast pieces following graphs. When background stitching and Overcasting are completed, work pearl cotton Backstitches and Straight Stitches.

3 Work apple highlight with full strand white. Using 1 ply country red, tie two tiny bows around base of pigtails, placing bow in front.

4 With wood glue, attach sawtooth hanger to back of frame. Cut ribbon in half, trimming ends in an inverted "V." Fold each length over at center to form "L" shapes; glue one fold to upper left-hand corner and one to lower right-hand corner.

5 Using photo as a guide and thick white glue through step 7, glue stitched boy and girl over ribbon folds at corners.

6 For ribbon lengths along top and bottom of frame, fold to form "L" shapes at remaining corners, leaving a 1¼-inch tail. Glue folds to corners and 1¼-inch tails to frame sides. Place dabs of glue on frame top and bottom under ribbon; press ribbon into glue to form ruffled streamers.

7 Glue ends of ribbon lengths along frame sides approximately 5¾ inches from folds at corners. Place dabs of glue on frame top and bottom under ribbon; press ribbon into glue to form ruffled streamers.

COLOR KEY	
SLATE	
Worsted Weight Yarn	**Yards**
❑ White #1	1
■ Orange #245	2
■ Sea coral #246	2
❑ Tan #334	1
■ Mid brown #339	1
■ Silver #412	1
❑ Light coral rose #749	1
■ True blue #822	1
■ Country red #914	2
⁄ White #1 Straight Stitch	
#5 Pearl Cotton	
✔ Black #310 Backstitch and Straight Stitch	5
● Black #310 French Knot	
Color numbers given are for Coats & Clark Red Heart Classic worsted weight yarn Art. E267 and DMC #5 pearl cotton.	

tote

✖ materials ✖

- ☐ 1 sheet Uniek Quick-Count Christmas red 7-count plastic canvas
- ☐ ½ sheet Uniek Quick-count clear 7-count plastic canvas
- ☐ Coats & Clark Red Heart Classic worsted weight yarn Art. E267 as listed in color key
- ☐ DMC #3 pearl cotton as listed in color key
- ☐ DMC #5 pearl cotton as listed in color key
- ☐ #16 tapestry needle
- ☐ Large-eye needle
- ☐ ½ yard 4mm twisted red satin cording
- ☐ Thick white glue

finished size:

5⅛ inches W x 6¾ inches H x ¾ inches D

COLOR KEY	
TOTE	
Worsted Weight Yarn	**Yards**
◯ White #1	1
◢ Black #12	7
◯ Yellow #230	2
◯ Orange #245	4
△ Sea coral #246	2
◢ Warm brown #336	2
◯ Silver #412	1
◢ Emerald green #676	3
△ Paddy green #686	2
◯ Light coral rose #749	1
◢ Skipper blue #848	
△ Cherry red #912	2
◢ Cardinal #917	1
Uncoded areas are Olympic blue #849 Continental Stitches	5
◢ White #1 Straight Stitch	
◢ Black #12 Straight Stitch	
◢ Orange #245 Straight Stitch	
◢ Warm brown #336 Straight Stitch	
#3 Pearl Cotton	
◢ White Backstitch and Straight Stitch	1
#5 Pearl Cotton	
◢ Black #310 Backstitch and Straight Stitch	7
● Black #310 French Knot	
Color numbers given are for Coats & Clark Red Heart Classic worsted weight yarn Art. E267 and DMC #3 pearl cotton and #5 pearl cotton.	

instructions

1 Cut tote front from clear plastic canvas according to graph.

2 From red plastic canvas, cut one 33-hole x 44-hole piece for toteback, two 18-hole x 44-hole pieces for tote sides, one 33-hole x 18-hole piece for tote bottom and two 5-hole x 5-hole pieces for handle reinforcements. All red plastic canvas pieces will remain unstitched.

3 Stitch tote front following graph, working uncoded areas with Olympic blue Continental Stitches.

4 Straight Stitch warm brown apple stem and cowlick on boy's head, white highlight on apple, black pencil tips and orange apple rays.

5 Stitch words at bottom of front with white #3 pearl cotton. Using black #5 pearl cotton, work embroidery on apple and children, stitching over eyes four times.

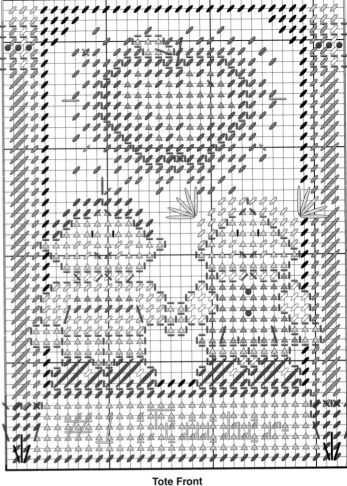

Tote Front
33 holes x 44 holes
Cut 1 from clear

6 Following graph, Whipstitch sides to front, then work black #5 pearl cotton Backstitches, Straight Stitches and French Knots on pencil, working stitches over edges where indicated.

7 Using black yarn throughout, Whipstitch bottom to sides and front; Whipstitch back to sides and bottom. Overcast top edges.

8 To attach handle, use large-eye needle to thread ends of twisted cording through sides, six holes from top and seven holes from front, threading through handle reinforcements on inside of bag at the same time. Knot ends, trim and glue to secure. ❑

Take-Along Hopscotch

Designs by Mary T. Cosgrove

Pass away those morning and afternoon school bus trips
with this colorful hopscotch game!

✶ materials ✶

- ❏ 1 sheet Uniek Quick-Count 7-count plastic canvas
- ❏ Uniek Needloft plastic canvas yarn as listed in color key
- ❏ #16 tapestry needle
- ❏ White pony bead
- ❏ Size 3-0 (¼-inch) sew-on snap
- ❏ Clear nylon thread
- ❏ White craft glue

finished size:

Hopscotch Board: 6⅞ inches W x 13⅝ inches L

Numbers Wheel: 4⅝ inches square

Player: 2¼ inches W x 3¼ inches H x 1¼ inches D

Marker: 1 inch W x 1 inch L

skill level
beginner

cutting & stitching

1 Cut plastic canvas according to graphs. Two markers and one spinner will remain unstitched.

2 Stitch player stands and two markers following graphs, working one stand and one marker as graphed and remaining stand and marker with bright orange.

3 Stitch players following graphs, working uncoded areas with pink Continental Stitches. Work one player as graphed and one replacing bright blue with bright orange.

4 Stitch numbers wheel, hopscotch board and one spinner following graphs, working uncoded areas on board with black Continental Stitches.

5 When background stitching is completed, work numbers, noses, mouths and eyes with black yarn following graphs.

6 Overcast numbers wheel and board with white. Overcast stands and players with adjacent colors.

assembly

1 Whipstitch one unstitched marker to each stitched marker with adjacent colors. Whipstitch unstitched spinner to stitched spinner with black.

2 For pigtail ties, cut two 3-inch lengths each of bright blue and bright orange yarn.

3 Using photo as a guide and matching dress color of player, thread yarn through holes indicated on heads. Tie yarn in a knot and trim ends to ¼ inch. Apply a small amount of glue on ends to prevent fraying.

4 Using pink and two stitches per hole, stitch bottom edges of players to matching stands where indicated on graph with pink lines.

5 Using clear nylon thread throughout, stitch white pony bead to center of wheel with one-half of sew-on snap on top of bead. Stitch remaining half of snap to center backside of spinner where indicated on graph. Snap spinner on wheel. ❏

Marker
6 holes x 6 holes
Cut 4, stitch 2
Stitch 1 as graphed
and 1 with bright orange

Stand
8 holes x 8 holes
Cut 4, stitch 2
Stitch 1 as graphed
and 1 with bright orange

```
COLOR KEY
Plastic Canvas Yarn                          Yards
■ Black #00                                    30
■ Maple #13                                     2
☐ White #41                                    14
■ Bright orange #58                             9
■ Bright blue #60                               8
  Uncoded areas are on hopscotch board
  are black #00 Continental Stitches
  Uncoded areas on players are
  pink #07 Continental Stitches                 4
⟋ Pink #07 Overcasting
⟋ Black #00 Backstitch and Straight Stitch
● Black #00 French Knot
○ Attach pigtail tie
● Attach snap
Color numbers given are for Uniek Needloft plastic canvas
yarn.
```

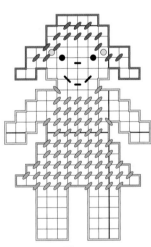

Player
14 holes x 21 holes
Cut 2
Stitch 1 as graphed
Stitch 1, replacing bright
blue with bright orange

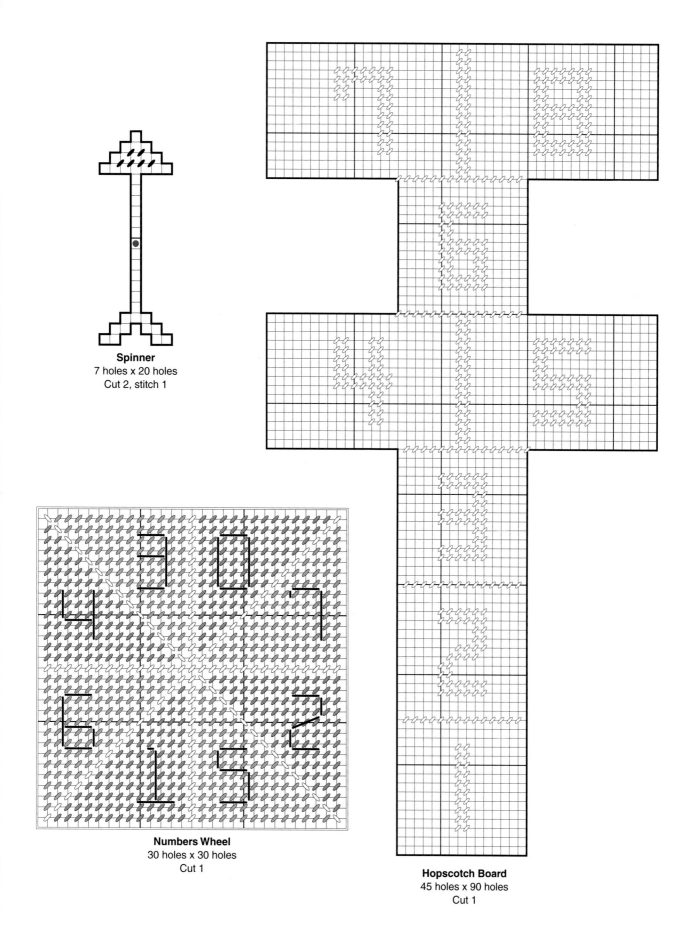

Spinner
7 holes x 20 holes
Cut 2, stitch 1

Numbers Wheel
30 holes x 30 holes
Cut 1

Hopscotch Board
45 holes x 90 holes
Cut 1

Li'l Punkin Frame

Design by Susan Leinberger

Display a favorite photo of your little sweetheart in this delightful magnetic frame!

skill level • beginner

graphs continued on page 116

✖ materials ✖

- ❑ ½ sheet Uniek Quick-Count 7-count plastic canvas
- ❑ Uniek Needloft plastic canvas yarn as listed in color key
- ❑ DMC #3 pearl cotton as listed in color key
- ❑ #16 tapestry needle
- ❑ 6 inches green chenille stem
- ❑ Pencil
- ❑ 2 (4-inch) lengths self-adhesive magnet strip
- ❑ Hot-glue gun

finished size:

3¾ inches W x 4 inches H

instructions

1 Cut plastic canvas according to graphs (this page and page 116). Frame back will remain unstitched.

2 Stitch frame front and leaves following graphs, working uncoded area on frame front with eggshell Continental Stitches.

3 Overcast leaves and stem with holly, then work Straight Stitches on leaves.

4 Work letters on front with black pearl cotton; work Backstitches around eggshell area with 1 ply holly.

5 Using bittersweet, Overcast top edges of front from dot to dot with bittersweet, then Whipstitch remaining edges of front to back around sides and bottom. Do not Overcast top edge of frame back.

6 For tendrils, insert ends of chenille stem from back to front through holes indicated on graph and pull through to front, keeping ends even. Wrap ends around pencil several times to form tendrils.

7 Using photo as a guide, glue leaves to front under stem, sliding bottom notch on leaves in place around chenille stems.

8 Attach self-adhesive magnet strips to frame back. ❑

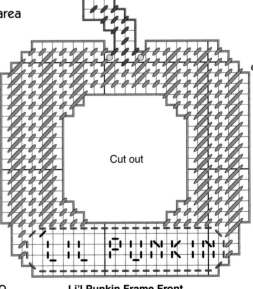

Li'l Punkin Frame Front
24 holes x 26 holes
Cut 1

Cut out

On-the-Go Kids' Bag Tags

Designs by Mary T. Cosgrove

Help your kids keep track of their bags by stitching them a set of these handy bag tags! They're perfect for backpacks and luggage.

skill level • beginner

✸ materials ✸

❑ ½ sheet Uniek Quick-Count 7-count plastic canvas
❑ Uniek Needloft plastic canvas yarn as listed in color key
❑ #16 tapestry needle
❑ Small amount white poster board
❑ Pen or permanent marker

finished size:
Airplane: 4¼ inches W x 3⅜ inches H, excluding hanger

School Bus: 3⅜ inches W x 2 inches H, excluding hangers

instructions

1 Cut plastic canvas according to graphs (page 110).

2 Stitch pieces following graphs, reversing one airplane before stitching.

3 For airplane, Overcast inside edges with white. Using bright blue, Overcast back edges from dot to dot; Whipstitch wrong sides together along remaining edges.

4 For school bus, Overcast inside edges and back edges from dot to dot with yellow. Whipstitch wrong sides together along remaining edges with yellow and black following graphs.

5 Cut a 2¾-inch x ¾-inch piece of white poster board for airplane. Cut a 2⅜-inch x 1¼-inch piece of white poster board for school bus.

6 On airplane tag, write the name on one side and the address on the other side. Insert through opening on back of airplane.

7 On school bus tag, add name and address to one side and school bus number to back side, making sure to place words so they can be seen in opening. Insert through opening on back of school bus.

8 Cut one 9-inch length of bright blue yarn. Attach to top of airplane wings with a Lark's Head Knot. Tie ends in a knot to form a loop for hanging.

9 Cut one 9-inch length of yellow yarn. Insert ends to inside of bus through hole indicated on graph. Tie ends in a knot to form a loop for hanging. Tuck knot inside bus. ❑

COLOR KEY
SCHOOL BUS

Plastic Canvas Yarn	Yards
■ Black #00	2
□ Yellow #57	4
● Attach hanger	

Color numbers given are for Uniek Needloft plastic canvas yarn.

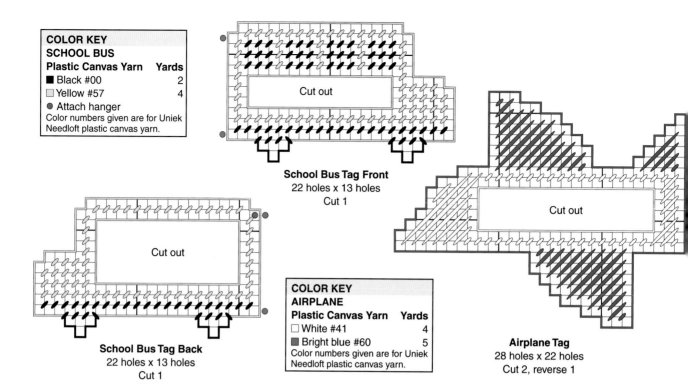

School Bus Tag Front
22 holes x 13 holes
Cut 1

School Bus Tag Back
22 holes x 13 holes
Cut 1

COLOR KEY
AIRPLANE

Plastic Canvas Yarn	Yards
□ White #41	4
■ Bright blue #60	5

Color numbers given are for Uniek Needloft plastic canvas yarn.

Airplane Tag
28 holes x 22 holes
Cut 2, reverse 1

Garden Miss Towel Topper

Design by Judy Collishaw

From the pretty red flower in her hair to the buckles on her dress, this sweet gal will add a charming touch to your kitchen!

skill level • beginner

Jumper Pocket
5 holes x 4 holes
Cut 2

Garden Miss Flower
3 holes x 3 holes
Cut 1

✷ materials ✷

- ❑ ½ sheet 7-count plastic canvas
- ❑ Worsted weight yarn as listed in color key
- ❑ DMC #3 pearl cotton as listed in color key
- ❑ DMC #5 pearl cotton as listed in color key
- ❑ #16 tapestry needle
- ❑ 1¼-inch round craft magnet
- ❑ 2 (⅜-inch x ⅝-inch) buckles
- ❑ Sewing needle and sewing thread to match denim blue yarn
- ❑ Small hand towel
- ❑ Low-temperature glue gun

finished size:
4⅜ inches W x 6¾ inches H, excluding hand towel

instructions

1 Cut plastic canvas according to graphs. Cut one 23-hole x 3-hole piece for towel bar. Towel bar will remain unstitched.

2 Following graphs through step 4, stitch and Overcast flower. Stitch remaining pieces, working uncoded background on face with peach Continental Stitches and uncoded areas on jumper and pockets with denim Continental Stitches.

3 Overcast girl, pockets and shovel, Whipstitching side edges of unstitched towel bar to wrong side of skirt from blue dot to blue dot on each side of skirt while Overcasting.

4 When background stitching and Overcasting are completed, work black French Knots, wrapping yarn around needle two times. Work red and yellow French Knots, wrapping yarn around needle one time. Work pearl cotton embroidery.

5 Using photo as a guide, through step 7, with sewing needle and sewing thread, sew one buckle to each jumper strap at bib.

6 Glue flower to hat where indicated on graph. Glue shovel to center of girl, placing hand on shovel over hand on girl. Glue one pocket at a slight angle to each side of skirt. Glue round magnet to backside of head.

7 Place towel over bar on backside of girl. ❑

COLOR KEY	
Worsted Weight Yarn	**Yards**
☐ White	4
☐ Yellow	3
◼ Red	3
☐ Peach	2
◼ Tan	2
☐ Gray	2
◼ Dark brown	1
Uncoded areas on jumper and pockets are demin blue Continental Stitches	7
Uncoded background on face is peach Continental Stitches	
╱ Demin blue Overcasting and Whipstitching	
○ Yellow French Knot	
● Red French Knot	
● Black French Knot	1
#3 Pearl Cotton	
╱ Very light carnation #894 Straight Stitch	1
#5 Pearl Cotton	
╱ White Running Stitch	
⋎ Red #321 Fly Stitch	1
╱ Black #310 Backstitch	1
● Attach flower	1
Color numbers given are for DMC pearl cotton.	

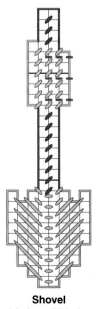

Shovel
8 holes x 26 holes
Cut 1

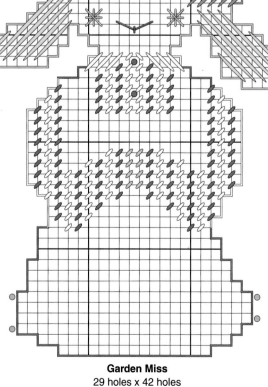

Garden Miss
29 holes x 42 holes
Cut 1

Silly Scarecrow

Design by Lee Lindeman

Add a whimsical touch to your dinner table or favorite side table with this charming scarecrow!

skill level • beginner

✹ materials ✹

- ❏ 1 sheet 7-count plastic canvas
- ❏ Coats & Clark Red Heart Super Saver worsted weight yarn Art. E301 as listed in color key
- ❏ #3 pearl cotton as listed in color key
- ❏ #16 tapestry needle
- ❏ Small amount red felt or imitation suede
- ❏ 2 (3mm) round black beads
- ❏ 3 (6mm) round black cabochons
- ❏ Straw hat 2 inches in diameter at crown
- ❏ Sewing needle and off-white sewing thread
- ❏ Small amount natural raffia
- ❏ 2 (3-inch-long) twigs
- ❏ Polyester fiberfill
- ❏ ¾-inch rock
- ❏ Hot-glue gun

finished size:

5¾ inches W x 8 inches H x 1¼ inches D

cutting & stitching

1 Cut plastic canvas according to graphs. Cut one 4-hole x 4-hole piece for pocket.

2 Using pattern given, cut four gloves from red felt or imitation suede.

3 Continental Stitch and Overcast pocket with skipper blue. Stitch remaining pieces following graphs, working head back entirely in Aran Continental Stitches.

4 When background stitching is completed, work black pearl cotton Backstitches for mouth and Aran French Knot for nose.

5 On body pieces, using bright yellow, Overcast top neck edges and arm edges from dot to dot.

assembly

1 Use photo as a guide throughout assembly. Using sewing needle and off-white thread, attach beads to head front where indicated on graph.

2 Whipstitch head front and back together with Aran, stuffing with fiberfill before closing.

3 Following graphs through step 4, with wrong sides facing, Whipstitch base to bottom edges of body front and back. Whipstitch body front and back together

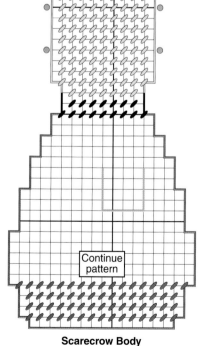

Scarecrow Body
18 holes x 35 holes
Cut 2

Continue pattern

along side edges up to waist, adding fiberfill and rock while Whipstitching.

4 Continue Whipstitching up side edges, bypassing Overcast areas. Stuff upper body with fiberfill.

5 Glue neck on head into neck opening of body. Glue twigs into arm openings. Glue cabochons to body front for buttons.

6 Matching edges, glue two gloves together over end of one twig. Repeat with remaining glove pieces, gluing to remaining twig.

7 Glue a small bunch of natural raffia to backside of pocket, allow-ing raffia to extend above top edge ½ inch to 1 inch . Glue raffia and pocket to lower body where indicated on graph with blue lines.

8 Glue raffia to head for hair. Thread a length of skipper blue yarn through base of straw hat; tie ends in a bow and trim as desired. Glue hat to head.

9 Tie two strands of raffia around neck in a bow. ❑

Scarecrow Glove
Cut 4 from red
felt or imitation suede

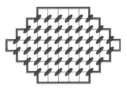

Scarecrow Head
10 holes x 15 holes
Cut 2
Stitch front as graphed
Stitch back entirely with
Aran Continental Stitche

Scarecrow Base
11 holes x 7 holes
Cut 1

COLOR KEY	
Worsted Weight Yarn	**Yards**
■ Black #312	1
☐ Aran #313	2
☐ Bright yellow #324	4
▦ Rose pink #372	1
■ Skipper blue #384	10
○ Aran #313 French Knot	
#3 Pearl Cotton	
╱ Black Backstitch	1
● Attach bead	
Color numbers given are for Coats & Clark Super Saver worsted weight yarn Art. E301.	

Black Cat Pin

Design by Kristine Loffredo

At work or at play, this easy-to-stitch pin will add a Halloween accent to any outfit!

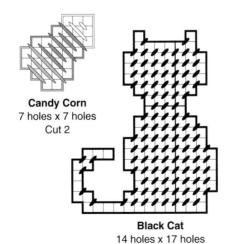

✖ materials ✖

- ☐ ¼ sheet 7-count plastic canvas
- ☐ Uniek Needloft plastic canvas yarn as listed in color key
- ☐ #16 tapestry needle
- ☐ 1-inch pin back
- ☐ Hot-glue gun

finished size:
2⅝ inches W x 3 inches H

COLOR KEY	
Plastic Canvas Yarn	**Yards**
■ Black #00	3
▦ Tangerine #11	1
☐ White #41	1
▦ Bittersweet #52	1
Color numbers given are for Uniek Needloft plastic canvas yarn.	

skill level beginner

Candy Corn
7 holes x 7 holes
Cut 2

Black Cat
14 holes x 17 holes
Cut 1

instructions

1 Cut plastic canvas according to graphs.

2 Stitch and Overcast pieces following graphs.

3 Using photo as a guide, glue candy corn pieces to lower right side of cat. Glue pin back to backside of cat. ❑

Happy Harvest

Design by Janna Britton

Country folk will love hanging this whimsical wall hanging
with Mr. Scarecrow driving the tractor!

skill level • beginner

✖ materials ✖

- ❑ 1 sheet 7-count plastic canvas
- ❑ Uniek Needloft plastic canvas yarn: ¼ yard royal and as listed in color key
- ❑ #16 tapestry needle
- ❑ 2-inch straw hat
- ❑ 5 long strands natural raffia
- ❑ 48 inches 20-gauge black wire
- ❑ Wire cutters
- ❑ Pencil
- ❑ 10¼-inch x 3½-inch piece wood
- ❑ Drill and 1⁄16-inch drill bit
- ❑ Sandpaper
- ❑ Low-temperature glue gun

finished size:

10¼ inches W x 19 inches L

cutting & stitching

1 Cut plastic canvas according to graphs (this page and pages 115 and 116).

2 Stitch pieces following graphs, working uncoded areas with eggshell Continental Stitches. Work embroidery over completed background stitching.

3 Overcast pieces following graphs. For hair, add Lark's Head Knots in desired lengths of yellow yarn where indicated on graph.

assembly

1 Use photo as a guide throughout assembly. For each hand, cut six 1-inch lengths yellow yarn. Place together in a bundle and attach to wrong side of wrist with bright blue yarn. Glue to secure.

2 Cut royal blue yarn in half. Tie one half around each wrist and knot on front side; trim ends as desired.

3 Glue hat to head, pushing hair down; trim hair as desired. Glue right arm to shoulder on left side of scarecrow.

4 With black, attach wheels to tractor through yarn on backside of each wheel, making sure bottom edges are even.

5 Drill four holes in corners of board ½ inch from top and bottom edges and ¾ inches from sides.

6 Cut wire into two 12-inch lengths and one 24-inch length. Wrap lengths around pencil to curl. Insert 12-inch lengths from back to front through bottom holes on board. Coil or twist ends tightly on front to secure.

7 Thread wire on left side from front to back through shoulder of scarecrow; wrap wire around itself on backside of scarecrow. Repeat with wire on right side, threading through top right corner of tractor front.

8 Glue letters to board front so they read "HAPPY HARVEST."

9 For hanger, thread ends of 24-inch length wire from back to front through top holes on board. Coil or twist ends tightly on front to secure. Place all five strands of natural raffia together, then tie in a bow around hanger. ❑

COLOR KEY	
Plastic Canvas Yarn	**Yards**
■ Black #00	10
■ Holly #27	2
▢ Christmas green #28	12
▢ Silver #37	3
▢ Yellow #57	10
■ Bright blue #60	3
Uncoded areas are eggshell #39 Continental Stitches	8
⁄ Eggshell #39 Overcasting	
⁄ Cinnamon #14 Backstitch	1
⁄ Yellow #57 Straight Stitch	
✖ Pink #07 Cross Stitch	1
● Cinnamon #14 French Knot	
○ Yellow #57 Lark's Head Knot	
Color numbers given are for Uniek Needloft plastic canvas yarn.	

Happy Harvest Letters
7 holes x 8 holes

Cut 2   Cut 2   Cut 2   Cut 1

Cut 1   Cut 1   Cut 1   Cut 1   Cut 1

Front Tractor Tire
12 holes x 12 holes
Cut 1

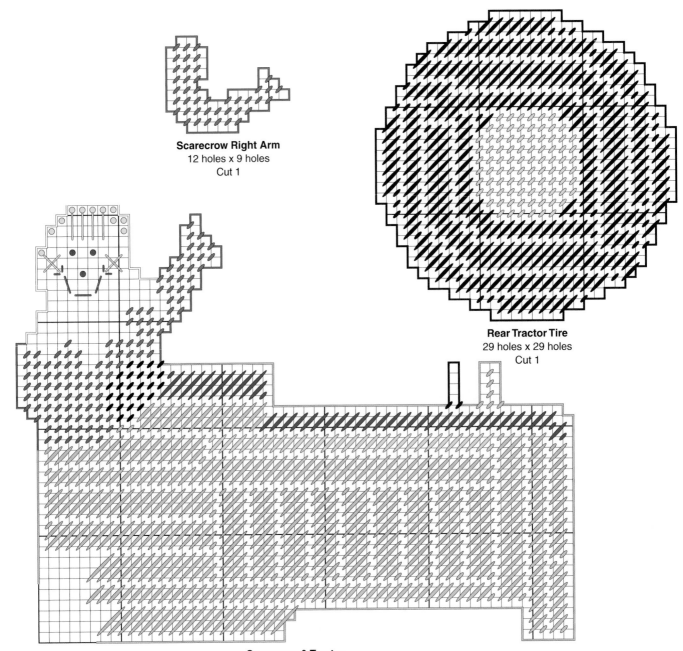

Scarecrow Right Arm
12 holes x 9 holes
Cut 1

Rear Tractor Tire
29 holes x 29 holes
Cut 1

Scarecrow & Tractor
54 holes x 41 holes
Cut 1

Pumpkin Frame continued from page 108

COLOR KEY

Plastic Canvas Yarn	Yards
■ Holly #27	4
■ Bittersweet #52	5
Uncoded area is eggshell #39 Continental Stitches	2
╱ Holly #27 Backstitch and Straight Stitch	
#3 Pearl Cotton	
╱ Black #310 Backstitch and Straight Stitch	1
○ Insert chenille stem	

Color numbers given are for Uniek Needloft plastic canvas yarn and DMC #3 pearl cotton.

Li'l Punkin Frame Leaf
9 holes x 11 holes
Cut 2

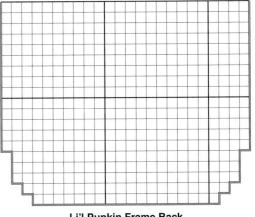

Li'l Punkin Frame Back
24 holes x 19 holes
Cut 1
Do not stitch

Autumn Favor Box

Design by Deborah Scheblein

Perfect for sharing with your Thanksgiving dinner guests, this clever box can be filled with a special note or treat!

skill level • beginner

✖ materials ✖

- ⅓ sheet 7-count plastic canvas
- Worsted weight yarn as listed in color key
- #16 tapestry needle
- Green cloth-covered wire
- Small paint brush
- Hot-glue gun

finished size:
1⅞ inches W x 3¼ inches H x 1⅞ inches D

instructions

1 Cut plastic canvas according to graphs. Cut one 11-hole x 9-hole piece for box bottom. Bottom will remain unstitched.

2 Stitch remaining pieces following graphs. Following graphs, Overcast around side and top edges of stem side and leaf side from dot to dot; Overcast top edges of short sides from dot to dot.

3 Using orange, Whipstitch leaf side and stem side to short sides along remaining side edges, then Whipstitch sides to bottom.

4 Glue wire to leaf where indicated on graph. Glue wire to stem and pumpkin where indicated on graph.

5 Curl desired length of wire around handle of small paint brush to form spiral. Remove handle and glue to stem side, placing one end near top of straight wire.

6 Close box by interlocking flaps on leaf and stem sides. ❑

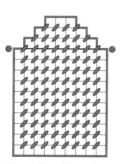

Favor Box Short Side
9 holes x 13 holes
Cut 2

COLOR KEY	
Plastic Canvas Yarn	**Yards**
■ Orange	9
■ Green	1
■ Medium copper	1
⁄ Wire placement	

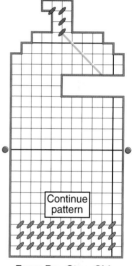

Continue pattern

Favor Box Stem Side
11 holes x 24 holes
Cut 1

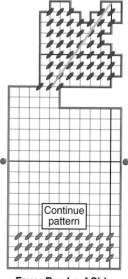

Continue pattern

Favor Box Leaf Side
11 holes x 25 holes
Cut 1

★ **materials** ★

- ❏ 1 sheet Uniek Needloft Quick-Count 7-count plastic canvas
- ❏ Uniek Needloft plastic canvas yarn as listed in color key
- ❏ DMC #5 pearl cotton as listed in color key
- ❏ DMC 6-strand embroidery floss as listed in color key
- ❏ #16 tapestry needle
- ❏ 1½ yards ⅜-inch-wide white grosgrain ribbon
- ❏ ¾ yards ⅜-inch-wide emerald green grosgrain ribbon
- ❏ Neon pony beads: 5 green and 9 purple
- ❏ Nylon thread
- ❏ Thick white glue

finished size:
8⅜ inches W x 18¼ inches H, excluding hanger

Friendly Ghost Wind Catcher

Design by Janelle Giese

Hang this friendly spook on your front porch and watch him flutter and swing with every breeze!

skill level • beginner

cutting & stitching

1 Cut plastic canvas according to graphs (page 120).

2 Stitch pieces following graphs, working uncoded areas on ghost with white Continental Stitches.

3 Overcast candy corn with adjacent colors. For ghost, Overcast only the inside edges on hand and skirt indicated on graph, working Straight Stitches between skirt cut outs while Overcasting; Overcast outside edges following graph.

4 Using 6-strand embroidery floss, embroider cheeks with 2-plies very light cranberry; work Smyrna Cross Stitches for white highlights on eyes with 6-strands.

Work remaining embroidery with black pearl cotton.

assembly

1 Use photo as a guide throughout assembly. For ribbon streamers, cut one 12-inch length, two 11-inch lengths and two 9-inch lengths from white ribbon.

2 Tie a knot near one end on each length. Thread one purple and one green bead onto each length, sliding beads down to knots.

3 Placing longest length in the center and shortest lengths on the outside and keeping ribbon flat, thread ribbon through skirt holes from back to front through bottom hole, then from front to back through top hole.

4 Adjust lengths so measurements between top beads and bottom edge of ghost are as follows: 7 inches at center, 6 inches at both sides of center and 5 inches at outside. Glue ribbon ends to back of ghost. Trim ends below knots; seal ends with glue.

5 For candy corn garland, thread one end of green ribbon through tapestry needle and thread on four purple pony beads. Thread ribbon ends from front to back through holes at hands.

6 Adjust length of garland, allowing tails to dangle. Evenly space beads, gluing candy corn between beads and placing large candy corn at center. Glue ribbon to back of hands. Trim ends, so they are even with top corner on widest part of skirt.

7 For hanger, cut a very long length of nylon thread. Double length twice to make four strands. Attach ends to top left corner of hat and to top left corner of hat brim on the right, allowing loop to extend several inches above top of hat. ❏

Small Candy Corn
8 holes x 10 holes
Cut 2

COLOR KEY

Plastic Canvas Yarn	Yards
■ Black #12	1
□ Tangerine #11	1
■ Pumpkin #12	2
■ Fern #23	1
■ Christmas green #28	1
■ Silver #37	1
□ White #41	35
■ Purple	4
□ Yellow	2
■ Bright purple #64	2

Uncoded areas are white #41
Continental Stitches

╱ White #41 Backstitch

6-Strand Embroidery Floss

╱ White Straight Stitch — 1
✕ Very light cranberry #605 Cross Stitch — 1

#5 Pearl Cotton

╱ Black #310 Backstitch and Straight Stitch — 3

Color numbers given are for Uniek Needloft plastic canvas yarn and DMC 6-strand embroidery floss and #5 pearl cotton.

Large Candy Corn
12 holes x 14 holes
Cut 1

Ghost
55 holes x 68 holes
Cut 1

Moonlit Magnets

Designs by Judy Collishaw

Tack reminders to yourself on the refrigerator or filing cabinet with this pair of eerie magnets!

skill level • beginner

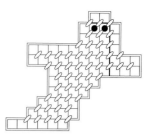

Ghost
13 holes x 11 holes
Cut 1

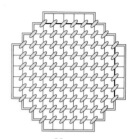

Moon
11 holes x 11 holes
Cut 2

✖ materials ✖

- ¼ sheet 7-count plastic canvas
- Worsted weight yarn as listed in color key
- #5 pearl cotton as listed in color key
- #16 tapestry needle
- 2 (⅝-inch) round craft magnets
- Low-temperature glue gun

finished size:
Ghost: 2¼ inches W x 2⅜ inches H

Bat: 2¼ inches W x 1⅜ inches H

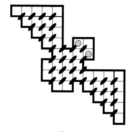

Bat
11 holes x 11 holes
Cut 1

COLOR KEY	
Worsted Weight Yarn	**Yards**
☐ Yellow	4
■ Black	2
☐ White	2
● Black French Knot	
#5 Pearl Cotton	
◯ Ecru French Knot	1

instructions

1 Cut plastic canvas according to graphs.

2 Stitch and Overcast pieces following graphs. Work ecru pearl cotton French Knots on bat. Work black French Knots on ghost using 2-plies black yarn.

3 Using photo as a guide, glue bat and ghost to moon pieces. Glue one craft magnet to back-side of each moon. ❏

Jolly Jack-o'-Lanterns

Designs by Celia Lange Designs

These silly jack-o'-lanterns are sure to scare up some stitching fun!

skill level • intermediate

✖ materials ✖

❑ 2 sheets 7-count plastic canvas
❑ Darice Nylon Plus plastic canvas yarn as listed in color key
❑ #16 tapestry needle
❑ 2 (18-inch) lengths 20-gauge green florist wire
❑ Pencil or 5⁄16-inch dowel
❑ Raffia straw
❑ Hot-glue gun

finished size:
Treat Bag: 6⅛ inches W x 9¾ inches H x 2 inches D

Tall Pumpkin Hanging: 4¾ inches W x 7¼ inches H

Short Pumpkin Hanging: 4¾ inches W x 6¾ inches H

cutting & stitching

1 Cut plastic canvas according to graphs (this page and page 124).

2 Stitch pieces following graphs, working uncoded areas on tall pumpkin with sundown Continental Stitches. Stitch bag back without moon, filling in with nautical blue pattern.

3 Overcast handle and top edges of bag front, back and sides with nautical blue. Overcast hats with beige, short pumpkins with rust and tall pumpkin with sundown.

4 Whipstitch bag front and back to sides with nautical blue. Whipstitch front, back and sides to bottom with fern.

assembly

1 Use photo as a guide throughout assembly. Wrap florist wire around pencil or dowel to form spirals. Attach one length to tall pumpkin and remaining length to one short pumpkin where indicated on graphs, wrapping wire around itself on backside of pumpkins.

2 Cut a 36-inch length of sundown. Secure one end and twist, or hold both ends of yarn in fingers and twist in opposite directions, until yarn begins to loop back on itself.

3 Place ends of twisted yarn together, folding yarn in half and allowing yarn halves to twist around each other. Knot ends so yarn will not untwist.

4 Tie twisted yarn around one hat, knotting in front. Tie a knot in yarn tails approximately 1 inch from knot on front; trim. Glue yarn to backside of hat. Glue hat to tall pumpkin.

5 Repeat steps 2–4 two more times, using bittersweet yarn and gluing hats to short pumpkins.

6 Center and glue short pumpkin without wire hanger to bag front. Center and glue handles inside bag front and back.

7 For each pumpkin hanging, tie several strands of raffia in a bow around center top of hanger. ❑

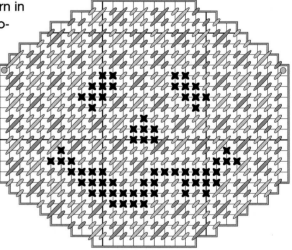

Short Pumpkin
28 holes x 23 holes
Cut 2

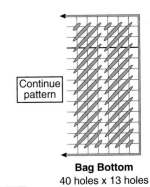

Continue pattern

Bag Bottom
40 holes x 13 holes
Cut 1

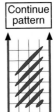

Continue pattern

Bag Handle
4 holes x 70 holes
Cut 1

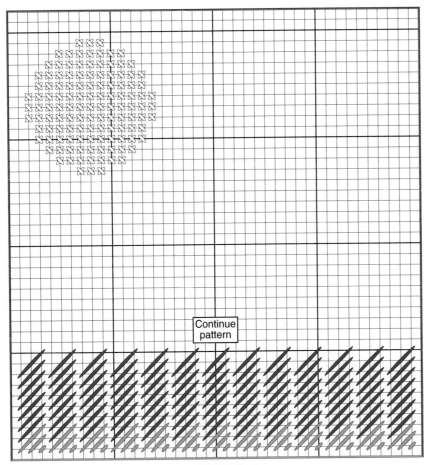

Continue pattern

Bag Front & Back
40 holes x 42 holes
Cut 2
Stitch front as graphed
Stitch back with fern and
nautical blue stitches only

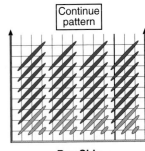

Continue pattern

Bag Side
13 holes x 42 holes
Cut 2

COLOR KEY

Plastic Canvas Yarn	Yards
Tangerine #15	14
Bittersweet #18	10
Brown #36	8
Baby yellow #42	5
Beige #43	17
Nautical blue #45	73
Rust #51	24
Fern #57	12
Uncoded areas are sundown #16 Continental Stitches	13

✎ Sundown #16 Overcasting
● Attach wire hanger
Color numbers given are for Darice Nylon Plus plastic
canvas yarn.

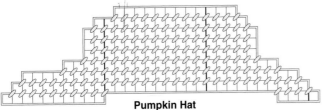

Pumpkin Hat
31 holes x 9 holes
Cut 3

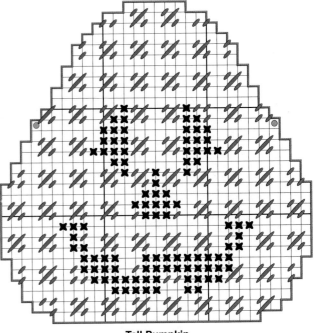

Tall Pumpkin
30 holes x 30 holes
Cut 1

Spooky Scents

Designs by Christina Laws

Each of these colorful spooks is sure
to liven up your Halloween party!
No one will know they are air-freshener covers!

skill level • beginner

✖ materials ✖

❏ 2 sheets 7-count plastic canvas

❏ Coats & Clark Red Heart Super
Saver worsted weight yarn Art.
E300: 35 inches amethyst #356
and as listed in color key

❏ #16 tapestry needle

❏ Hot-glue gun

finished size:
Witch: 3⅞ inches W x 7⅞ inches
H x 3¾ inches D

Jack-o'-Lantern: 3⅞ inches W
x 6⅞ inches H x 3¾ inches D

cutting & stitching

1 Cut plastic canvas according to graphs. Cut one 11-hole x 11-hole piece each for witch top and for jack-o'-lantern top.

2 Continental Stitch witch top with black and jack-o'-lantern top with vibrant orange.

3 Following graphs through step 7, stitch witch front, back and sides, working uncoded area on front with kiwi Continental Stitches, but leaving bars highlighted with blue unworked at this time.

4 When background stitching is completed, add lavender Straight Stitches and hot red Backstitches to face.

5 Stitch jack-o'-lantern front, working uncoded areas with black Continental Stitches. Work back and sides entirely in vibrant orange

pattern, eliminating black eyes, nose and mouth.

6 Stitch nose pieces, reversing one before stitching. Stitch hat, arms, leaves and stem following graphs, working uncoded areas on hat with black Continental Stitches.

7 Overcast witch hat and arms. Overcast jack-o'-lantern stem and leaves.

assembly

1 Use photo as a guide throughout assembly. Whipstitch wrong sides of witch nose pieces together, leaving back edges unworked, then Whipstitch back edges to front where indicated with blue lines.

2 Whipstitch witch front to sides with kiwi and black. Using black, Whipstitch sides to back, then

Whipstitch front, back and sides to top; Overcast bottom edges.

3 For hair, cut amethyst yarn into 10 (3½-inch) lengths. Glue five lengths to each side of hat on backside along bottom edge.

4 Glue hat to top of witch's head and arms just below face.

5 Using vibrant orange, Whipstitch jack-o'-lantern front and back to sides, then Whipstitch front, back and sides to top; Overcast bottom edges.

6 Glue stem to top of jack-o'-lantern front, then glue leaves to bottom of stem. ❏

Jack-o'-Lantern Leaf
7 holes x 7 holes
Cut 2

Jack-o'-Lantern Stem
7 holes x 7 holes
Cut 1

COLOR KEY
JACK-O'-LANTERN

Worsted Weight Yarn	Yards
■ Mid brown #339	1
▨ Vibrant orange #354	46
■ Paddy green #368	2
Uncoded areas are black #312	
Continental Stitches	2

Color numbers given are for Coats & Clark Red Heart Super Saver worsted weight yarn Art E300.

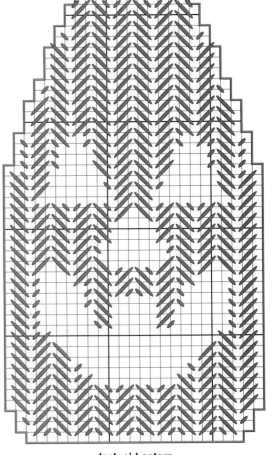

Jack-o'-Lantern
25 holes x 42 holes
Cut 4
Stitch front as graphed
Stitch sides and back entirely
in vibrant orange pattern

Witch Nose
6 holes x 4 holes
Cut 2, reverse 1

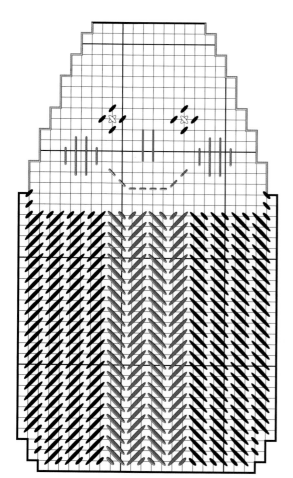

Witch Front
25 holes x 42 holes
Cut 1

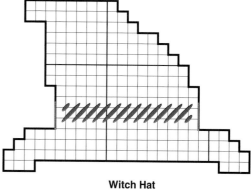

Witch Hat
24 holes x 16 holes
Cut 1

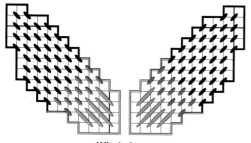

Witch Arms
11 holes x 12 holes
Cut 1 set

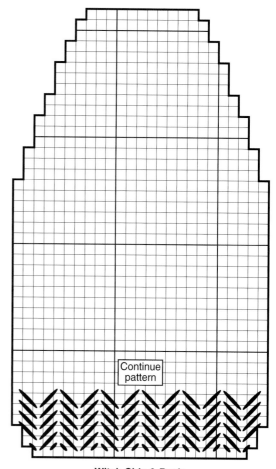

Continue pattern

Witch Side & Back
25 holes x 42 holes
Cut 3

COLOR KEY
WITCH

Worsted Weight Yarn	Yards
☐ White #311	1
◼ Black #312	39
◼ Lavender #358	4
◼ Kiwi #651	6

Uncoded areas on hat and arms are
black #312 Continental Stitches.
Uncoded area on witch front is kiwi #651
Continental Stitches.
⁄ Lavender #358 Straight Stitch
⁄ Hot red #390 Backstitch
Color numbers given are for Coats & Clark Red Heart Super
Saver worsted weight yarn Art E300.

Jack-o'-Lantern Basket & Ornament

Design by Angie Arickx

Fill the basket with your favorite Halloween treats, and hang the ornament in your window for a festive decoration!

skill level • beginner

✖ materials ✖

- ☐ 1½ sheets Uniek Quick-Count 7-count plastic canvas
- ☐ Uniek Needloft plastic canvas yarn as listed in color key
- ☐ #16 tapestry needle

finished size:

Basket: 6½ inches W x 5¾ inches H x 2⅝ inches D

Ornament: 6⅜ inches W x 5¾ inches H

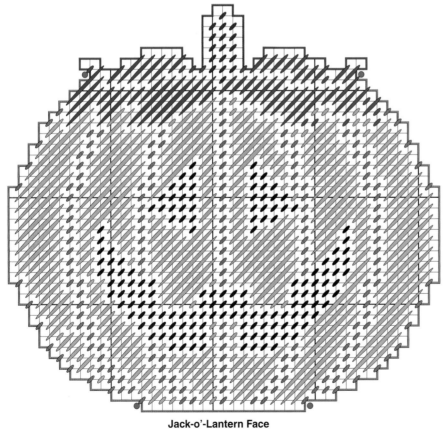

Jack-o'-Lantern Face
42 holes x 38 holes
Cut 2 for basket
Cut 1 for ornament

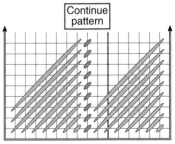

Continue pattern

Jack-o'-Lantern Basket Side
16 holes x 40 holes
Cut 2

1 Cut and stitch plastic canvas according to graphs. Cut one 16-hole x 16-hole piece for basket bottom. Basket bottom will remain unstitched.

2 Following graphs throughout,

Whipstitch basket sides to two faces between blue dots on each side of face. Whipstitch unstitched bottom to faces and sides. Overcast top edges.

3 Overcast ornament following graph. Hang as desired. ❑

COLOR KEY	
Plastic Canvas Yarn	**Yards**
■ Black #00	9
□ Pumpkin #12	41
■ Cinnamon #14	2
■ Christmas green #28	8
■ Bittersweet #52	16
Color numbers given are for Uniek Needloft plastic canvas yarn.	

Cornucopia Pin

Design by Mary T. Cosgrove

Dress up any outfit with this sparkling cornucopia-of-fruits-and-vegetables pin!

skill level • beginner

✖ materials ✖

❑ Small amount Uniek Quick-Count 10-count plastic canvas

❑ Small amount 14-count gold perforated paper

❑ Kreinik ⅛-inch Ribbon as listed in color key

❑ Kreinik Heavy (#32) Braid as listed in color key

❑ Kreinik Medium (#16) Braid as listed in color key

❑ #18 tapestry needle

❑ ¾-inch pin back

❑ Jewel glue

finished size:
2½ inches W x 2¼ inches H

instructions

1 Cut plastic canvas according to graph. Using plastic canvas as a template, trace and cut shape on white side of perforated paper.

2 Stitch plastic canvas following graph, working uncoded area with misty gold Continental Stitches.

3 Work French Knots for grapes and two green Turkey Loop Stitches. Overcast following graph, then work bronze Backstitches and Straight Stitches.

COLOR KEY	
Plastic Canvas Yarn	**Yards**
■ Red #003	½
■ Green #008	½
□ Chartreuse #015	½
╱ Purple Hi Lustre #12HL Overcasting	½
○ Purple Hi Lustre #12HL French Knot	
● Green #008 Turkey Loop Stitch	
Heavy (#32) Braid	
■ Orange #027	1
□ Star yellow #091	½
Uncoded area is misty gold #071 Continental Stitches	½
● Purple #12 French Knot	1
Medium (#16) Braid	
■ Bronze Hi Lustre #052	2
╱ Bronze Hi Lustre #052 Backstitch and Straight Stitch	
Color numbers given are for Kreinik ⅛-inch Ribbon, Heavy (#32) Braid and Medium (#16) Braid.	

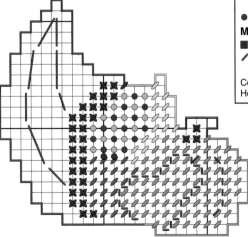

Cornucopia Pin
24 holes x 22 holes
Cut 1

4 Glue white side of perforated paper to wrong side of stitched piece. Allow to dry.

5 Glue pin back to center back of completed piece. Allow to dry. ❑

Acorn Wind Chime

Design by Celia Lange Designs

Catch autumn breezes with this attractive acorn wind chime
by hanging it in your kitchen window.

skill level • beginner

★ materials ★

❏ 1 sheet 7-count plastic canvas
❏ Coats & Clark Red Heart Super Saver worsted weight yarn Art. E300 as listed in color key
❏ 7 inches tan #3 pearl cotton
❏ #16 tapestry needle
❏ 1¾-inch silk sunflower
❏ Assorted autumn silk leaves
❏ 5 (6mm) gold-tone wind chimes
❏ Nylon fishing line
❏ Hot-glue gun

finished size:
5⅛ inches W x 8 inches H, excluding hanger

instructions

1 Cut plastic canvas according to graphs (page 132).

2 Stitch pieces following graphs. Using brown, Overcast bottom and inside edges of cap pieces, then Whipstitch wrong sides together along remaining edges. Using warm brown, Whipstitch inside edges of acorn together.

3 Using nylon fishing line, attach first chime by securing fishing line on inside of acorn then bring fishing line down between plastic canvas pieces where indicated at first arrow. Thread on chime and come up at second arrow, leaving ½ inch between chime and edge.

continued on page 132

Owl Wind Chime

Design by Janelle Giese

Perched on a maple tree branch, this wise old owl and his golden chimes will catch every breeze!

skill level • beginner

Owl
45 holes x 43 holes
Cut 1

COLOR KEY	
Plastic Canvas Yarn	**Yards**
■ Black #00	1
□ Red #01	1
■ Burgundy #03	2
■ Rust #09	3
□ Tangerine #11	1
■ Cinnamon #14	4
□ Gold #17	1
□ Gray #38	2
□ Eggshell #39	4
□ Camel #43	3
Uncoded areas are beige #40 Continental Stitches	4
╱ Eggshell #39 Straight Stitch	
✗ Black #00 Cross Stitch	
Metallic Craft Cord	
■ Solid gold #55020	1
╱ Solid gold #55020 Straight Stitch	
#5 Pearl Cotton	
╱ Ultra dark coffee brown #938 Backstitch and Straight Stitch	6
● Attach wind chime	
● Attach hanger	
Color numbers given are for Uniek Needloft plastic canvas yarn and metallic craft cord and DMC #5 pearl cotton.	

✖ materials ✖

- ❏ ½ sheet Uniek Quick-Count stiff 7-count plastic canvas
- ❏ Uniek Needloft plastic canvas yarn as listed in color key
- ❏ Uniek Needloft metallic craft cord as listed in color key
- ❏ DMC #5 pearl cotton as listed in color key
- ❏ #16 tapestry needle
- ❏ 5 (6mm) gold wind chimes
- ❏ Nylon thread

finished size:
6¾ inches W x 6⅝ inches H, excluding hanger and chimes

instructions

1 Cut plastic canvas according to graph (page 131).

2 Stitch piece following graph, working uncoded areas with beige Continental Stitches.

3 When background stitching is completed, work large solid gold Straight Stitches over center of eye, then work black Cross Stitch over top of solid gold stitches. Work eggshell Straight Stitch for beak highlight.

4 Overcast piece following graph. When Overcasting is completed, work Backstitches and Straight Stitches with ultra dark coffee brown pearl cotton.

5 Using nylon thread, attach chimes where indicated on graph, keeping tops of chimes 1 inch below lowest point of motif.

6 For hanger, thread a double strand of nylon thread through holes indicated on graph. Allowing hanger to extend 3 inches to 4 inches above motif. ❏

Acorn Wind Chime continued from page 130

4 Thread line down at third arrow, repeating procedure until all five charms are attached. Secure fishing line on inside.

5 Whipstitch outside edges of acorn together with warm brown.

6 Thread tan pearl cotton through hole at top of cap; tie

ends in a knot to form a loop for hanging.

7 Glue top of acorn inside cap. Glue sunflower and leaves to cap. ❏

COLOR KEY	
Worsted Weight Yarn	**Yards**
■ Brown #328	13
▨ Warm brown #336	26
▦ Mid brown #339	8
Color numbers given are for Coats & Clark Red Heart Super Saver worsted weight yarn Art E300.	

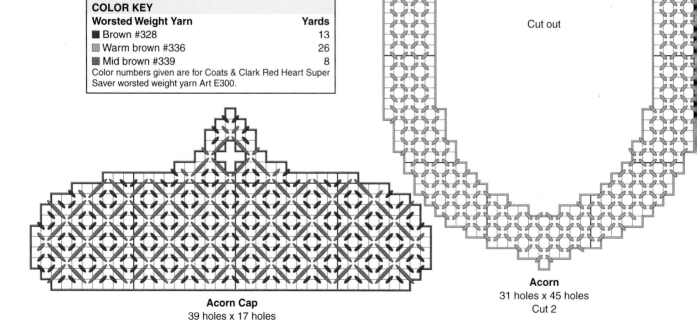

Acorn Cap
39 holes x 17 holes
Cut 2

Cut out

Acorn
31 holes x 45 holes
Cut 2

Autumn Basket

Design by Lee Lindeman

Celebrate autumn's splendor with this vibrant basket adorned with oak leaves and acorns!

skill level • beginner

✖ materials ✖

- ❏ 2 sheets 7-count plastic canvas
- ❏ Worsted weight yarn as listed in color key
- ❏ #16 tapestry needle
- ❏ 25–30 dried acorns
- ❏ Clear nail polish
- ❏ Sheer wire-edged golden beige ribbon
- ❏ Basket with handle (sample is 8¾ inches W x 10¾ inches H x 7½ inches D)
- ❏ Hot-glue gun

finished size:
8¾ inches W x 12½ inches H x 9¼ inches D

instructions

1 Cut leaves from plastic canvas according to graphs (page 134).

2 Following graphs throughout, Stitch one large leaf with rust as graphed, reverse one and stitch with burgundy. Stitch both medium leaves with medium coral, reversing one before stitching. Stitch two small leaves with gold, one with burgundy and one with rust, reversing one before stitching.

3 Overcast leaves with adjacent colors. Using photo as a guide, glue one small leaf to bottom of handle on both sides. Glue remaining leaves as desired below handles to basket front and back.

4 Coat acorns with clear nail polish; allow to dry. Glue acorns in clusters to basket around leaves and to base of handle on both sides of basket.

5 Make a multilooped bow from ribbon and glue to top of handle. ❑

COLOR KEY	
BASKET	
Worsted Weight Yarn	**Yards**
☐ Medium coral	14
Burgundy	12
■ Rust	12
☐ Gold	10

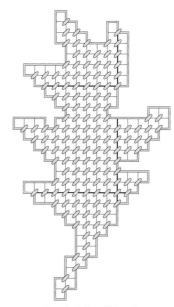

Basket Small Leaf
15 holes x 27 holes
Cut 4, reverse 1
Stitch 2 as graphed
Stitch 1 with burgundy and
1 with rust

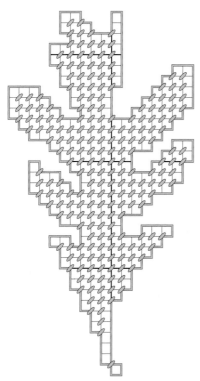

Basket Medium Leaf
18 holes x 34 holes
Cut 2, reverse 1

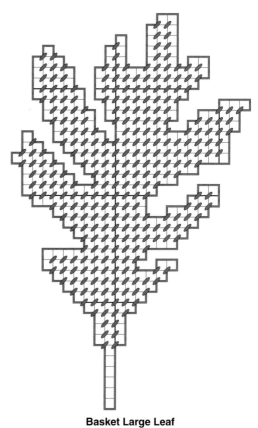

Basket Large Leaf
23 holes x 37 holes
Cut 2
Stitch 1 as graphed
Reverse 1 and stitch with
burgundy

Acorn Necklace

Design by Lee Lindeman

Add a handsome touch of autumn color to any outfit with this quick-to-sitch necklace!

skill level • beginner

✳ necklace materials ✳

- ❑ Small amount 7-count plastic canvas
- ❑ Worsted weight yarn as listed in color key
- ❑ 6-strand embroidery floss as listed in color key
- ❑ DMC 6-strand metallic embroidery floss as listed in color key
- ❑ #16 tapestry needle
- ❑ Large dried acorn
- ❑ Clear nail polish
- ❑ 2 gold eye pins: 1 long enough to fit through acorn
- ❑ Small round-nose pliers
- ❑ 32 inches black satin rattail cord
- ❑ Tacky glue

finished size:

Leaf: 1⅜ inches W x 1⅛ inches H

Necklace Pendant: 1⅜ inches W x 3⅜ inches L

instructions

1 Cut two leaves from plastic canvas according to graph.

2 Stitch leaves following graph.

COLOR KEY	
NECKLACE	
Worsted Weight Yarn	**Yards**
■ Burgundy	1
■ Rust	1
■ Burnt orange	1
▢ Medium coral	1
6-Strand Embroidery Floss	
✏ Black Backstitch and Straight Stitch	1
6-Strand Metallic Embroidery Floss	
✏ Gold #5282 Whipstitching	3
Color numbers given are for DMC 6-strand metallic embroidery floss.	

Attach eye pin

Necklace Leaf
9 holes x 12 holes
Cut 2

Embroider veins on leaves with black 6-strand embroidery floss. Whipstitch wrong sides of leaves together with gold metallic embroidery floss.

3 Insert and glue one eye pin through gold floss and between plastic canvas leaf pieces where indicated on graph, cutting length of pin in half if desired.

4 Remove acorn cap. Carefully poke a hole at top of acorn cap and at top and bottom of acorn. Push remaining eye pin into hole at bottom of acorn up through top of acorn. Insert pin through cap; glue cap on acorn to secure.

5 Use pliers to make a loop from pin at top of acorn cap, cutting pin as necessary to fit.

6 Apply two coats of clear nail polish to acorn; allow to dry between coats.

7 When polish is dry, slightly open loop on stitched leaf and slip on loop at bottom of acorn. Close loop.

8 Thread rattail through loop. Tie ends in a knot. ❑

Grapes Basket

Design by Janelle Giese

Quick and easy to stitch, this handsome basket makes a lovely gift!

skill level intermediate

✖ materials ✖

- ¼ sheet 7-count plastic canvas
- Coats & Clark Red Heart Classic worsted weight yarn Art. E267 as listed in color key
- DMC #3 pearl cotton as listed in color key
- #16 tapestry needle
- Basket with handle (sample used 7 inches W x 10 inches H x 6 inches D)
- 2 yards 2-inch-wide wire-edge craft ribbon in color complimenting 1½-inch-wide ribbon
- 2 yards 1½-inch-wide wire-edge craft ribbon in color complimenting 2-inch-wide ribbon
- Carpet thread
- Spanish moss or other filler
- Thick white glue

finished size:

Stitched Motif: 5 inches W x 4 inches H

cutting & stitching

1 Cut plastic canvas according to graph (page 136).

2 Stitch piece following graph, working uncoded areas with new berry Continental Stitches.

3 Overcast following graph. Work pearl cotton Backstitches and Straight Stitches.

4 For grape highlights, work eggshell Pin Stitches, coming up through motif, splitting a Continental Stitch, then drawing needle back through point of entry.

assembly

1 Use photo as a guide throughout assembly. For large bow, make a triple-looped bow with 2-inch-wide ribbon by pinching even lengths of ribbon at center to form loops. Wrap center with carpet thread; knot to secure and leave ends.

2 For smaller bow, cut a 24-inch length of 1½-inch-wide ribbon; make a double-looped bow following instructions in step 1. Place smaller bow over larger bow and wrap carpet thread around center of both bows to join. Knot, leaving ends.

3 Using remaining length of 1½-inch-wide ribbon for streamer, pinch streamer at center, placing against back of bow assembly. Draw ends of carpet thread through basket to inside; knot off.

continued on page 138

Maple Leaf Coasters

Design by Linda Wyszynski

Capture the beauty of autumn leaves with this set of colorful maple leaf coasters!

skill level • beginner

✖ materials ✖

- ❑ 2 sheets Uniek Quick-Count 7-count plastic canvas
- ❑ Coats & Clark Red Heart Super Saver worsted weight yarn Art. E300 as listed in color key
- ❑ DMC #3 pearl cotton as listed in color key
- ❑ #16 tapestry needle
- ❑ 4-pound-test fishing line or invisible thread
- ❑ Small paint brush

finished size:

Coasters: 4 inches W x 4⅛ inches H

Coaster Holder: 5¾ inches W x 4⅛ inches H

instructions

1 Cut plastic canvas according to graphs (page 138). Cut one 30-hole x 9-hole piece for holder bottom.

2 Holder bottom, 6 coasters and liner pieces, which are two holder sides and one each of holder front and back, will remain unstitched.

3 Using medium sage through step 4, Continental Stitch one front, one back and two sides.

4 Place unstitched liner pieces behind corresponding stitched pieces; working through all thicknesses, Whipstitch front and back to sides, then Whipstitch front, back and sides to bottom. Whipstitch unstitched liner pieces to stitched pieces along top edges.

5 Following graph, Continental Stitch one leaf with gold and one with medium sage. Reverse four leaves and Continental Stitch two leaves with amethyst, one with medium sage and one with burgundy. Stitch all stems with blue green pearl cotton.

6 Work pearl cotton Backstitches for leaf veins using graph as a guide, but stitching veins on each leaf differently, following the general vein lines.

7 Matching edges, Whipstitch one unstitched leaf to each stitched leaf, working all edges with adjacent colors.

8 Using photo as a guide, securely attach one amethyst leaf and one medium sage leaf to holder front with fishing line, making sure bottom edges of leaves are not below bottom edge of holder.

9 Place maple leaf coasters in holder. ❑

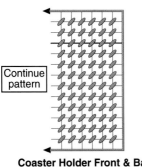

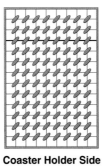

Coaster Holder Front & Back
30 holes x 13 holes
Cut 4, stitch 2

Coaster Holder Side
9 holes x 13 holes
Cut 4, stitch 2

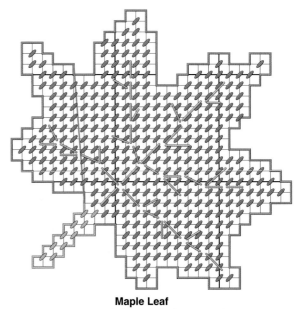

Maple Leaf
27 holes x 26 holes
Cut 12, stitch 6
Stitch 1 with gold and
1 with medium sage
Reverse 4
Stitch 2 with amethyst,
1 with burgundy and
1 with medium sage

COLOR KEY	
Worsted Weight Yarn	**Yards**
■ Gold #321	22
Amethyst #356	22
Burgundy #376	22
■ Medium Sage #632	35
#5 Pearl Cotton	
□ Blue green #502	27⅓
⁄ Blue green #502 Backstitch	
Color numbers given are for Coats & Clark Red Heart Super Saver worsted weight yarn Art. E300 and DMC #5 pearl cotton.	

Grapes Basket continued from page 136

4 Place stitched grapes over bow assembly and attach with carpet thread, drawing ends to inside of basket and knotting off.

5 Arrange streamer ends at baskets sides by bending wire edges to form loops; tack in place with glue. Wrap ends of streamers up around handle, gluing in place. Trim ends to match.

6 Fill basket with Spanish moss or other filler. ❑

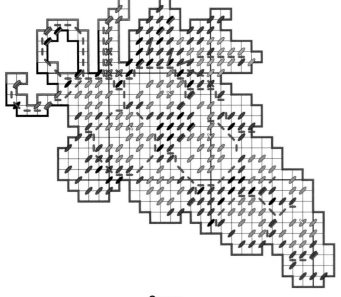

Grapes
32 holes x 27 holes
Cut 1

COLOR KEY	
Worsted Weight Yarn	**Yards**
■ Black #12	2
▧ Nickel #401	2
▨ Medium sage #632	1
■ Dark sage #633	2
▨ Light berry #761	2
■ Claret #762	3
Uncoded areas are new berry #760 Continental Stitches	2
⁄ Eggshell #111 Pin Stitch	1
#3 Pearl Cotton	
⁄ Black #310 Backstitch and Straight Stitch	5
Color numbers given are for Coats & Clark Red Heart Classic worsted weight yarn Art. E267 and DMC #3 pearl cotton.	

Autumn Bears Wreath

Design by Janelle Giese

Stitch this friendly autumn decoration for your home
to add a feeling of warmth and hospitality!

skill level • beginner

✸ materials ✸

- ❏ ½ sheet 7-count plastic canvas
- ❏ Coats & Clark Red Heart Classic worsted weight yarn Art. E267 as listed in color key
- ❏ DMC #3 pearl cotton as listed in color key
- ❏ #16 tapestry needle
- ❏ 12-inch grapevine wreath
- ❏ Twisted paper ribbon in 2 coordinating colors (sample used a tan-and-brick gingham and a solid tan)
- ❏ Raffia straw
- ❏ 24-gauge green craft wire
- ❏ Wire cutters
- ❏ Pliers
- ❏ Thick white glue

finished size:

Leaf Bear: 4⅜ inches W x 6¼ inches H

Apple Bear: 3 inches W x 4 inches H

Pumpkin Bear: 3¼ inches W x 4 inches H

instructions

1 Cut plastic canvas according to graphs.

2 Stitch pieces following graphs, working uncoded areas with tan Continental Stitches.

3 Overcast two leaves with cardinal. Overcast pumpkin and remaining leaf with bronze. Overcast bears with mid brown.

4 When background stitching and Overcasting are completed, work black yarn Straight Stitches for eyes on all three bears and for mouth on leaf bear. Stitch apple stems and pumpkin vine with light sage yarn.

5 Work all remaining embroidery with black pearl cotton following graphs.

assembly

1 Use photo as a guide throughout assembly. Cut a 10-inch length of craft wire and bend into a semicircle.

2 Thread ends of wire under two stitches on each side of leaf bear where indicated with blue lines, going from outer edge toward center. Bend ends into small curlicues. Dab a small amount of glue between wire and side edges of paws to secure.

3 Using black pearl cotton, attach wire to yarn on backside of leaves. Make sure leaves are evenly spaced at center of wire, then glue to secure.

4 Untwist a generous length of twisted paper ribbon and wrap around wreath, gluing ends together on backside.

5 Make a bow with both shades of paper ribbon and with raffia straw, allowing long tails of raffia straw. Secure at center with craft wire. Wrap a small length of paper ribbon around center of bow; glue on backside. Attach bow to bottom of wreath with craft wire.

6 Form a small wire loop at top back of wreath for hanger. Glue bears to wreath. ❏

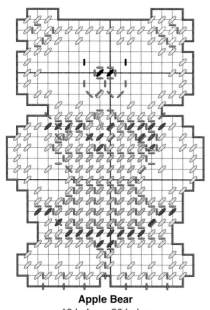

Apple Bear
19 holes x 26 holes
Cut 1

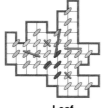

Leaf
9 holes x 9 holes
Cut 3
Overcast 2 as graphed
Overcast 1 with bronze

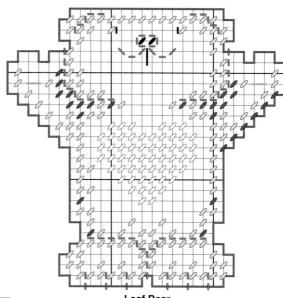

Leaf Bear
27 holes x 26 holes
Cut 1

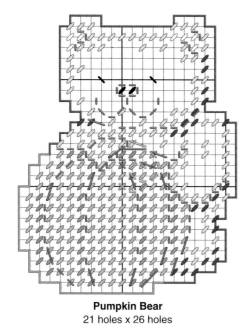

Pumpkin Bear
21 holes x 26 holes
Cut 1

COLOR KEY	
Worsted Weight Yarn	**Yards**
■ Black #12	1
□ Eggshell #111	2
▨ Medium clay #280	3
▨ Bronze #286	3
▨ Warm brown #336	8
■ Mid brown #339	6
▨ Light sage #631	2
▨ Country red #914	1
▨ Cardinal #917	1
Uncoded areas are tan #334 Continental Stitches	7
⁄ Black #12 Straight Stitch	
⁄ Light sage #631 Backstitch and Straight Stitch	
#3 Pearl Cotton	
⁄ Black #310 Backstitch and Straight Stitch	5

Color numbers given are for Coats & Clark Red Heart Classic worsted weight yarn Art. E267 and DMC #3 pearl cotton.

CHAPTER FOUR
Winter Wonders

Add holiday fun and cheer

to your booth and home

with these easy crafts!

Winter brings along with it many of the year's most beloved characters and motifs. Friendly snowmen, jolly Santas, sparkling snowflakes, heavenly angels and more abound during these months. Stitch dozens of ornaments, stocking stuffers and winter decorations to add sparkle and life to your bazaar booth, and money to your pocket!

Snow Globe

Design by Lee Lindeman

Dress up an end table throughout the winter season with this simply delightful project!

skill level • intermediate

✖ materials ✖

- ❑ 3 sheets 7-count plastic canvas
- ❑ Worsted weight yarn as listed in color key
- ❑ #16 tapestry needle
- ❑ Small amount orange craft foam
- ❑ Small amount red felt
- ❑ Small amount natural raffia
- ❑ 2 (3mm) round black beads
- ❑ 5 black seed beads
- ❑ 3 (6mm) round black cabochons
- ❑ Small red star button
- ❑ 10 inches ⅛-inch-wide blue satin ribbon
- ❑ 10-inch long strip plaid fabric
- ❑ 2 (2½-inch-long) tree twigs
- ❑ 3-inch-long tree twig
- ❑ Child's red knit sock cuff
- ❑ Sewing needle and red and white sewing thread
- ❑ Tiny basket
- ❑ Miniature pinecones
- ❑ White acrylic paint
- ❑ Small paintbrush
- ❑ Small amount Styrofoam plastic foam
- ❑ Small amount fiberfill
- ❑ Fish bowl approximately 6 inches H with 5¼-inch opening
- ❑ Hot-glue gun

finished size:

9 inches H x 8½ inches D

cutting & stitching

1 Cut plastic canvas according to graphs (pages 146 and 147). *Note: Globe base top has an opening slightly smaller than opening of fish bowl in order to keep bowl secure enough without gluing it to the base.*

2 For carrot nose, cut a narrow ⅜-inch-long strip from orange craft foam, cutting one end to a point. Cut four mittens from red felt using pattern given (page 146).

3 Stitch pieces following graphs, working head back entirely with white Continental Stitches and reversing one small tree base before stitching.

4 With sewing needle and white sewing thread, attach 3mm beads to head front for eyes and seeds beads to head front for mouth where indicated on graph.

5 Overcast bottom edges of trees, then Whipstitch wrong sides of corresponding trees together with adjacent colors, stuffing a bit of fiberfill into bottom opening.

6 Using white through step 7,

Overcast inside edges of globe base top. Whipstitch wrong sides of small tree base pieces together.

7 On body front and back, Overcast neck edges and arm edges between arrows.

snowman assembly

1 Using white through step 2, Whipstitch head front and back together, stuffing with a small amount of fiberfill before closing.

2 Whipstitch wrong sides of body front and back together along unstitched side edges, then Whipstitch body base to bottom edges, stuffing with fiberfill before closing.

3 Use photo as a guide through step 6. Glue neck of head into opening at top of body. Glue cabochons to body front for coal buttons. Glue star button to the right of cabochons.

4 For hat, from top of sock, cut a 2-inch-wide piece long enough to fit snugly around snowman's head. Using red thread, sew seam along 2-inch edge. Use a running stitch to gather hat ¼ inch from top of hat. Turn up cuff; glue hat to snowman's head.

5 Tie plaid fabric around neck for scarf. Glue to secure.

6 Matching edges, glue two mittens together over one end of one 2½-inch twig. Repeat with remaining 2½-inch twig. Glue twigs into arm openings on body.

globe assembly

1 Using photo as a guide throughout assembly, paint white "snow" dots on globe. Allow to dry.

2 Whipstitch wrong sides of winter scene base together with white. Glue snowman to center right of base top. Glue large tree to base behind snowman.

3 For broom, glue several short

lengths of natural raffia around one end of 3-inch twig. Wrap a short length of blue satin ribbon around raffia near top of raffia. Glue broom to base and snowman.

4 Glue tiny basket to base on left side of snowman, then glue miniature pinecones in basket and a few to base. Tie remaining length of satin ribbon in a bow around basket handle; trim ends.

5 Cut four bean-size balls from plastic foam and glue in a pile in front of basket and snowman.

6 Whipstitch wrong sides of globe base pieces together with white. Place winter scene inside center hole

of globe base and glue in place.

7 Turn fish bowl upside down and carefully place over winter scene, bringing lip of globe base over lip of fish bowl.

8 Glue small tree to small tree base, then glue to top of globe. ❏

Globe Snowman Mitten
Cut 4 from red felt

Back Edge

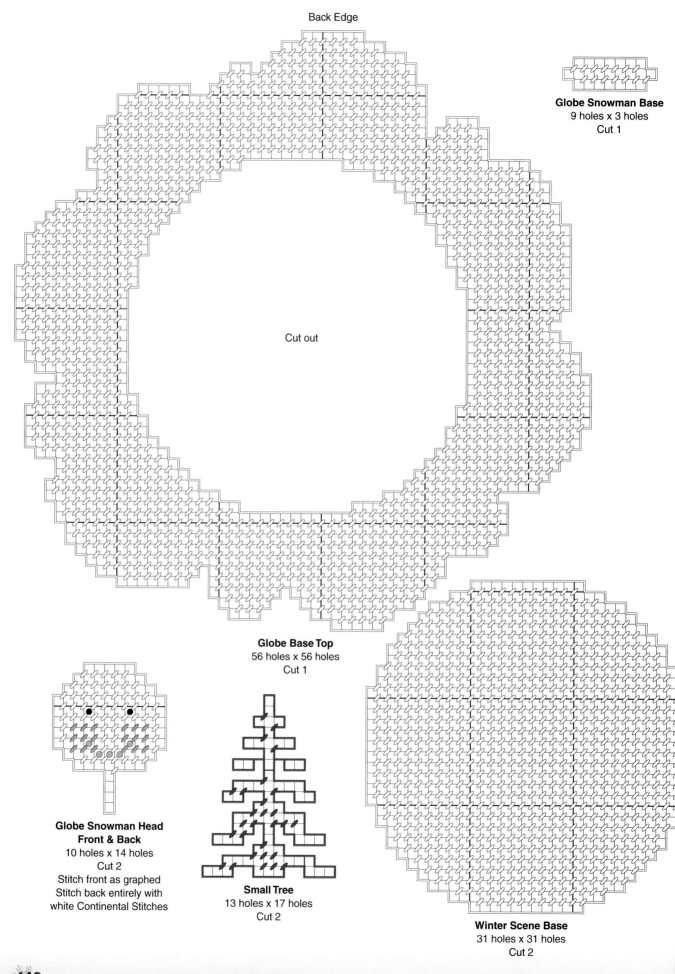

Globe Snowman Base
9 holes x 3 holes
Cut 1

Cut out

Globe Base Top
56 holes x 56 holes
Cut 1

Globe Snowman Head
Front & Back
10 holes x 14 holes
Cut 2
Stitch front as graphed
Stitch back entirely with
white Continental Stitches

Small Tree
13 holes x 17 holes
Cut 2

Winter Scene Base
31 holes x 31 holes
Cut 2

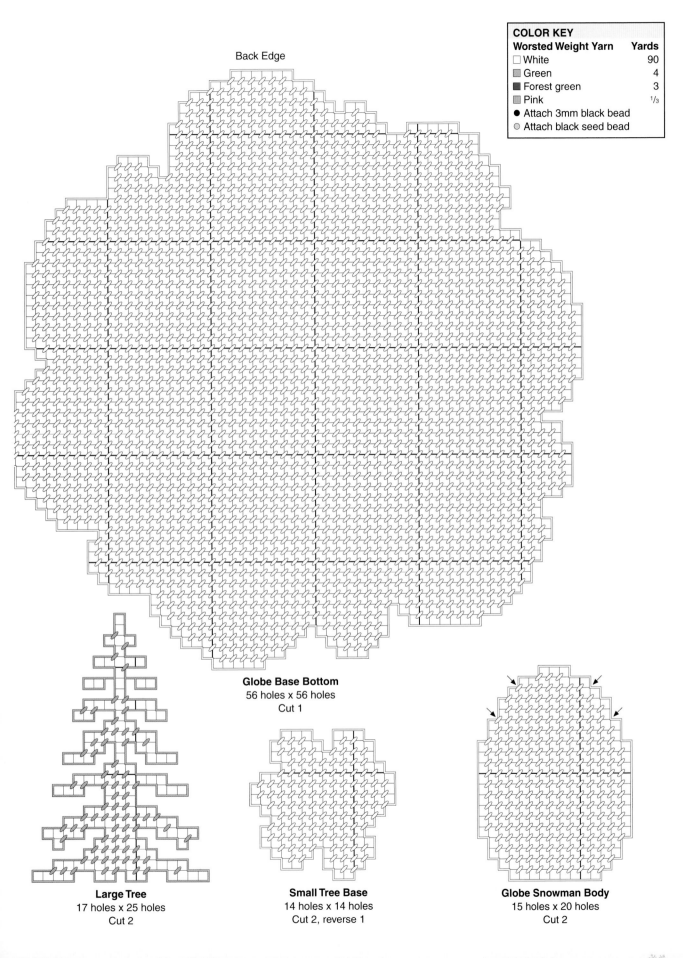

Back Edge

COLOR KEY
Worsted Weight Yarn	Yards
☐ White	90
▨ Green	4
■ Forest green	3
▨ Pink	1/3
● Attach 3mm black bead	
○ Attach black seed bead	

Globe Base Bottom
56 holes x 56 holes
Cut 1

Large Tree
17 holes x 25 holes
Cut 2

Small Tree Base
14 holes x 14 holes
Cut 2, reverse 1

Globe Snowman Body
15 holes x 20 holes
Cut 2

Winter Fun Magnets

Designs by Joyce Keklock

Tack all those miscellaneous notes and shopping lists to your refrigerator with this set of four wintry magnets!

skill level • beginner

materials

- ⅓ sheet 7-count plastic canvas
- Uniek Needloft plastic canvas yarn: 7 inches eggshell #39 and as listed in color key
- #16 tapestry needle
- 3 (¼-inch) white pompoms
- 1 yard white crochet cotton
- 6½ inches ½-inch-wide magnetic strip
- Hot-glue gun

finished size:

Each Mitten: 1¾ inches W x 1½ inches H

Pair of Ice Skates: 3 inches W x 2¼ inches H

Shovel: 1½ inches W x 3½ inches H

Sled: 1¾ inches W x 2⅞ inches H, excluding handle

cutting & stitching

1 Cut plastic canvas according to graphs. Cut one 7-hole x 8-hole piece for sled bottom and two 7-hole x 2 hole pieces for sled braces. Sled bottom will remain unstitched.

2 Cut magnetic strip into four 1¼-inch lengths and one 1½-inch length. Set aside.

3 Using black through step 4, Continental Stitch and Overcast top edges of sled braces. Following

graphs, stitch and Overcast sled runners around bottom, sides and top from dot to dot, reversing one runner before stitching.

4 Whipstitch braces to runners where indicated with blue lines on runner graph, then Whipstitch unstitched bottom to bottom edges of braces and remaining bottom edges of runners.

5 Stitch and Overcast remaining pieces following graphs, reversing one mitten before stitching.

assembly

1 Use photo as a guide throughout assembly. Tie ends of three 20-inch lengths of lemon yarn together in a knot, leaving 2-inch tails. Braid lengths to measure 12 inches, then tie another knot. Weave tails

through yarn on back of mittens.
Tie center of braid in a bow.

2 Cut crochet cotton in half.
Using one length for each skate,
lace crochet cotton through holes
indicated with blue dots; tie ends
in a bow at top. Glue skates
together as in photo.

3 Glue pompoms to shovel.

4 Glue sled runner assembly to
bottom of sled. Thread a 7-inch
length of eggshell yarn from top to
bottom through holes indicated on
steering bar with a green dot. Tie
ends in a knot on bottom side.
Glue steering bar to top of sled
along front edge.

5 Glue one 1¼-inch magnetic
strip to back of shovel, to back of
each mitten and to bottom of sled.
Glue 1½-inch magnetic strip to back
of ice skates. ❏

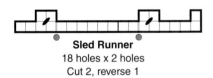

Sled Runner
18 holes x 2 holes
Cut 2, reverse 1

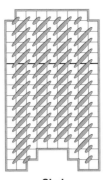

Sled
9 holes x 15 holes
Cut 1

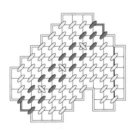

Ice Skate
15 holes x 13 holes
Cut 2

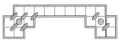

Sled Steering Bar
11 holes x 3 holes
Cut 1

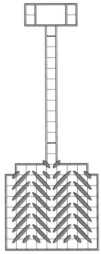

Shovel
9 holes x 23 holes
Cut 1

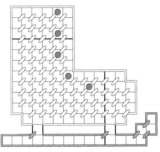

Mitten
11 holes x 10 holes
Cut 2, reverse 1

COLOR KEY	
Plastic Canvas Yarn	**Yards**
■ Black #00	3
■ Christmas red #02	3
□ Lemon #20	7
■ Christmas green #28	1
▨ Silver #37	1
□ White #41	4
▨ Camel #43	4
Color numbers given are for Uniek Needloft plastic canvas yarn.	

Cool Penguins Wall Hanging

Design by Kimberly A. Suber

Hang this whimsical project on a wall or door to chase away those winter blues!

skill level • beginner

✿ materials ✿

- ⅓ sheet 7-count plastic canvas
- Worsted weight yarn as listed in color key
- #16 tapestry needle
- Hot-glue gun

finished size:
9½ inches W x 4½ inches H

instructions

1 Cut plastic canvas according to graphs.

2 Stitch and Overcast penguins and sign following graphs, working uncoded areas on penguins with white Continental Stitches and uncoded area on sign with light blue Continental Stitches.

3 Stitch and Overcast wings, feet and snowflakes following graphs. Stitch two wings as graphed for left penguin; reverse two before stitching for right penguin.

4 Work bright blue Backstitches around eyes when background stitching is completed.

5 Stitch beaks following graph. Overcast beaks along two sides from dot to dot. Whipstitch wrong sides of two beak pieces together along remaining edges. Repeat with remaining two beak pieces.

6 Stitch and Overcast hats, scarves and scarf tails following graphs, working one hat, one scarf and one set of tails as graphed. Work Lark's Head Knots in bottom holes of scarf tails with bright green; separate plies for fringe.

7 Work remaining hat and scarf pieces, replacing bright blue with purple, bright green with yellow and tangerine with fuchsia.

assembly

1 Using photo as a guide throughout assembly, glue Whipstitched corner of beaks to penguin faces. Glue feet along bottom edges of penguins.

2 For left penguin, glue one wing behind right shoulder, extending out, and second wing to left shoulder front. For right penguin, glue one wing behind left shoulder, extending out, and remaining wing to right shoulder front.

3 Glue bright green hat and scarf pieces to one penguin; glue yellow hat and scarf pieces to remaining penguin.

4 Glue sign between penguins to wings. Glue on snowflakes as desired.

5 Hang as desired. ❏

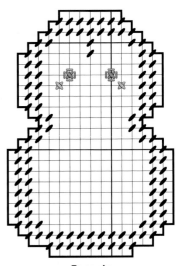

Penguin
16 holes x 23 holes
Cut 2

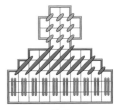

Hat
10 holes x 9 holes
Cut 2
Stitch 1 as graphed
Stitch 1, replacing bright blue with purple, bright green with yellow and tangerine with fuchsia

Penguin Foot
5 holes x 4 holes
Cut 4

Penguin Beak
3 holes x 3 holes
Cut 4

Snowflake
7 holes x 7 holes
Cut 4

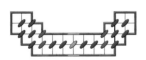

Scarf
12 holes x 4 holes
Cut 2
Stitch 1 as graphed
Stitch 1, replacing
bright blue with purple,
bright green with yellow
and tangerine with fuchsia

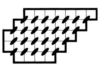

Penguin Wing
9 holes x 5 holes
Cut 4, reverse 2

Scarf Tails
2 holes x 6 holes
Cut 1 set for each penguin
Stitch 1 set as graphed
Stitch 1 set, replacing
bright blue with purple,
bright green with yellow
and tangerine with fuchsia

COLOR KEY	
Worsted Weight Yarn	**Yards**
☐ White	14
■ Black	8
■ Bright blue	2
■ Bright green	2
Yellow	2
■ Tangerine	2
■ Pink	1
Fuchsia	1
Purple	1
Uncoded area on penguin is white	
Continental Stitches	
Uncoded area on sign is light blue	
Continental Stitches	2
✎ Bright blue Backstitch	
● Bright green Lark's Head Knot	

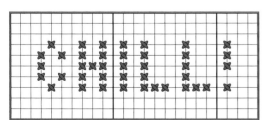

Sign
24 holes x 10 holes
Cut 1

Let It Snow Frame

Design by Kimberly A. Suber

Celebrate the season with this bright and cheery winter frame dressed up with snowflakes, a snowman and a cardinal!

skill level • beginner

✴ materials ✴

- ¼ sheet 7-count plastic canvas
- Small amount 10-count plastic canvas
- Worsted weight yarn: 4 inches each yellow and fuchsia and as listed in color key
- #16 tapestry needle
- #18 tapestry needle
- 3½-inch x 5-inch horizontal acrylic photo frame
- Hot-glue gun

finished size:
6⅝ inches W x 4¼ inches H

instructions

1 Cut snowflakes from 10-count plastic canvas; cut all remaining pieces from 7-count plastic canvas according to graphs.

2 Using #18 tapestry needle and 2 plies white yarn, stitch and Overcast snowflakes following graphs (this page and page 154).

3 Following graphs and using #16 tapestry needle and 4 plies yarn throughout, Overcast berries. Stitch and Overcast all remaining pieces, working uncoded background on frame with bright blue Continental Stitches and reversing one tree branch before stitching.

4 When background stitching is completed, work French Knots and Straight Stitches following graphs.

5 Using photo as a guide through step 8, glue stitched frame to front of plastic frame. Glue wing to cardinal. Glue tree branches, holly berries, holly leaves and cardinal to upper right corner of frame.

6 Twist 4-inch lengths of yellow and fuchsia yarn together; knot ends. Tie around snowman's neck for scarf.

7 Glue snowman and Christmas tree to lower left corner of frame.

8 Glue snowflakes as desired on remaining frame edges. ❑

Holly Leaf
3 holes x 3 holes
Cut 1 from 7-count

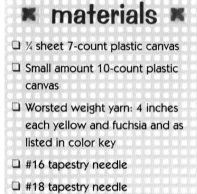

Frame Snowflake
7 holes x 7 holes
Cut 4 from 10-count

Christmas Tree
7 holes x 10 holes
Cut 1 from 7-count

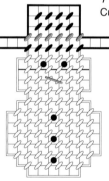

Frame Snowman
9 holes x 16 holes
Cut 1 from 7-count

COLOR KEY	
Worsted Weight Yarn	**Yards**
☐ White	2
■ Red	2
■ Green	
■ Bright green	
■ Black	1
Uncoded background on frame is bright blue Continental Stitches	
⁄ Bright blue Overcasting	
⁄ Brown Overcasting	1⁄
⁄ Tangerine Straight Stitch and Overcasting	
⁄ Orange Straight Stitch	1⁄
○ White French Knot	
● Red French Knot	
● Black French Knot	

graphs continued on page 154

Winter Miss Basket

Design by Janelle Giese

This sweet basket is sure to chase away those winter chills!
It makes a lovely centerpiece or gift basket!

skill level • intermediate

✖ materials ✖

- ¼ sheet 7-count plastic canvas
- Honeysuckle Yarns rayon chenille yarn from Elmore-Pisgah Inc. as listed in color key
- Coats & Clark Red Heart Classic worsted weight yarn Art. E267 as listed in color key
- DMC #3 pearl cotton as listed in color key
- DMC #5 pearl cotton as listed in color key
- DMC 6-strand embroidery floss as listed in color key
- #16 tapestry needle
- Basket with handle (sample used basket 10 inches in diameter x 5 inches H, not including handle)
- 12 Mill Hill Products platinum violet #03023 antique glass seed beads from Gay Bowles Sales Inc.
- Beading needle
- 1 yard each 2½-inch-wide wire-edged craft ribbon in 2 coordinating colors
- Sewing needle and carpet thread
- Thick white glue

finished size:

Stitched Motif: 4⅛ inches W x 6¼ inches H

instructions

1 Cut plastic canvas according to graph (page 154).

2 Continental Stitch piece following graph, using a double strand chenille yarn and working ivory first.

Work uncoded area on face with light clay Continental Stitches and uncoded areas on coat with dark plum Continental Stitches.

3 Overcast piece with a single strand of ivory and blackberry following graph.

4 When background stitching and Overcasting are completed, Cross Stitch cheeks and Backstitch "fur dimples" with 2 plies floss. Backstitch coat below muff with #3 pearl cotton. Embroider upper collar and face with #5 pearl cotton, stitching over vertical stitch on eyes four times.

5 For coat buttons, attach three seed beads at each attachment point, using beading needle and one ply dark dark violet floss.

6 Using photo as a guide through step 9, for background bow, slightly overlap two lengths of ribbon laid side by side, then make a four-loop bow. Using carpet thread, work a running stitch through all layers at center.

7 Make top bow with coordinating ribbon, keeping loops slightly smaller so background color extends at edges. Using remaining length of coordinating ribbon for tails, place center of this length below smaller bow, then work a running stitch through center of tails and bow with carpet thread.

8 Place top bow over background bow; draw carpet thread at top and bottom in center of bows to gather. Place bows on basket side below handle and draw thread to inside of basket; knot to secure.

9 With carpet thread, tack stitched motif over center of bows; draw thread to inside of basket, knotting to secure. Glue tail ends to basket; trim as desired. ❑

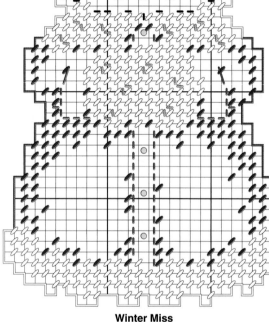

Winter Miss
27 holes x 41 holes
Cut 1

COLOR KEY

Rayon Chenille Yarn	Yards
☐ Ivory #03	14
■ Blackberry #49	8
Uncoded areas on coat are dark plum #46 Continental Stitches	10
Worsted Weight Yarn	
■ Mid brown #339	1
■ Coffee # 365	1
Uncoded area on face is light clay #275 Continental Stitches	2
#3 Pearl Cotton	
✎ Black #310 Backstitch	1
#5 Pearl Cotton	
✎ Black #310 Backstitch	1
6-Strand Embroidery Floss	
✎ Dark dark violet #327 Backstitch	1
✖ Very dark dusty rose #3731 Cross Stitch	1
○ Attach seed beads	

Color numbers given are for Elmore-Pisgah Inc. Honeysuckle Yarns rayon chenille yarn, Coats & Clark Red Heart Classic worsted weight yarn Art. E267 and DMC pearl cotton and 6-strand embroidery floss.

Let It Snow Frame continued from page 152 ────────

Holly Berry
1 hole x 1 hole
Cut 2 from 7-count

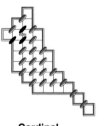

Cardinal
9 holes x 10 holes
Cut 1 from 7-count

Tree Branch
8 holes x 3 holes
Cut 2, reverse 1, from 7-count

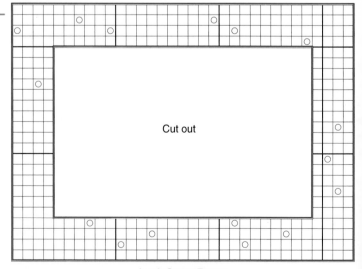

Cut out

Let It Snow Frame
33 holes x 24 holes
Cut 1 from 7-count

Snowflake Starburst Ornament

Design by Ruby Thacker

Add a golden sparkle to your Christmas tree with this beautiful, beaded ornament!

skill level • beginner

materials

- 5-inch plastic canvas hexagon by Uniek
- ⅛-inch-wide metallic yarn as listed in color key
- #16 tapestry needle
- 6 (14mm x 10mm) gold large hole oval jewelry bead by The Beadery
- 18mm x 13mm gold oval acrylic cabochon by The Beadery
- 6 inches gold lamé thread
- Hot-glue gun

finished size:

3¼ inches W x 3¾ inches H, excluding hanger

instructions

1 Cut plastic canvas hexagon according to graph, cutting away gray area and leaving bar at end of points three holes long.

2 Stitch and Overcast snowflake following graph.

3 Place glue in five beads and insert one unstitched point of snowflake in each bead.

4 For remaining bead, fold gold lamé thread in half; insert ends of thread into one end of bead, forming a hanging loop. Place glue inside bead and insert remaining point of snowflake into other end of bead.

5 Glue cabochon to center front of snowflake. ❑

Snowflake
Cut 1,
cutting away gray area

COLOR KEY	
⅛-Inch Metallic Yarn	**Yards**
▢ Gold	3
∕ Gold Straight Stitch	

Angel in the Snow

Design by Lee Lindeman

Delight a special friend with this enchanting project! She's just the right size for setting on a desk or in a cubicle!

skill level
beginner

✖ materials ✖

- ❏ 1 sheet 7-count plastic canvas
- ❏ Coats & Clark Red Heart Classic worsted weight yarn Art. E267 as listed in color key
- ❏ 6-strand embroidery floss as listed in color key
- ❏ #16 tapestry needle
- ❏ 15 inches GlissenGloss Estaz white #ES 01 fuzzy garland fiber from Source Marketing Inc.
- ❏ 2 (3mm) round black beads
- ❏ ⅝ inch gold star button
- ❏ 3½ inch x 1½ inch piece white craft foam
- ❏ Small amount jute mini-curl doll hair
- ❏ Sewing needle and white sewing thread
- ❏ Small amount fiberfill
- ❏ Hot-glue gun

finished size:
6 inches H x 4¾ inches D

cutting & stitching

1 Cut plastic canvas according to graphs. Cut one pair of wings from white craft foam using pattern given.

2 Stitch pieces following graphs, reversing two sleeves before stitching. When background stitching is completed, work lily pink French

Knot for nose and red floss Straight Stitch for mouth.

3 With sewing needle and white sewing thread, attach 3mm beads to head front for eyes where indicated on graph.

assembly

1 Using emerald green, Overcast bottom edges of trees, then Whipstitch wrong sides of tree pieces together. Stuff a small amount of fiberfill into bottom opening.

2 Using white through step 4, Whipstitch wrong sides of foundation pieces together.

3 Overcast top edge of robe, then Whipstitch wrong sides together along side edges. Stuff with fiberfill, then Whipstitch robe base to bottom edges.

4 Overcast bottom edges of sleeves. For each sleeve, Whipstitch wrong sides of two pieces together.

5 Using lily pink throughout, Whipstitch wrong sides of head front and back together, stuffing with a small amount of fiberfill before closing. For each arm and foot, Whipstitch wrong sides of two pieces together.

6 Using photo as a guide through

step 8, glue neck of head into opening at top of robe. Cut jute mini curl hair into short pieces; glue to head. Glue gold star button to hair on head front.

7 Glue hands inside sleeves. Glue feet to front edge of robe. Glue white fuzzy garland fiber around bottom edge of sleeves and robe. Glue one length around collar. Glue wings to robe back.

8 Glue angel and tree to foundation. ❑

Angel in the Snow Tree
17 holes x 25 holes
Cut 2

COLOR KEY	
Worsted Weight Yarn	**Yards**
☐ White #1	40
■ Emerald green #676	16
☐ Lily pink #719	6
▨ Pale rose #755	1/3
○ Lily pink #719 French Knot	
6-Strand Embroidery Floss	
╱ Red Straight Stitch	1/4
● Attach 3mm black bead	
Color numbers given are for Coats & Clark Red Heart Classic worsted weight yarn Art. E267.	

Angel in the Snow Sleeve
7 holes x 10 holes
Cut 4, reverse 2

Angel in the Snow Head Front & Back
9 holes x 12 holes
Cut 2
Stitch front as graphed
Stitch back entirely with lily pink Continental Stitches

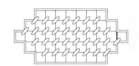

Angel in the Snow Body Base
11 holes x 5 holes
Cut 1

Angel in the Snow Hand
2 holes x 5 holes
Cut 4

Angel in the Snow Foot
3 holes x 3 holes
Cut 4

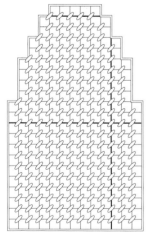

Angel in the Snow Robe
13 holes x 21 holes
Cut 2

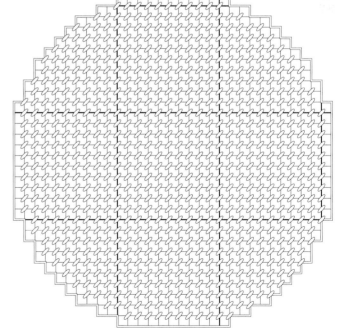

Angel in the Snow Foundation
31 holes x 31 holes
Cut 2

Angel in the Snow Wings
Cut 1 from craft foam

Snow Friends Ornaments

Designs by Lee Lindeman

Add winter cheer to your home with this set of three ornaments. Hang one or all in a window, on your Christmas tree, or even around your rearview mirror in your car!

skill level • beginner

teddy bear ✖ materials ✖

- ❏ 1 sheet 7-count plastic canvas
- ❏ Worsted weight yarn as listed in color key
- ❏ Metallic craft cord as listed in color key
- ❏ 6-strand embroidery floss as listed in color key
- ❏ #18 tapestry needle
- ❏ 2 (9mm) brown crystal eyes from Westrim Crafts
- ❏ 8mm round black cabochon
- ❏ 1-inch off-white or beige pompom
- ❏ Red ultrasuede or felt
- ❏ Pinking shears
- ❏ Small amount fiberfill
- ❏ Hot-glue gun

finished size:
3⅜ inches W x 6½ inches H, excluding hanger

cutting & stitching

1 Cut plastic canvas according to graphs (page 160).

2 From red ultrasuede or felt, cut one 7¼-inch x ½-inch strip for scarf. Cut into each end approximately ⅜ inches several times to make fringe. Cut out skirt circle with pinking shears using pattern given (page 162); use regular scissors to cut out center hole.

3 Stitch ice skates, reversing two before stitching. Whipstitch wrong sides of two skates together. Repeat with remaining two skates.

4 Stitch ears following graphs, working ear fronts with off-white as graphed and ear backs with tan.

5 Stitch remaining pieces following graphs, working uncoded areas with tan Continental Stitches. Stitch body back and head back entirely with tan Continental Stitches. Reverse two arms and two legs before stitching.

6 When background stitching is completed, work black floss Backstitches and Straight Stitches on head front.

assembly

1 Using tan through step 3, for each ear, Whipstitch wrong sides of one front and one back together.

2 Whipstitch wrong sides of head front and back together, stuffing with fiberfill before closing. Overcast top and bottom edges of body front and back; Whipstitch wrong sides together along remaining edges.

3 For each arm, match edges and Whipstitch wrong sides of two arm pieces together. Repeat for legs.

4 Using photo as a guide through step 9, glue neck of head into opening at top of body. Glue ears to head. Glue cabochon to face for nose. Glue eyes to face.

5 Glue one arm to shoulder area on right side of body back; glue remaining arm to shoulder area on left side of body front.

6 Stuff body with a small amount of fiberfill, then glue legs into opening at bottom of body. Glue one ice skate to bottom of each leg.

7 Slip skirt onto bear and glue to waist. Tie scarf around neck and glue to secure.

8 Glue 1-inch pompom to center body back under skirt.

9 Thread a 10½-inch length of silver craft cord through center top hole of head. Tie ends in a knot to form a loop for hanging.

continued on page 160

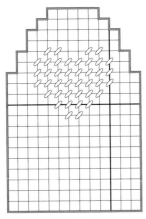

Teddy Bear Body Front & Back
13 holes x 19 holes
Cut 2
Stitch front as graphed
Stitch back entirely with
tan Continental Stitches

COLOR KEY
TEDDY BEAR

Worsted Weight Yarn	Yards
☐ Off-white	5
▨ Pink	1
Uncoded areas are tan Continental Stitches	20
⁄ Tan Whipstitching	
Metallic Craft Cord	
☐ Silver	2
6-Strand Embroidery Floss	
⁄ Black Straight Stitch	¼

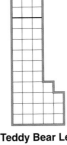

Teddy Bear Leg
5 holes x 12 holes
Cut 4, reverse 2

Teddy Bear Arm
6 holes x 10 holes
Cut 4, reverse 2

Teddy Bear Ear Front & Back
3 holes x 3 holes
Cut 4
Stitch 2 as graphed for fronts
Stitch 2 with tan for backs

Teddy Bear Ice Skate
8 holes x 3 holes
Cut 4, reverse 2

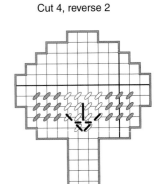

Teddy Bear Head Front & Back
13 holes x 15 holes
Cut 2
Stitch front as graphed
Stitch back entirely with
tan Continental Stitches

angel
✖ materials ✖

- ❏ 1 sheet 7-count plastic canvas
- ❏ Worsted weight yarn as listed in color key
- ❏ #18 tapestry needle
- ❏ 10½ inches silver metallic craft cord
- ❏ 2 (3mm) round black beads
- ❏ 22mm crystal star-shaped acrylic jewel
- ❏ 2 (13mm–15mm) crystal star jewels
- ❏ 15 inches ½-inch-wide white lace trim
- ❏ Sewing needle and white and black sewing thread
- ❏ 4-inch x 2-inch piece white craft foam
- ❏ Pinking shears
- ❏ Small amount jute mini-curl doll hair
- ❏ Small amount fiberfill
- ❏ Hot-glue gun

finished size:
4 inches W x 5½ inches H, excluding hanger

cutting & stitching

1 Cut plastic canvas according to graphs (pages 161 and 162).

2 Using pinking shears, cut angel wings from white craft foam using pattern given.

3 Stitch pieces following graphs, reversing two legs before stitching and working head back entirely with light pink Continental Stitches.

assembly

1 Using sewing needle and black thread, attach black beads for eyes where indicated on graph.

2 Whipstitch wrong sides of head front and back together with light pink, stuffing with a small amount of fiberfill before closing.

3 With white, Overcast top and bottom edges of body front and back; Whipstitch wrong sides together along remaining edges.

4 Whipstitch wrong sides of arms together with white and light pink following graphs. Using light pink,

Whipstitch wrong sides of one leg front and one leg back together. Repeat for remaining leg.

5 Using photo as a guide through step 9, glue neck of head into opening at top of body. Glue arms to shoulder area on back of body. Stuff body with a small amount of fiberfill, then glue legs into opening at bottom of body.

6 Thread a 10½-inch length of silver craft cord through center top hole of head. Tie ends in a knot to form a loop for hanging.

7 Cut jute mini curl hair into short pieces; glue to head front and back around hanging loop.

8 Gather a 6-inch length of lace trim using sewing needle and white sewing thread. Tie securely around neck for ruffled collar. Glue remaining length around bottom of body; trim to fit and glue in back.

9 Glue large star to top of hair in front of hanger. Glue two smaller stars to body front. Glue on wings.

snowman materials

- ❑ 1 sheet 7-count plastic canvas
- ❑ Worsted weight yarn as listed in color key
- ❑ #18 tapestry needle
- ❑ 10½ inches silver metallic craft cord
- ❑ 2 (4mm) round black beads
- ❑ 3 (6mm) black faceted beads
- ❑ 8-inch-long strip plaid fabric
- ❑ Sewing needle and white and black sewing thread.
- ❑ Small amounts black and red ultrasuede or felt
- ❑ Small piece orange craft foam
- ❑ 3-inch Christmas sprig
- ❑ Small amount fiberfill
- ❑ Hot-glue gun

finished size:

4¼ inches W x 6½ inches H, excluding hanger

cutting & stitching

1 Cut plastic canvas according to graphs (page 162).

2 Cut a narrow ⅜-inch long piece from orange craft foam for carrot nose, cutting one end to a point. Cut a 4-inch x ⅜-inch strip from red ultrasuede or felt for hatband.

3 From black ultrasuede or felt, cut a ⅜-inch wide mouth; cut one hat brim using pattern given (page 162), cutting out center as shown.

4 Stitch pieces following graphs, reversing two legs and two arms before stitching.

assembly

1 For eyes, attach 4mm black beads with sewing needle and black thread to head front where indicated on graph. For coal buttons, attach 6mm black beads with sewing needle and white thread to body front where indicated on graph.

2 Whipstitch wrong sides of head front and back together with white and black following graphs, stuffing with a small amount of fiberfill before closing.

3 With white, Overcast top and bottom edges of body front and back; Whipstitch wrong sides together along remaining edges.

4 Whipstitch wrong sides of arms together with white. Whipstitch wrong sides of one leg front and one leg back together with red and white following graph. Repeat for remaining leg.

5 Using photo as a guide through step 8, glue neck of head into opening at top of body. Glue arms to shoulder area on back of body. Stuff body with a small amount of fiberfill, then glue legs into opening at bottom of body.

6 Slip hat brim over head and glue in place where black and white stitching meet. Glue hatband around head just above hat brim. Glue mouth and nose in place on head front.

7 Tie plaid fabric scarf around neck; glue to secure. Glue Christmas sprig to one arm.

8 Thread a 10½-inch length of silver craft cord through a center top hole of head. Tie ends in a knot to form a loop for hanging. ❑

COLOR KEY	
ANGEL	
Worsted Weight Yarn	Yards
☐ White	20
▢ Light pink	8
▦ Pink	½
● Attach black bead	

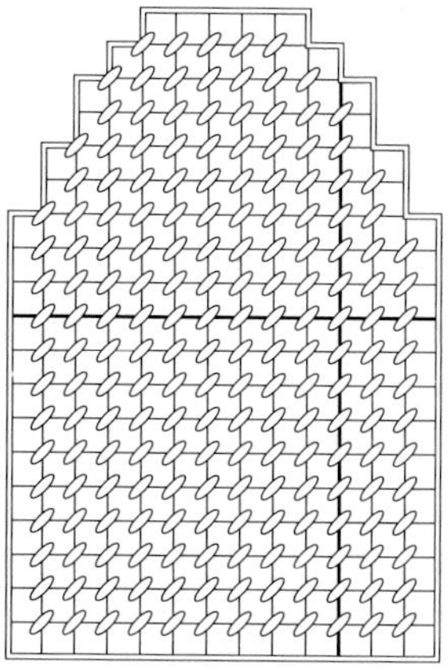

Angel Body
13 holes x 19 holes
Cut 2

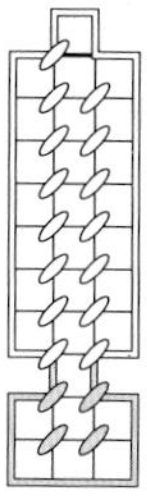

Angel Arm
3 holes x 11 holes
Cut 4

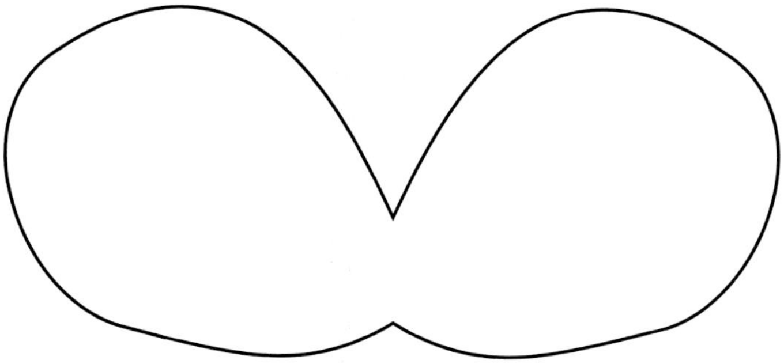

Angel Wings
Cut 1 from
white craft foam

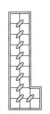

Angel Leg
3 holes x 9 holes
Cut 4, reverse 2

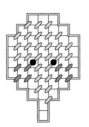

Angel Head Front & Back
7 holes x 10 holes
Cut 2
Stitch front as graphed
Stitch back entirely with
light pink Continental Stitches

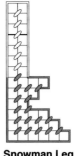

Snowman Leg
6 holes x 13 holes
Cut 4, reverse 2

COLOR KEY SNOWMAN	
Worsted Weight Yarn	**Yards**
☐ White	25
■ Black	2
▨ Red	2
▢ Pink	1
● Attach 4mm black bead	
○ Attach 6mm black bead	

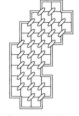

Snowman Arm
6 holes x 10 holes
Cut 4, reverse 2

Snowman Head Front
12 holes x 19 holes
Cut 1

Snowman Hat Brim
30 holes x 50 holes
Cut 1 from black
ultrasuede or felt

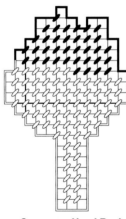

Snowman Head Back
12 holes x 19 holes
Cut 1

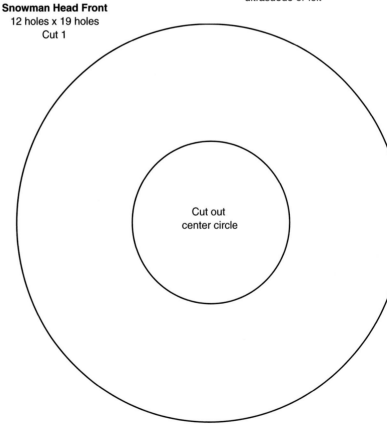

Cut out
center circle

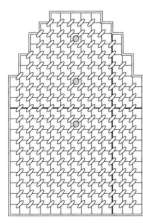

Snowman Body
13 holes x 19 holes
Cut 2

Teddy Bear Skirt
Cut 1 from red
ultrasuede or felt

Rudolph Lollipop Ornament

Design by Deborah Scheblein

Tuck a yummy lollipop into this friendly character for a special holiday ornament

skill level • beginner

✖ materials ✖

- ½ sheet 7-count plastic canvas
- Worsted weight yarn as listed in color key
- #16 tapestry needle
- 10 inches ⅛-inch-wide red satin ribbon
- 12mm movable eyes
- ⅝-inch red pompom
- Hot-glue gun

finished size:
5 inches H x 1¾ inches in diameter

instructions

1 Cut plastic canvas according to graph.

2 Stitch reindeer following graph, leaving overlapped sections unworked at this time.

3 Overcast all edges following graph. Overlap where indicated on graph, forming reindeer into a cone shape. Straight Stitch overlapped sections together with brown as indicated on graph.

4 Thread red satin ribbon through hole indicated at center top of Rudolph's head. Tie in a knot to form a loop for hanging.

5 Using photo as a guide, glue movable eyes to tan area. For nose, center and glue red pompom along bottom edge. ❑

COLOR KEY	
Worsted Weight Yarn	**Yards**
■ Brown	8
☐ Off-white	3
▨ Tan	1
╱ Brown Straight Stitch	
● Attach red satin ribbon	

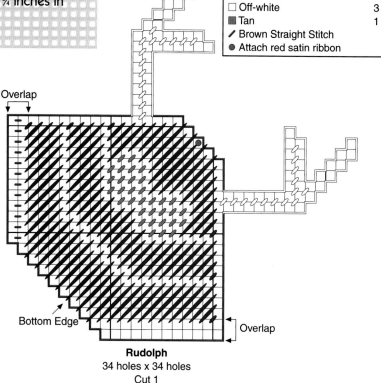

Overlap

Bottom Edge

Overlap

Rudolph
34 holes x 34 holes
Cut 1

Sparkle Paper Ornaments

Designs by Ruby Thacker

This set of six simple-to-stitch ornaments has extra sparkle and color!

skill level • beginner

✳ materials ✳

- ☐ 1 sheet 7-count plastic canvas
- ☐ Uniek Needloft plastic canvas yarn as listed in color key
- ☐ Uniek Needloft metallic craft cord as listed in color key
- ☐ #16 tapestry needle
- ☐ 2 (6-inch) lengths ⅛-inch-wide red satin ribbon
- ☐ 2 yards gold lamé thread
- ☐ 2 sheets Funky Film holographic paper from Grafix
- ☐ Hot-glue gun

finished size:

Square Ornaments: 2¾ inches W x 3 inches H, excluding hanger

Oval Ornaments: 2⅝ inches W x 3⅜ inches H, excluding hanger

instructions

1 Cut plastic canvas according to graphs (this page and pages 165 and 184). Cut two inserts from holographic paper for each ornament following patterns given.

2 Following graphs, stitch pieces. Overcast inside edges.

3 Whipstitch wrong sides of corresponding ornament pieces together around part of each ornament. Place holographic paper back to back and slip between ornament pieces, then complete Whipstitching.

4 Tie each length of red ribbon in a bow and glue to top of each wreath.

5 For each ornament, cut a 12-inch length of gold lamé thread. Fold in half and insert through center top hole of ornament. Tie in a knot to form a loop for hanging. ❏

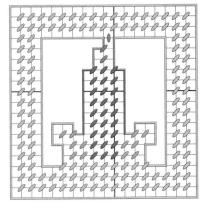

Candle Ornament
18 holes x 18 holes
Cut 2

COLOR KEY	
Plastic Canvas Yarn	**Yards**
■ Christmas red #02	13
■ Christmas green #28	9
■ Royal #32	13
■ Eggshell #39	13
╱ Cinnamon #14 Overcasting	1
Metallic Craft Cord	
■ Green #55004	8
■ Solid gold #55020	2
☐ Solid silver #55021	4
Color numbers given are for Uniek Needloft plastic canvas yarn and metallic craft cord.	

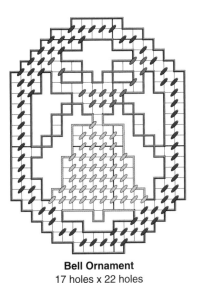

Bell Ornament
17 holes x 22 holes
Cut 2

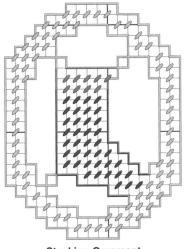

Stocking Ornament
17 holes x 22 holes
Cut 2

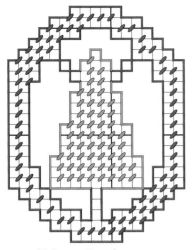

Christmas Tree Ornament
17 holes x 22 holes
Cut 2

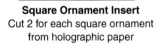

Square Ornament Insert
Cut 2 for each square ornament
from holographic paper

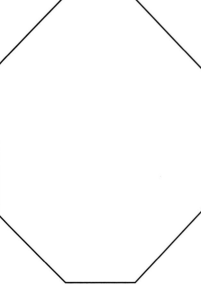

Oval Ornament Insert
Cut 2 for each oval ornament
from holographic paper

Graphs continued on page 184

Little Animals Treat Holders

Designs by Christina Laws

Welcome kids home from school with one of these friendly animals! Tuck a treat inside each for a daily after-school surprise!

skill level • intermediate

instructions

1 Cut plastic canvas according to graphs (this page and page 168).

2 Stitch dog pieces following graphs, working uncoded areas on front and feet with pale yellow Continental Stitches. Reverse dog back and stitch with Reverse Continental Stitches, working ears and tail with dark brown, and body and head back entirely with pale yellow.

3 When background stitching is completed, work Backstitches on face front.

4 Following graphs, Overcast dog feet from dot to dot around bottom, side and top. Whipstitch wrong sides of front and back together following graph, Whipstitching unstitched edge of dog feet to dog sides between dots, working through all three thicknesses.

5 Using adjacent color, stitch feet together in the middle. For eyes, glue two black cabochons to face where indicated on graph. Insert treat between feet and body.

6 Stitch cat pieces following graphs and steps 2–5, working uncoded areas with gold Continental Stitches. Work cat back entirely with gold Reverse Continental Stitches.

7 Stitch mouse pieces following graphs and steps 2–5, working uncoded areas with gray Continental Stitches. Work mouse back entirely with gray Reverse Continental Stitches.

8 Stitch bear pieces following graphs and steps 2–5, working uncoded areas with tan Continental Stitches. Work bear back entirely with tan Reverse Continental Stitches.

9 Stitch frog pieces following graphs and steps 2–5, working uncoded areas on front with green Continental Stitches. Work frog back entirely with green Reverse Continental Stitches Overcast frog feet around top, side and bottom edges. ❏

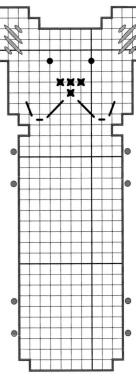

Bear Treat Holder
16 holes x 34 holes
Cut 2
Stitch front as graphed
Stitch back with medium brown
Reverse Continental Stitches

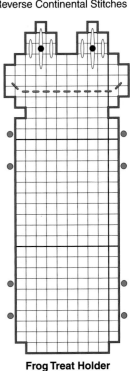

Frog Foot
5 holes x 3 holes
Cut 4

Frog Treat Holder
12 holes x 31 holes
Cut 2
Stitch front as graphed
Stitch back with green
Reverse Continental Stitches

✖ **materials** ✖

☐ 1 sheet 7-count plastic canvas

☐ Worsted weight yarn as listed in color key

☐ #16 tapestry needle

☐ 10 (5mm) round black cabochons

☐ Hot-glue gun

finished size:

Dog: 3⅜ inches W x 6⅛ inches H

Cat: 2⅜ inches W x 6⅜ inches H

Mouse: 3⅛ inches W x 6¼ inches H

Bear: 2½ inches W x 5¼ inches H

Frog: 2 inches W x 4¾ inches H

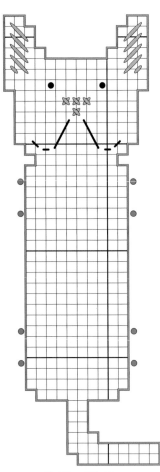

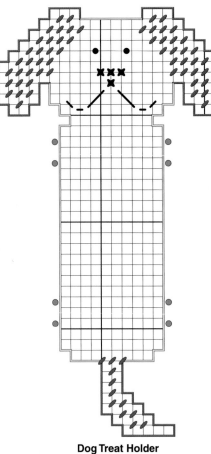

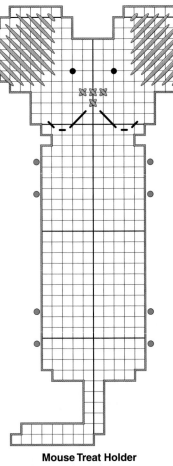

Cat Treat Holder
15 holes x 42 holes
Cut 2
Stitch front as graphed
Reverse back and stitch with
Reverse Continental Stitches

Dog Treat Holder
22 holes x 40 holes
Cut 2
Stitch front as graphed
Reverse back and stitch with
Reverse Continental Stitches

Mouse Treat Holder
20 holes x 41 holes
Cut 2
Stitch front as graphed
Reverse back and stitch with
Reverse Continental Stitches

COLOR KEY
DOG

Worsted Weight Yarn	Yards
■ Dark brown	3
■ Black	1
Uncoded areas are pale yellow Continental Stitches	10
∕ Pale yellow Overcasting and Whipstitching	
∕ Black Backstitch	
● Attach black cabochon	

COLOR KEY
BEAR

Worsted Weight Yarn	Yards
■ Tan	1
■ Black	1
Uncoded areas are medium brown Continental Stitches	11
∕ Medium brown Overcasting and Whipstitching	
∕ Black Backstitch	
● Attach black cabochon	

Animal Feet
5 holes x 4 holes
Cut 16
Stitch 4 with
pale yellow for dog,
4 with gold for cat,
4 with gray for mouse and
4 with medium brown for bear

COLOR KEY
MOUSE

Worsted Weight Yarn	Yards
■ Pink	1
Uncoded areas are gray Continental Stitches	11
∕ Gray Overcasting and Whipstitching	
∕ Black Backstitch	1
● Attach black cabochon	

COLOR KEY
FROG

Worsted Weight Yarn	Yards
■ Green	8
□ White	1
Uncoded areas are green Continental Stitches	1
∕ Red Backstitch	
● Attach black cabochon	

COLOR KEY
CAT

Worsted Weight Yarn	Yards
■ Pink	1
Uncoded areas are gold Continental Stitches	10
∕ Gold Overcasting and Whipstitching	
∕ Black Backstitch	
● Attach black cabochon	

Holiday Soap & Scents

Designs by Susan Leinberger

Treat **your** guests to holiday cheer, even in the bathroom,
with a soap dispenser cover and potpourri box!

✖ materials ✖

- 1 sheet Uniek Quick-Count clear 7-count plastic canvas
- 1 sheet Uniek Quick-Count Christmas green 7-count plastic canvas
- Uniek Needloft plastic canvas yarn as listed in color key
- Uniek Needloft solid metallic craft cord as listed in color key
- #16 tapestry needle
- 3 yards ¼-inch wide metallic gold ribbon
- Seam sealant or clear nail polish
- Hot-glue gun

finished size:

Soap Dispenser Cover: 3 inches W x 5⅛ inches H x 2 inches D

Potpourri Box: 3¼ inches square x 3⅛ inches H

project note

To prevent fraying, use seam sealant or clear nail polish on ends of ribbon and metallic craft cord.

instructions

1 Cut dispenser cover side, dispenser cover bottom, box lid top and box lid sides from clear plastic canvas according to graphs (pages 170 and 171). Cover bottom will remain unstitched.

skill level • beginner

2 Cut box sides from green plastic canvas according to graph. Also cut one 19-hole x 19-hole piece from green plastic canvas for box bottom. Box bottom will remain unstitched.

3 Stitch remaining pieces following graphs, working uncoded areas on cover side and lid top with red Continental Stitches. Overcast inside edges of lid sides and cover side with holly.

4 Using red through step 6, Overcast bottom edges of lid sides and top edges of box sides and cover side.

5 Whipstitch short edges of cover side together, forming a circle, then Whipstitch side to unstitched cover bottom.

6 Whipstitch box sides together, then Whipstitch box sides to unstitched box bottom. Whipstitch lid sides together, then Whipstitch lid sides to lid top.

finishing

1 Cut one 10-inch length and one 14-inch length of ¼-inch-wide gold metallic ribbon.

2 Glue one end of 10-inch length to inside seam of cover side, then thread ribbon from back to front through first hole along upper edge of side. Weave ribbon in and out through holes around side until starting point is reached. Trim end as necessary and glue over inside seam.

3 Glue one end of 14-inch length ribbon to an inside corner of box lid. Weave ribbon through holes as in step 2, trimming end and gluing in place at starting point.

4 For each of the two bows, cut a 32-inch length and an 8-inch length of ¼-inch-wide gold metallic ribbon.

5 Using photo as a guide through step 6, using 32-inch length, make a bow with four 2-inch loops on each side of center. Tie 8-inch length around center and secure with a square knot.

6 Glue one bow to center front of cover along top edge and one to center of lid top. Trim tails as desired. ❏

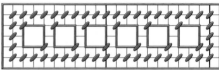

Potpourri Box Lid Side
21 holes x 6 holes
Cut 4 from clear

COLOR KEY	
Plastic Canvas Yarn	**Yards**
■ Holly #27	20
Uncoded areas on cover side and lid top are red #01 Continental Stitches	21
⁄ Red #01 Overcasting and Whipstitching	
Metallic Craft Cord	
■ Solid gold #55020	14
Color numbers given are for Uniek Needloft plastic canvas yarn and metallic craft cord.	

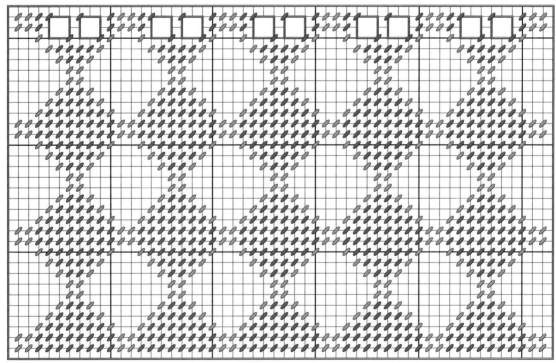

Soap Dispenser Cover Side
53 holes x 33 holes
Cut 1 from clear

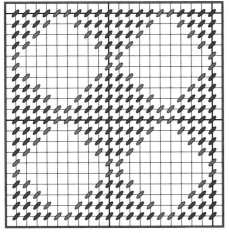

Potpourri Box Lid Top
21 holes x 21 holes
Cut 1 from clear

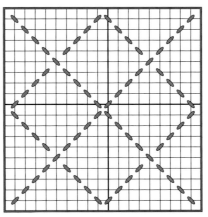

Potpourri Box Side
19 holes x 19 holes
Cut 4 from green

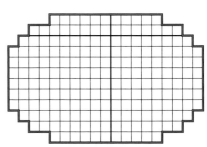

Soap Dispenser Cover Bottom
19 holes x 12 holes
Cut 1 from clear
Do not stitch

Wiggly Worm

Design by Mary T. Cosgrove

This squiggly, wiggly worm makes
a great stocking stuffer for kids!

skill level • beginner

instructions

1 Cut plastic canvas according to graph.

2 Stitch and Overcast worm following graph.

3 Glue eyes to worm's head where indicated.

4 Twist chenille stems together for body. Stitch one end of body to wrong side of head with green metallic ribbon; bend ends of chenille stems over stitches to secure. Bend curves into body as desired. ❏

✖ materials ✖

❏ Small amount 10-count plastic canvas

❏ Kreinik ⅛-inch ribbon as listed in color key

❏ #22 tapestry needle

❏ 6-inch chenille stems: 1 red, 1 green

❏ 2 (7mm) round black movable eyes

❏ Craft glue

finished size:

Stitched Motif: 1⅛-inch square

Finished Worm: 3⅜ inches L

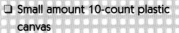

COLOR KEY	
⅛-Inch Ribbon	**Yards**
■ Red #003	⅙
■ Green #008	1½
● Attach movable eye	
Color numbers given are for Kreinik ⅛-inch Ribbon.	

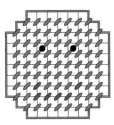

Wiggly Worm
10 holes x 10 holes
Cut 1

Granny Square Coasters

Design by Robin Howard-Will

Stitched on light brown canvas, this set of coasters will work up in a snap!

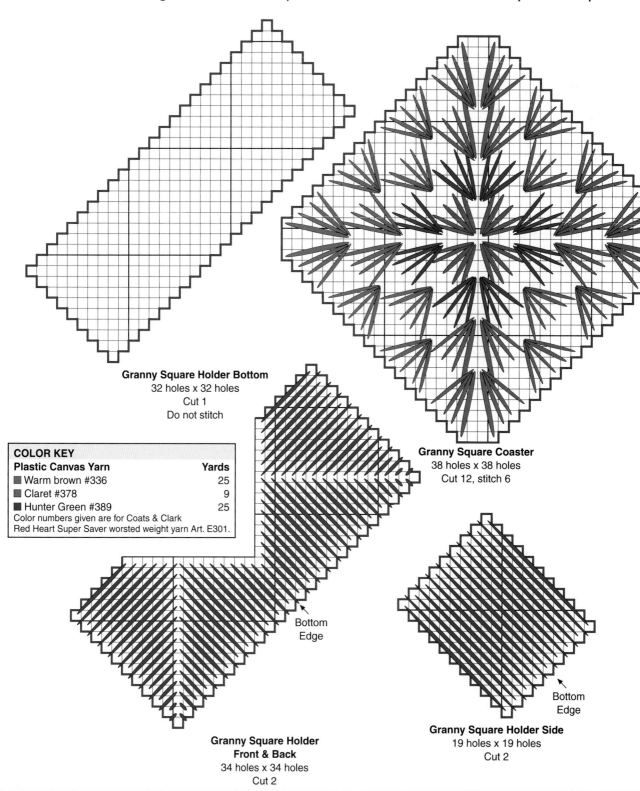

Granny Square Holder Bottom
32 holes x 32 holes
Cut 1
Do not stitch

Granny Square Coaster
38 holes x 38 holes
Cut 12, stitch 6

Bottom
Edge

Bottom
Edge

**Granny Square Holder
Front & Back**
34 holes x 34 holes
Cut 2

Granny Square Holder Side
19 holes x 19 holes
Cut 2

COLOR KEY	
Plastic Canvas Yarn	**Yards**
■ Warm brown #336	25
■ Claret #378	9
■ Hunter Green #389	25
Color numbers given are for Coats & Clark	
Red Heart Super Saver worsted weight yarn Art. E301.	

✖ materials ✖

❑ 9 sheets light brown 7-count plastic canvas

❑ Coats & Clark Red Heart Super Saver worsted weight yarn Art. E301 as listed in color key

❑ #16 tapestry needle

finished size:

Coasters: 4⅛ inches square

Coaster Holder: 5¼ inches W x 2⅜ inches H x 2⅛ inches D

skill level • beginner

instructions

1 Cut plastic canvas according to graphs.

2 Stitch pieces following graphs.. Six coasters and holder bottom will remain unstitched.

3 Using hunter green through step 4, Whipstitch one unstitched coaster to backside of each stitched coaster.

4 Whipstitch holder front and back to holder sides, then Whipstitch front, back and sides to unstitched holder bottom. Overcast all uneven top edges, but do not Overcast center "V" straight edges on front and back. ❑

Toy Chest Magnet

Design by Ronda Bryce

Dress up your refrigerator with this delightful toy chest magnet with miniature ducky, sailboat and blocks!

skill level • beginner

✖ materials ✖

- ¼ sheet 7-count plastic canvas
- Uniek Needloft plastic canvas yarn as listed in color key
- DMC 6-strand embroidery floss as listed in color key
- #16 tapestry needle
- Sewing needle and beige sewing thread
- 3 (10mm) gold jump rings
- 10 (2mm) gold beads
- 1-inch brass hinge #9142-25 from Darice
- 2¼ inches ½-inch-wide magnetic strip
- Hot-glue gun

finished size:

3⅜ inches W x 2¾ inches H

instructions

1 Cut plastic canvas according to graphs.

2 Stitch and Overcast pieces following graphs, working uncoded background on toy chest with beige Continental Stitches.

3 When background stitching and Overcasting are completed, work French Knot with black floss; work Straight Stitches and Backstitches with yarn.

4 Using sewing needle and beige sewing thread, attach gold beads to toy chest.

5 Use photo as a guide through

step 7. For handles on toy chest, make loops with a double strand camel four holes from top on each side.

6 Using sewing needle and beige sewing thread, center and sew hinge to toy chest just under top edge; attach green block behind "A" block.

7 Following graphs, attach jump ring to duck, sailboat and "A" block, then attach each to toy chest.

8 Glue magnetic strip to back of toy chest. ❑

Duck
8 holes x 5 holes
Cut 1

Green Block
4 holes x 4 holes
Cut 1

"A" Block
4 holes x 4 holes
Cut 1

Sailboat
9 holes x 7 holes
Cut 1

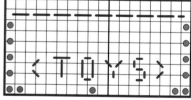

Toy Chest
18 holes x 9 holes
Cut 1

COLOR KEY	
TOY TIME	
Plastic Canvas Yarn	**Yards**
■ Holly #27	1
■ Royal #32	1
□ White #41	1
□ Yellow #57	1
Uncoded area is beige #40 Continental Stitches	3
╱ Red #01 Straight Stitch and Overcasting	1
╱ Camel #43 Backstitch and Overcasting	2
╱ Bright orange #58 Overcasting	1
╱ Brown #15 Backstitch	1
╱ Beige #40 Backstitch and Straight Stitch	
6-Strand Embroidery Floss	
● Black #310 French Knot	¼
● Attach gold bead	
● Attach jump ring	
Color numbers given are for Uniek Needloft plastic canvas yarn and DMC 6-strand embroidery floss.	

Hobby Horses

Designs by Ronda Bryce

Children will play for hours with these unique projects!
Let your child select the colors for his or her very own horse!

✖ materials ✖

Each Horse
- ❏ 1 sheet Uniek Needloft 7-count plastic canvas
- ❏ Uniek Needloft plastic canvas yarn as listed in color key
- ❏ #16 tapestry needle
- ❏ 10 inches ⅜-inch dowel
- ❏ Small amount fiberfill
- ❏ Sewing needle
- ❏ Craft glue

Paint
- ❏ 1¼ yards ¼-inch-wide black satin ribbon
- ❏ ½ yard 1½-inch-wide red fringe
- ❏ 2 (1½ inch) silver conchos
- ❏ 6 (5mm) silver beads
- ❏ 2 (10mm) silver jump rings
- ❏ Black and red sewing thread

Rosey
- ❏ 2½ yards ⁷⁄₁₆-inch-wide white flat lace trim
- ❏ ½ yard 1-inch-wide white lace trim
- ❏ 2 (½-inch-wide) mauve ribbon roses with leaves
- ❏ 1½-inch wide mauve petal ribbon rose with center pearls
- ❏ 2 (10mm) gold jump rings
- ❏ Mauve silk miniature rosebud bouquet
- ❏ White sewing thread

finished size:
7½ inches W x 9¼ inches H, excluding dowel

cutting & stitching

1 Cut plastic canvas according to graphs.

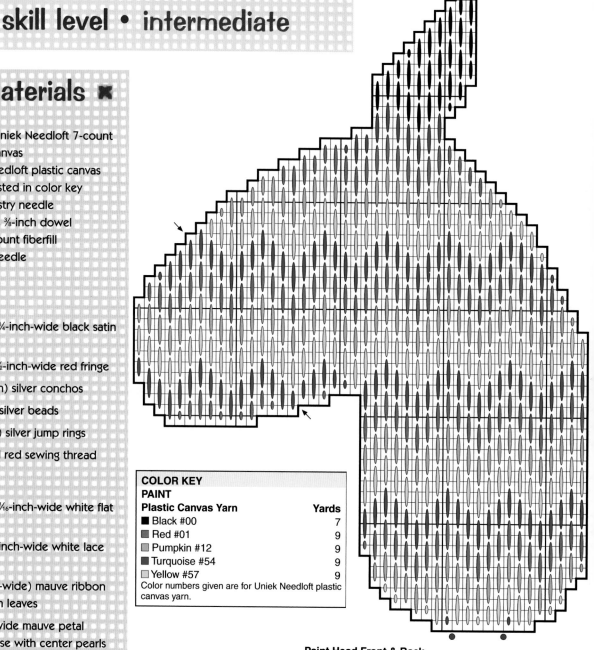

COLOR KEY	
PAINT	
Plastic Canvas Yarn	**Yards**
■ Black #00	7
■ Red #01	9
■ Pumpkin #12	9
■ Turquoise #54	9
☐ Yellow #57	9
Color numbers given are for Uniek Needloft plastic canvas yarn.	

Paint Head Front & Back
44 holes x 61 holes
Cut 2, reverse 1

2 Stitch pieces following graphs, reversing one of each head before stitching.

3 Using photo as a guide through step 4, for Paint's eyes, stitch silver conchos to head front and back with black yarn.

4 For Rosey's eyes, stitch

1½-inch mauve petal roses to head front and back with sewing needle and white sewing thread.

5 Following graphs throughout, Overcast bottom edges between dots. Whipstitch wrong sides of corresponding head pieces together along remaining edges, stuffing lightly with fiberfill before completing the Whipstitching.

paint assembly

1 Using photo as a guide throughout assembly, for Paint's harness, wrap a 9-inch length of black ribbon around nose at arrows; turn raw edges under and overlap, then stitch to head using sewing needle and black sewing thread.

2 Thread one end of a 13-inch length of black ribbon through silver jump ring; fold over about ¾ inches and tack down with black sewing thread. Repeat with remaining end.

3 Place midpoint of ribbon over back of head, then tack to horse front and back where it crosses nose ribbon.

4 For reins, cut a 21-inch length of black ribbon. Thread ends through jump rings, fold 1 inch under and tack with black sewing thread.

5 Using sewing needle and black sewing thread, attach three silver beads to harness on each side of Paint's head, placing first bead where nose and head pieces meet.

6 For mane, with red sewing thread, Whipstitch red fringe to head back, turning edges under and trimming to fit.

7 Glue wooden dowel into opening at bottom edge. Allow to dry.

rosey assembly

1 For Rosey's harness and reins, repeat steps 1–4 of Paint assembly, using ⁷⁄₁₆-inch-wide lace trim, gold jump rings and white sewing thread.

2 Using sewing needle and white sewing thread, attach ½-inch-wide mauve ribbon roses to harness on

each side of head where nose and head pieces meet.

3 For mane, with white sewing thread, Whipstitch 1-inch-wide white lace trim to head back, turning edges under and trimming to fit.

4 Glue wooden dowel into opening at bottom edge. Allow to dry.

5 Make a bow with a 12-inch length of white lace trim. Place stems of rose bouquet on at bottom edge of head, then wrap remaining ⁷⁄₁₆-inch-wide trim around stems and dowel to hold bouquet in place; glue ribbon end to dowel. Glue bow just below rosebuds. ❏

COLOR KEY
ROSEY

Plastic Canvas Yarn	Yards
■ Lavender #05	15
□ Pink #07	28

Color numbers given are for Uniek Needloft plastic canvas yarn.

Rosey Head Front & Back
44 holes x 61 holes
Cut 2, reverse 1

Frosty's "Snowbank"

Design by Vicki Blizzard

Kids will love putting their pennies into this whimsical bank!

materials

- 2 sheets 7-count plastic canvas
- Coats & Clark Red Heart Classic worsted weight yarn Art. E267 as listed in color key
- Uniek Needloft solid metallic craft cord as listed in color key
- #16 tapestry needle
- Hot-glue gun

finished size:

Bank: 7 inches W x 5¼ inches H x 2¼ inches D

Sled: 2⅝ inches W x 3⅝ inches L x 1½ inches H, excluding yarn handle

skill level • beginner

cutting & stitching

1 Cut plastic canvas according to graphs (pages 179 and 189). Cut one 40-hole x 13-hole piece for bank bottom. Bank bottom will remain unstitched.

2 Stitch and Overcast sled runners with cherry red, reversing one before stitching. Stitch and Overcast arms with mid brown.

3 Stitch remaining pieces following graphs, working uncoded area on snowman with white Continental Stitches. Do not stitch top bars of lower back as indicated.

4 Overcast holly leaf, heart, coins, sled and sled steering bar with adjacent colors. Overcast snowman following graph. Overcast scarf A and side and top edges of scarf B with paddy green.

5 Thread one 3-inch length of paddy green yarn through each hole along bottom edge of scarf B. Tie each length in an overhand knot; trim to ⅜ inch.

6 Using 4 plies yarn, work paddy green Straight Stitch and cherry red French Knot on holly leaf; work black Backstitches around buttons.

7 Work black French Knots for eyes and cherry red Couch Stitch for mouth with 2 plies yarn.

8 Whipstitch wrong sides of nose pieces together with tangerine.

assembly

1 Using white through step 3, Overcast coin slot opening and bottom edge of upper back. Whipstitch short edges of coin slot to top edges of front and upper back.

2 Whipstitch bottom edges of front and lower back to long sides of unstitched bottom, then Whipstitch sides to coin slot and to bottom.

3 Whipstitch sides to curved edges of front, easing sides to fit curves. Overlap upper back over unworked holes of lower back, then Whipstitch lower and upper backs to sides, easing sides to fit curves and Whipstitching through all three thicknesses at overlap.

4 Use photo as a guide through step 9. Glue sled runners to bottom of sled where indicated on sled graph with blue lines. Glue steering bar to top of sled along front edge.

5 For rope handle, cut a 9-inch length of warm brown yarn. Thread ends from top to bottom through holes indicated with blue dots on steering bar. Pull ends through to desired length and tie knots on wrong side; trim ends.

6 Glue three coins to top of sled.

7 Glue holly leaf to hat. and nose to face. Glue scarf B at a slight angle to body, then glue scarf A over top of scarf B. Glue heart to body.

8 Glue one arm to each side of body on backside. Glue one coin to each hand.

9 Glue snowman to front of snowbank. ❑

Holly Leaf
3 holes x 4 holes
Cut 1

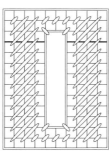

Snowbank Coin Slot
10 holes x 13 holes
Cut 1

Snowman Straight Arm
7 holes x 14 holes
Cut 1

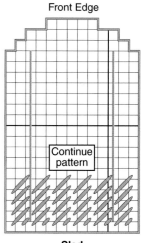

Front Edge

Continue pattern

Sled
13 holes x 20 holes
Cut 1

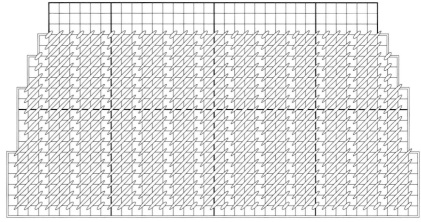

Continue pattern

Snowbank Front
40 holes x 30 holes
Cut 1

Snowbank Lower Back
40 holes x 20 holes
Cut 1

graphs continued on page 189

Snowman Kit

Design by Susan Leinberger

Add the finishing touches to your snowman with this innovative set of snowman features!

skill level • beginner

materials

- 1 sheet Uniek Quick-Count country blue 7-count plastic canvas
- Small amounts Uniek Quick-Count Christmas 7-count plastic canvas: red, black, orange, green
- Uniek Needloft plastic canvas yarn as listed in color key
- Uniek Needloft metallic craft cord as listed in color key
- Uniek Needloft solid metallic craft cord as listed in color key
- Uniek Needloft iridescent craft cord as listed in color key
- #16 tapestry needle
- 9 (3-inch) lengths ³⁄₁₆ inch wooden dowels
- Hot-glue gun

finished size:

Eyes: 1¾ inches W x 3⅛ inches H

Nose: 1¼ inches W x 5⅛ inches L

Mouth: 4⅞ inches W x 1⅛ inches H

Heart: 4½ inches W x 3⅝ inches H

Buttons: 2⅜ inches in diameter

Box: 11½ inches W x 4 inches H x 5⅞ inches D, including handles

snowman features

1 Following graphs (pages 181-182) through step 4, cut two mouth pieces and two heart pieces from red plastic canvas, six buttons from green plastic canvas, three nose sides and one nose base from orange plastic canvas and four eyes from black plastic canvas.

2 For each of the three buttons, two eyes, mouth and heart, place two pieces of plastic canvas together and stitch through both thicknesses following graphs, whipstitching inside and outside edges together on buttons.

3 Work gold Backstitches on heart. Using a double strand Christmas red; work Cross Stitch on each button.

4 Continental Stitch nose base. Nose sides will remain unstitched. Whipstitch nose sides together, then Whipstitch nose base to open end of nose.

5 Glue one dowel to center back of eyes, nose, buttons and heart. Glue one dowel to back of mouth on each end.

box

1 Cut box short sides, box lid top and box lid sides from country blue plastic canvas according to graphs (page 182).

2 Also from country blue plastic

canvas, cut one 60-hole x 36-hole piece for box bottom, two 31-hole x 3-hole pieces for box handles and two 60-hole x 25-hole pieces, one each for box front and back. Box front, back, sides, bottom and handles will remain unstitched.

3 Stitch lid top and lid sides following graphs.

4 Using blue through step 5, Overcast long sides of handles, then Whipstitch ends of handles to short sides where indicated

on graph. Whipstitch box front and back to box short sides, then Whipstitch front, back and sides to box bottom.

5 Whipstitch one lid short side to each end of lid long side, then Whipstitch lid sides to front and side edges of lid top. Whipstitch back edge of lid top to top edge of box back. Overcast all remaining edges of lid sides. ❏

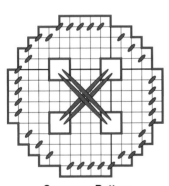

Snowman Button
15 holes x 15 holes
Cut 6 from green

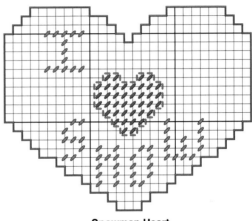

Snowman Heart
29 holes x 23 holes
Cut 2 from red

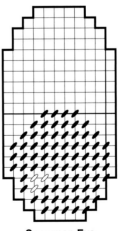

Snowman Eye
11 holes x 20 holes
Cut 4 from black

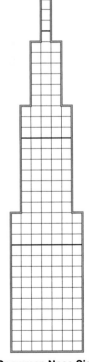

Snowman Nose Side
7 holes x 33 holes
Cut 4 from orange
Do not stitch

COLOR KEY

Plastic Canvas Yarn	Yards
■ Black #00	5
■ Christmas red #02	5
■ Holly #27	6
╱ Bright orange #58 Whipstitching	2
Metallic Craft Cord	
■ Solid gold #55020	2
╱ Blue #55002 Overcasting and Whipstitching	10
╱ Solid gold #55020 Backstitch	
Iridescent Craft Cord	
☐ White #55033	11
╱ Attach handle	

Color numbers given are for Uniek Needloft plastic canvas yarn, metallic craft cord and iridescent craft cord.

Box Lid Long Side
62 holes x 4 holes
Cut 1 from country blue

Box Lid Short Side
38 holes x 4 holes
Cut 2 from country blue

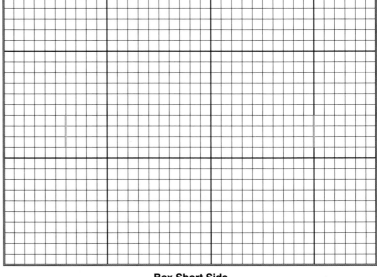

Box Short Side
36 holes x 25 holes
Cut 2 from country blue
Do not stitch

Snowman Nose Base
7 holes x 6 holes
Cut 1 from orange

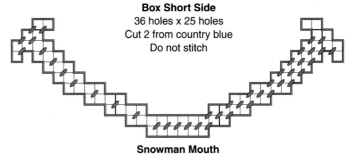

Snowman Mouth
32 holes x 11 holes
Cut 2 from red

Back Edge

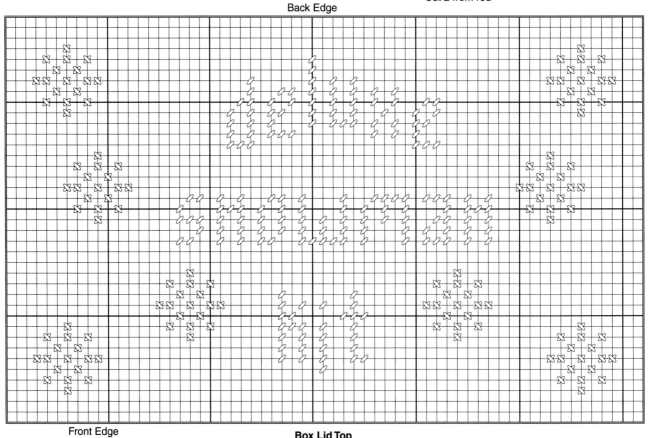

Front Edge

Box Lid Top
62 holes x 38 holes
Cut 1 from country blue

Jack Frost Suncatcher

Design by Janelle Giese

Soft pastel yarn accented with sparkling metallic thread, and beautiful crystals make this a keepsake winter project!

skill level • beginner

✖ materials ✖

- ☐ ½ sheet 7-count plastic canvas
- ☐ Uniek Needloft plastic canvas yarn as listed in color key
- ☐ Kreinik Tapestry (#12) Braid as listed in color key
- ☐ Kreinik Medium (#16) Braid as listed in color key
- ☐ DMC #8 pearl cotton as listed in color key
- ☐ #16 tapestry needle
- ☐ 5 (15mm) acrylic crystal round beads #0639-32 from Darice
- ☐ 26mm x 51mm acrylic crystal drop bead #0639-60 from Darice
- ☐ 4 (6mm) aluminum wind chimes
- ☐ 8 inches silver chain
- ☐ 2 (7mm) nickel jump rings
- ☐ Nylon monofilament thread

finished size:
Stitched Motif: 6½ inches W x 6¼ inches H

project note

Because chimes and crystal beads easily tangle, we recommend the finished project be hung on a door, wall or closed window.

instructions

1 Cut plastic canvas according to graph (page 184).

2 Stitch and Overcast piece following graph, working uncoded areas with white Continental Stitches. Work orchid French Knot for nose.

3 When background stitching and Overcasting are completed, work black pearl cotton embroidery, going over eye and eyelid two times and wrapping pearl cotton around needle two times for French Knot mouth.

4 Work silver braid Pin Stitch where indicated on graph, coming up near edge of eye and going down through center of pupil.

5 Stitch remaining embroidery with metallic braids, wrapping needle two times for silver French Knots and one time for star pink and star blue French Knots.

finishing

1 Attach jump rings to ends of chain and to stitched piece where indicated on graph.

2 Where indicated on graph, attach each of the four outside round crystal beads with monofilament, allowing beads to hang 3 inches from bottom edge; tie ends of

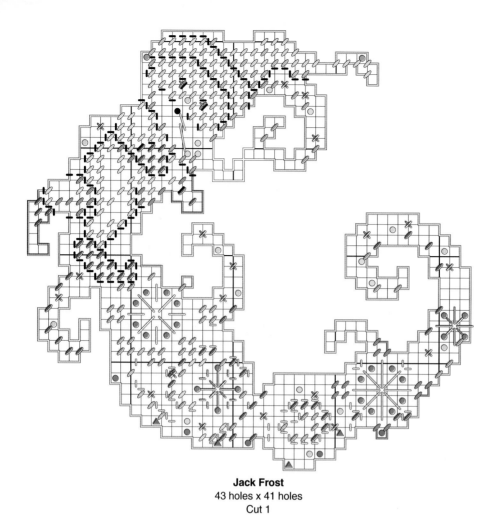

Jack Frost
43 holes x 41 holes
Cut 1

COLOR KEY

Plastic Canvas Yarn	Yards
☐ Moss #25	1
☐ Baby blue #36	8
☐ Silver	1
☐ Orchid #44	2
■ Lilac #45	3
☐ Flesh tone #56	1
■ Bright blue #60	1

Uncoded areas are white
#41 Continental Stitches
╱ White #41 Overcasting
● Orchid #44 French Knot

Tapestry (#12) Braid
╱ Silver #001 Straight
  Stitch and Pin Stitch   3
● Silver #001 French Knot

Medium (#16) Braid
╱ Star pink #092 Backstitch
  and Straight Stitch
╱ Star blue #094 Backstitch
  and Straight Stitch
○ Star pink #092 French Knot
○ Star blue #094 French Knot

#8 Pearl Cotton
╱ Black #310 Backstitch
  and Straight Stitch
● Black #310 French Knot
○ Attach jump ring
● Attach crystal
▲ Attach wind chime

Color numbers given are for Uniek Needloft
plastic canvas yarn, Kreinik Tapestry (#12)
Braid and Medium (#16) Braid and DMC #8
pearl cotton.

monofilament in a knot on backside.

3 For middle crystals, thread monofilament through center attachment hole, thread on round bead 4 inches from bottom edge. Wrap monofilament around bead once, bringing needle down through bead again.

4 Thread on drop bead 1 inch below round bead. Tie a knot in monofilament just above drop bead. Bring needle back up through round bead; tie a knot just above this bead. Bring monofilament back up to starting point; tie ends of monofilament in a knot on backside.

5 Attach wind chimes following step 2, allowing outside chimes to hang 2¼ inches from bottom edge and inside chimes to hang 2¾ inches from bottom edge. ❑

Sparkle Paper Ornaments continued from page 165

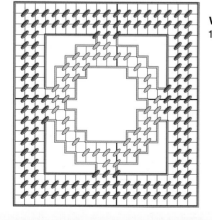

Wreath Ornament
18 holes x 19 holes
Cut 2

Candy Cane Ornament
18 holes x 19 holes
Cut 2

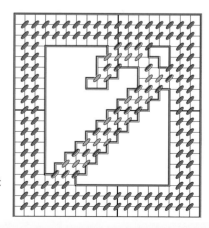

Fancy Hearts Basket & Hanger

Design by Lee Lindeman

These projects are perfect for sharing with friends and co-workers at the office! Fill the basket with Valentine treats to share, and display the hanger to add fun and cheer to the day!

skill level • beginner

basket
✖ materials ✖

- ❏ 2 sheets 7-count plastic canvas
- ❏ Coats & Clark Red Heart Classic worsted weight yarn Art. E267 as listed in color key
- ❏ #16 tapestry needle
- ❏ Basket with handle 8½-inches in diameter
- ❏ 8 (1-inch) pink ribbon roses
- ❏ Natural raffia
- ❏ Eucalyptus
- ❏ Hot-glue gun

finished size:

Large Hearts: 2⅝ inches W x 2¼ inches H

Small Hearts: 1¾ inches W x 1½ inches H

instructions

1 Cut eight large hearts and 12 small hearts from plastic canvas according to graphs.

2 Stitch large hearts following graph, working two with cherry red as graphed, two with lily pink and four with grenadine. Stitch four small hearts with cherry red as graphed, four with lily pink and four with grenadine.

3 Overcast large hearts with adjacent colors. Using photo as a guide through step 7, glue hearts around basket side, placing cherry red hearts under handles, lily pink hearts on opposite sides and grenadine hearts between cherry red and lily pink hearts.

4 Glue one ribbon rose at center top of each heart. Glue a 1½-inch to 1⅝-inch length of eucalyptus to basket on each side of each rose.

5 For each rose, place three 4-inch lengths of raffia together and tie a knot in center. Glue above rose.

6 For small hearts, place two of each color together, then Whipstitch wrong sides together with adjacent colors.

7 Cut three 13½-inch lengths of raffia. Glue end of one length into top of one cherry red heart. Glue

opposite end into remaining cherry red heart. Repeat for lily pink hearts and grenadine hearts. Tie lengths together in a knot around handle.

instructions

1 Cut plastic canvas according to graph.

2 Stitch large hearts following graph, then Whipstitch wrong sides of hearts together with cherry red.

3 Attach red tassel to bottom hole of heart with a Lark's Head Knot.

4 Using photo as a guide through step 5, for hanger, wrap and glue dark green ribbon around center top of heart, allowing loop to extend above top of heart.

5 Cut eucalyptus into four 2-inch to 4-inch lengths. Arrange and glue eucalyptus and baby's breath over ribbon at center top of heart; center and glue ribbon rose on top of arrangement. ❏

hanger ✖ materials ✖

- ❏ ½ sheet 7-count plastic canvas
- ❏ Coats & Clark Red Heart Classic worsted weight yarn Art. E267 as listed in color key
- ❏ #16 tapestry needle
- ❏ 12 inches ⅝-inch-wide dark green satin ribbon
- ❏ 1¼-inch pink ribbon rose
- ❏ 1½-inch red tassel
- ❏ Baby's breath
- ❏ Eucalyptus
- ❏ Hot-glue gun

finished size:

4⅛ inches W x 9⅝ inches H

Small Basket Heart
11 holes x 9 holes
Cut 12
Stitch 4 as graphed,
4 with lily pink and
4 with grenadine

Large Basket Heart
17 holes x 14 holes
Cut 8
Stitch 2 as graphed,
2 with lily pink and
4 with grenadine

Hanger Heart
32 holes x 30 holes
Cut 2

COLOR KEY	
BASKET	
Worsted Weight Yarn	**Yards**
	15
Grenadine #730	15
Lily pink #719	15
▪ Cherry red #912	
Color numbers given are for Coats & Clark Red Heart Classic worsted weight yarn Art. E267.	

COLOR KEY	
HANGER	
Worsted Weight Yarn	**Yards**
	20
▪ Cherry red #912	
Color number given is for Coats & Clark Red Heart Classic worsted weight yarn Art. E267.	

Victorian Hearts Ensemble

Designs by Susan Leinberger

Delight a favorite friend with this sweet Valentine set including a frame, mini basket and two magnets!

skill level • intermediate

instructions

1 Cut frame front, mini basket sides and magnets from clear plastic canvas; cut mini basket bottom from pastel pink plastic canvas according to graphs (page 188). Basket bottom will remain unstitched.

2 Cut one 31-hole x 37-hole piece for frame back and two 11-hole x 26-hole pieces for frame

stand from pastel pink plastic canvas. Back and stand pieces will remain unstitched.

3 Stitch frame front following graph. Overcast outer edge with orchid and inside edges with burgundy.

4 Using orchid throughout, Whipstitch frame stand pieces together around side and bottom

edges, then center and Whipstitch top edge to frame back, making sure bottom edges are even. Whipstitch frame front and back together around side and bottom edges.

✖ materials ✖

- ❑ 1 sheet Uniek Quick-Count clear 7-count plastic canvas
- ❑ ⅔ sheet Uniek Quick-Count pastel pink 7-count plastic canvas
- ❑ Uniek Needloft plastic canvas yarn as listed in color key
- ❑ ¼-inch-wide satin ribbon as listed in color key
- ❑ #16 tapestry needle
- ❑ 2 heavy duty ceramic button magnets
- ❑ Hot-glue gun

finished size:

Frame: 4¾ inches W x 5⅝ inches H

Mini Basket: 3⅛ inches square x 3½ inches H

Magnets: 3 inches W x 3⅓ inches H

5 Whipstitch basket sides following graph. When background stitching is completed, work Lazy Daisy Stitches with green satin ribbon, then work each rose with 1 yard burgundy ribbon following Fig. 1.

6 Using burgundy throughout, Whipstitch basket sides together along side edges from dot to dot; Overcast remaining edges. Tack corners of unstitched bottom to bottom points of each side; Overcast remaining edges of bottom.

7 Stitch and Overcast magnet A following graph. Work Lazy Daisy Stitches, then following Fig. 1, work rose with 1 yard burgundy ribbon. Repeat for magnet B, reversing burgundy and orchid and using 1 yard pink ribbon for rose.

8 Glue ceramic button magnet to center back of each stitched magnet. ❏

Fig. 1

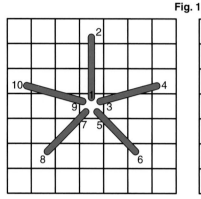 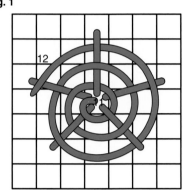

First, work five spokes from the same center hole. Next, bring needle up through center hole and begin weaving over and under spokes, keeping tension slightly loose. Continue weaving from center out until all spokes are covered. Draw ribbon slightly, so ribbon will resemble petals. Bring needle to backside and fasten off.

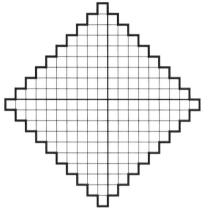

Basket Bottom
19 holes x 19 holes
Cut 1 from pastel pink
Do not stitch

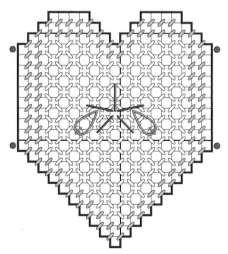

Basket Side & Magnet
19 holes x 22 holes
Cut 4 from clear for basket
Cut 1 from clear for magnet A
Stitch as graphed
Cut 1 from clear for magnet B
Stitch, reversing burgundy and orchid
Stitch rose with pink ribbon

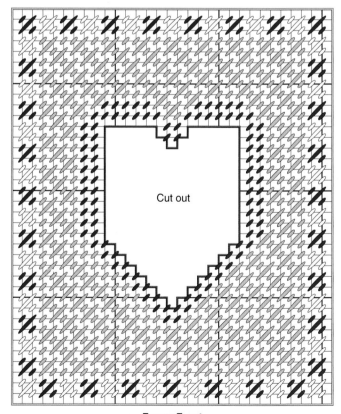

Cut out

Frame Front
31 holes x 37 holes
Cut 1 from clear

COLOR KEY
MAGNETS

Plastic Canvas Yarn	Yards
■ Burgundy #03	3
□ White #41	6
▨ Orchid #44	3
¼-Inch Satin Ribbon	
Pink Rose Stitch	1
✎ Burgundy Rose Stitch	1
✐ Green Lazy Daisy Stitch	2

Color numbers given are for Uniek Needloft plastic canvas yarn.

COLOR KEY
MINI BASKET

Plastic Canvas Yarn	Yards
■ Burgundy #03	4
□ White #41	10
▨ Orchid #44	7
¼-Inch Satin Ribbon	
✎ Burgundy Rose Stitch	2
✐ Green Lazy Daisy Stitch	2

Color numbers given are for Uniek Needloft plastic canvas yarn.

COLOR KEY
FRAME

Plastic Canvas Yarn	Yards
■ Burgundy #03	4
□ White #41	2
▨ Orchid #44	10

Color numbers given are for Uniek Needloft plastic canvas yarn.

Frosty's "Snowbank" continued from page 179

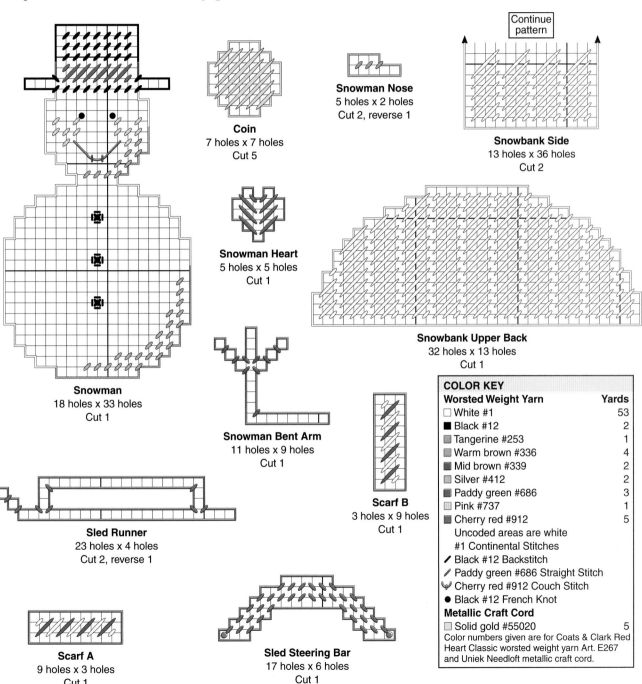

Coin
7 holes x 7 holes
Cut 5

Snowman Nose
5 holes x 2 holes
Cut 2, reverse 1

Continue pattern

Snowbank Side
13 holes x 36 holes
Cut 2

Snowman Heart
5 holes x 5 holes
Cut 1

Snowbank Upper Back
32 holes x 13 holes
Cut 1

Snowman
18 holes x 33 holes
Cut 1

Snowman Bent Arm
11 holes x 9 holes
Cut 1

Scarf B
3 holes x 9 holes
Cut 1

Sled Runner
23 holes x 4 holes
Cut 2, reverse 1

Scarf A
9 holes x 3 holes
Cut 1

Sled Steering Bar
17 holes x 6 holes
Cut 1

COLOR KEY

Worsted Weight Yarn	Yards
□ White #1	53
■ Black #12	2
▨ Tangerine #253	1
▨ Warm brown #336	4
■ Mid brown #339	2
▨ Silver #412	2
■ Paddy green #686	3
□ Pink #737	1
■ Cherry red #912	5

Uncoded areas are white
#1 Continental Stitches
✎ Black #12 Backstitch
✎ Paddy green #686 Straight Stitch
⌣ Cherry red #912 Couch Stitch
● Black #12 French Knot

Metallic Craft Cord

▨ Solid gold #55020	5

Color numbers given are for Coats & Clark Red Heart Classic worsted weight yarn Art. E267 and Uniek Needloft metallic craft cord.

Stitch Guide

Use the following diagrams to expand your plastic canvas stitching skills. For each diagram, bring needle up through canvas at the red number one and go back down through the canvas at the red number two. The second stitch is numbered in green. Always bring needle up through the canvas at odd numbers and take it back down through the canvas at the even numbers.

Background Stitches

The following stitches are used for filling in large areas of canvas. The Continental Stitch is the most commonly used stitch. Other stitches, such as the Condensed Mosaic and Scotch Stitch, fill in large areas of canvas more quickly than the Continental Stitch because their stitches cover a larger area of canvas.

Continental Stitch

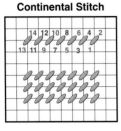

Condensed Mosaic

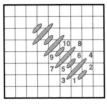

Alternating Continental

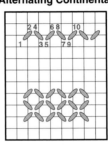

Cross Stitch

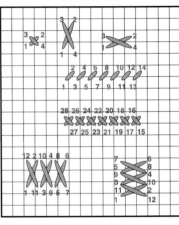

Long Stitch

Slanting Gobelin

Scotch Stitch

Embroidery Stitches

These stitches are worked on top of a stitched area to add detail to the project. Embroidery stitches are usually worked with one strand of yarn, several strands of pearl cotton or several strands of embroidery floss.

Lattice Stitch

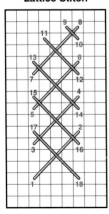

Chain Stitch

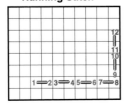

Straight Stitch

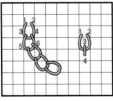

Fly Stitch

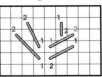

Running Stitch

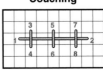

Couching

Backstitch

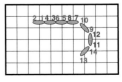

Embroidery Stitches

French Knot

Bring needle up through canvas.

Wrap yarn around needle 2 or 3 times, depending on desired size of knot; take needle back through canvas through same hole.

Lazy Daisy

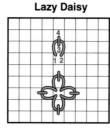

Bring yarn needle up through canvas, then back down in same hole, leaving a small loop.

Then, bring needle up inside loop; take needle back down through canvas on other side of loop.

Loop Stitch or Turkey Loop Stitch

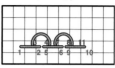

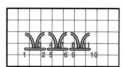

The top diagram shows this stitch left intact. This is an effective stitch for giving a project dimensional hair. The bottom diagram demonstrates the cut loop stitch. Because each stitch is anchored, cutting it will not cause the stitches to come out. A group of cut loop stitches gives a fluffy, soft look and feel to your project.

Specialty Stitches

The following stitches can be worked either on top of a previously stitched area or directly onto the canvas. Like the embroidery stitches, these too add wonderful detail and give your stitching additional interest and texture.

Diamond Eyelet

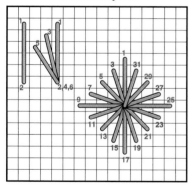

For each stitch, bring needle up at odd numbers around outside and take needle down through canvas at center hole.

Smyrna Cross

Satin Stitches

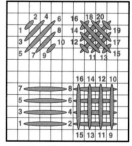

This stitch gives a "padded" look to your work.

Finishing Stitches

Overcast/Whipstitch

Overcasting and Whipstitching are used to finish the outer edges of the canvas. Overcasting is done to finish one edge at a time. Whipstitching is used to stitch two or more pieces of canvas together along an edge. For both Overcasting and Whipstitching, work one stitch in each hole along straight edges and inside corners, and two or three stitches in outside corners.

Lark's Head Knot

The Lark's Head Knot is used for a fringe edge or for attaching a hanging loop.

Special Thanks

We would like to acknowledge and thank the following designers whose original work has been published in this collection. We appreciate and value their creativity and dedication to designing quality plastic canvas projects!

Angie Arickx
Ballooning Bear, Miss Bunny Tissue Topper, Jack-o'-Lantern Basket & Ornament, Tulip Tote, Watermelon Napkin Holder

Nancy Barrett
Butterflies & Blooms Magnet

Vicki Blizzard
Frosty's "Snowbank," Pet ID Tags

Janna Britton
Happy Harvest

Ronda Bryce
Baby Carriage Pins, Hobby Horses, Tie Clip, Toy Chest Magnet, Tiny Treasures Pins, Victorian Pretties

Judy Collishaw
Craft Room Accents, Dresden Tea Bag Caddy, Garden Miss Towel Topper, Ewes Special Eyeglasses Case, Moonlit Magnets

Mary T. Cosgrove
Cornucopia Pin, On-the-Go Kids' Bag Tags, Take-Along Hopscotch, Wiggly Worm

Janelle Giese
Autumn Bears Wreath, Beach Bear Sunglasses Case, Cottage Note Holder, Friendly Ghost Wind Catcher, Grapes Basket, Jack Frost Suncatcher, Kitchen Cows, Owl Wind Chime, Rocky Coast Basket, Schoolkids Slate & Tote, Sun & Moon Wind Chimes, Sunbonnet Sweethearts Door Chime, Winter Miss Basket, Wishing Well Tote

Joan Green
Fun Frames

Robin Howard-Will
Granny Square Coasters

Joyce Keklock
Winter Fun Magnets

Carol Krob
Pansy Button Bookmark

Celia Lange Designs
Acorn Wind Chime, Jolly Jack-o'-Lanterns, Patriotic Bear Welcome Sign, Spring Welcome

Christina Laws
Bee & Butterfly Suncatchers,

Fridgie Clips, Little Animals Treat Holders, Spooky Scents

Susan Leinberger
Bookworm Book Holder, Floral Gingham Keepsakes, Gardener's Plant Pokes, Holiday Soap & Scents, Li'l Punkin Frame, Picnic Time Memo Magnets, Road Royalty Key Chains, Snowman Kit, Tea-Time Wind Chime, Tulip Candle Ring, Victorian Hearts Ensemble

Lee Lindeman
Angel in the Snow, Acorn Necklace, Autumn Basket, Fancy Hearts Basket & Hanger, Friendly Finger Puppets, Fun on Wheels, Silly Scarecrow, Snow Friends Ornaments, Spring Harvest Bunny, Snow Globe, Tulip Party Favor

Kristine Loffredo
Black Cat Pin

Alida Macor
God Bless Card

Nancy Marshall
Buggy Bag Clips

Terry Ricioli
Daisy Pincushion

Deborah Scheblein
Autumn Favor Box, Rudolph Lollipop Ornament, Wedding Accents, Wedding Hearts Sachets

Debi Schmitz
Loopy Flowers Frame

Nanette Seale
Tropical Fish Accents

Kimberly A. Suber
Cool Penguins Wall Hanging, Let It Snow Frame

Marianne Telesca
Carryall Baskets

Cera Thacker
Miniature Teddy Bear Ornaments, Teddy Bear Plant Poke

Ruby Thacker
Snowflake Starburst Ornament, Sparkle Paper Ornaments

Linda Wyszynski
Maple Leaf Coasters

Buyer's Guide

When looking for a specific material, first check your local craft and retail stores. If you are unable to locate a product locally, contact the manufacturers listed below for the closest retail source in your area or a mail-order source.

The Beadery
P.O. Box 178
Hope Valley, RI 02832
(401) 539-2432

Coats & Clark
Consumer Service
P.O. Box 12229
Greenville, SC 29612-0229
(800) 648-1479
www.coatsandclark.com

Darice
Mail-order source:
Schrock's International
P.O. Box 538
110 Water St.
Bolivar, OH 44612
(330) 874-3700

DMC Corp.
Hackensack Ave. Bldg. 10A
South Kearny, NJ 07032-4688
(800) 275-4117
www.dmc-usa.com

Elmore-Pisgah Inc.
P.O. Box 311
Rutherfordton, NC 28139
(800) 633-7829

**Gay Bowles Sales Inc./
Mill Hill Products**
P.O. Box 1060
Janesville, WI 53545
(800) 447-1332
www.millhill.com

Grafix
19499 Miles Rd.
Cleveland, OH 44128
(216) 581-9050

JHB International Inc.
1955 S. Quince St.
Denver, CO 80231
(303) 751-8100

Kreinik Mfg. Co. Inc.
3106 Timanus Ln., #101
Baltimore, MD 21244-2871
(800) 537-2166

Kunin Felt Co./Foss Mfg. Co. Inc.
P.O. Box 5000
Hampton, NH 03842-5000
(800) 292-7900
www.kuninfelt.com

Rainbow Gallery
Mail-order source:
Designs by Joan Green
3897 Indian Ridge Woods
Oxford, OH 45056
(513) 523-0437
(Mon.–Fri., 9:00 a.m.–5:00 p.m.)

Source Marketing Inc.
600 E. Ninth St.
Michigan City, IN 46360-3655
(219) 873-1000

Spinrite Inc.
P.O. Box 435
Lockport, NY 14094-0435
(800) 265-2864
Box 40
Listowel, Ontario N4W 3H3
Canada
(519) 291-3780

Uniek
Mail-order source:
Annie's Attic Catalog
1 Annie Ln.
Big Sandy, TX 75755
(800) 582-6643

**Westrim Crafts/Western
Trimming Corp.**
9667 Canoga Ave.
P.O. Box 3879
Chatsworth, CA 91311
(818) 998-8550

Yarn Tree Designs Inc.
P.O. Box 724
Ames, IA 50010
(800) 247-3952
www.yarntree.com